THE DRAMATIC TEXT WORKBOOK AND VIDEO

THE DRAMATIC TEXT WORKBOOK AND VIDEO

Practical Tools for Actors and Directors

SECOND EDITION

DAVID CAREY AND REBECCA CLARK CAREY

methuen | drama
LONDON • NEW YORK • OXFORD • NEW DELHI • SYDNEY

METHUEN DRAMA
Bloomsbury Publishing Plc
50 Bedford Square, London, WC1B 3DP, UK
1385 Broadway, New York, NY 10018, USA

BLOOMSBURY, METHUEN DRAMA and the Methuen Drama
logo are trademarks of Bloomsbury Publishing Plc

First published as *The Verbal Arts Workbook* by Methuen Drama 2010
This edition published in Great Britain 2019

Copyright © David Carey and Rebecca Clark Carey, 2019

David Carey and Rebecca Clark Carey have asserted their right
under the Copyright, Designs and Patents Act, 1988, to be identified
as authors of this work.

For legal purposes the Acknowledgements on p. xi constitute an
extension of this copyright page.

Cover design: Louise Dugdale
Cover image: Ensemble from *The Odyssey* at
the Oregon Shakespeare Festival. © Kim Budd

All rights reserved. No part of this publication may be reproduced or transmitted in any form or by any means, electronic or mechanical, including photocopying, recording, or any information storage or retrieval system, without prior permission in writing from the publishers.

Bloomsbury Publishing Plc does not have any control over, or responsibility for, any third-party websites referred to or in this book. All internet addresses given in this book were correct at the time of going to press. The author and publisher regret any inconvenience caused if addresses have changed or sites have ceased to exist, but can accept no responsibility for any such changes.

A catalogue record for this book is available from the British Library.

A catalog record for this book is available from the Library of Congress.

ISBN:	HB:	978-1-350-05504-9
	PB:	978-1-350-05505-6
	ePDF:	978-1-350-05507-0
	eBook:	978-1-350-05506-3

Series: Theatre Arts Workbooks

Typeset by Integra Software Services Pvt. Ltd.

To find out more about our authors and books visit www.bloomsbury.com
and sign up for our newsletters.

To the next generation:

Joanna Carey and Liam Carey

For whom words are not enough …

CONTENTS

Foreword *Jeannette Nelson* ix
Acknowledgements xi
Permissions xii

Introduction 1
The Dramatic Text Workbook and you 1
The Dramatic Text Workbook: An overview 2
Working with *The Dramatic Text Workbook* 10
Conclusion 14

1 Sound 15
Framework 15
Exploration 17
Exercises 18
Follow-up 47
Suggested texts 48
Further reading 49

2 Image 51
Framework 51
Exploration 53
Exercises 54
Follow-up 75
Suggested texts 76
Further reading 79

3 Sense 81
Framework 81
Exploration 83
Exercises 85
Follow-up 110
Suggested texts 111
Further reading 114

4 Rhythm 115
Framework 115
Exploration 118
Exercises 120
Follow-up 152
Suggested texts 152
Further reading 157

5 Argument 159
Framework 159
Exploration 160
Exercises 161
Follow-up 188
Suggested texts 189
Further reading 194

6 Putting It All Together 195
Macbeth 196
An Ideal Husband 206
Further reading 213

Appendix 1   Vocal Warm-Up 215
Appendix 2   Rudolf Laban 219
Appendix 3   Punctuation and Parts of Speech 221
Appendix 4   Curriculum Choices 225
Appendix 5   Professional Histories 229
Bibliography 235
Links to Workbook Video 242
Index 243

FOREWORD

Rehearsing a play can be the most stimulating part of being an actor. It's when you spend time exploring and examining the text; when you dig deeply into the language of the play to develop your character and uncover the detail of how they think, speak, relate to other characters and respond to the events of the play. It's when you and the writer seem to be working hand in hand.

Much of this work happens in the rehearsal room with the director or voice coach and the other actors, but most actors will also do some work alone, alongside rehearsal and perhaps even before they begin.

In *The Dramatic Text Workbook and Video*, David and Rebecca's exercises are suitable for the actor working alone, directors in the rehearsal room and for voice coaches who support them both. They help to take the actor right to the very centre of the texts, bringing clarity not only through developing precise speech but also by showing how dramatic language communicates thought and ideas.

Essential to their approach is the need for actors to make the language and the ideas it conveys their own. In our modern information-soaked world, eloquence is mistrusted and there is often a sense that if an emotion is real it leaves us speechless, taking from us the ability to speak coherently. In truth the opposite is usually the case. Today we sadly witness the aftermath of many terrible events, and in news programmes we hear from people eager to tell what they have seen; to say what they feel; to bear witness to the unthinkable. In these circumstances we hear speech that is honest, uninhibited and graphic: where metaphor, repetition and alliteration are often used. All because of the need to recreate for us the true drama and horror of what has been seen.

Plays don't always require actors to express extreme feelings, but they always require them to understand that language, when it is owned and honest, changes people and situations. Rebecca and David's exercises are designed to unlock the rhetoric of dramatic texts and thus empower actors to make informed, personal connections with the language of their character, which in turn allows them to speak it freely, confidently and, when needed, powerfully.

David Carey was my first teacher, and the humility and intelligence with which he approached teaching have been a guiding influence in my own work. We see that here: it is never the ego of the teacher that is important but the revelation of the work.

Part of what makes a great theatre practitioner is the understanding that the best of theatre is made through collaboration. This is particularly true of theatre voice coaching where the best 'teachers' guide actors to make discoveries of their own. This is exactly how David and Rebecca Carey approach their work. Not only do they demonstrate this in their exercises but are doing it themselves, bringing their individual experiences together to create an energetic and inspirational work.

Jeannette Nelson
Head of Voice
Royal National Theatre

ACKNOWLEDGEMENTS

For this revised edition of our book, previously titled *The Verbal Arts Workbook*, we would like to thank John O'Donovan, our former editor at Methuen Drama, for his encouragement and support.

We would like to acknowledge wholeheartedly the contribution that our teachers and our students have made to our understanding of language through the years. In particular, David would like to thank Cicely Berry for her passion for language, and Rebecca would like to thank Dudley Knight and Robert Cohen for their inspirational teaching.

We also want to thank Jim Long for his help in creating the video that accompanies this book. And our thanks also go to Emily, Savanna, Vinecia, Galen, Jeremy and Jon for their enthusiastic participation and excellent contributions in the workshop that forms the content of the video.

David wishes to thank the Higher Education Authority for the award of a National Teaching Fellowship, which enabled him to begin work on the first edition of this book, and for support provided through the 'Performing Classical and Modern Playtexts' research project under the supervision of Professor Mary Luckhurst of the University of York.

Our thanks go also to all at Bloomsbury; in particular, Jenny Ridout, Camilla Erskine, Anna Brewer and Lucy Brown for their support and enthusiasm.

PERMISSIONS

The authors gratefully acknowledge permission to use the following:

An extract from *Serious Money* ©1990 Caryl Churchill, Bloomsbury Methuen Drama, an imprint of Bloomsbury Publishing Plc.

An extract from *The Life and Adventures of Nicholas Nickleby* (stage adaptation) ©1982 David Edgar, Bloomsbury Methuen Drama, an imprint of Bloomsbury Publishing Plc.

An extract from *Hannah and the Dread Gazebo* © 2017 by Jiehae Park, published by Samuel French. All rights reserved. CAUTION: Professionals and amateurs are hereby warned that **'Hannah and the Dread Gazebo'** is subject to a royalty. It is fully protected under the copyright laws of the United States and of all countries covered by the International Copyright Union (including the Dominion of Canada and the rest of the British Commonwealth), the Berne Convention, the Pan-American Copyright Convention and the Universal Copyright Convention as well as all countries with which the United States has reciprocal copyright relations. All rights, including professional/amateur stage rights, motion picture, recitation, lecturing, public reading, radio broadcasting, television, video or sound recording, all other forms of mechanical or electronic reproduction, such as CD-ROM, CD-I, information storage and retrieval systems and photocopying, and the rights of translation into foreign languages, are strictly reserved. Particular emphasis is laid upon the matter of readings, permission for which must be secured from the Author's agent in writing. Inquiries concerning rights should be addressed to: William Morris Endeavor Entertainment, LLC, 11 Madison Avenue, 18th Floor, New York, New York 100190. Attn: **Michael Finkle.** *Hannah and the Dread Gazebo* premiered at the Oregon Shakespeare Festival in Ashland, OR in March 2017 under the direction of Chay Yew.

PERMISSIONS

Extracts from *Man and Superman* ©1957 Bernard Shaw, published by Penguin, reproduced by kind permission of The Society of Authors on behalf of the Bernard Shaw Estate.

An extract from *Under Milk Wood* by Dylan Thomas, copyright ©1952 by Dylan Thomas. Reprinted by permission of New Directions Publishing Corp. for the United States, its territories and Canada; and by permission of David Higham Associates Ltd on behalf of Dylan Thomas and Phoenix publishers throughout the world excluding North America.

An extract from *Ameriville* © UNIVERSES reproduced by kind permission of Steven Sapp, Mildred Ruiz-Sapp and William Ruiz, a.k.a. Ninja.

An extract from *Our Country's Good* ©2015 Timberlake Wertenbaker reproduced by kind permission of the author.

INTRODUCTION

The Dramatic Text Workbook and you

A number of years ago, we were working with a student on a Shakespeare speech for a voice project. The work was coming along reasonably well: the student was finding flexibility and range in his voice and a connection to breath support. We had gone over the speech, and he had established a good understanding of the character's situation and intentions. The speech, however, just wasn't coming to life. It lacked shape and specificity, and progress on these fronts was slow. One afternoon, however, the student came into class and declared that while settling into a lunch time cat nap, he had suddenly realized that he actually needed to think about *what he was saying* in the speech, not just about the circumstances surrounding it. This proved to be the golden key!

In our work as voice and text coaches with actors and drama students in the rehearsal process, we often find, as with this student, that acting problems can be solved by an investigation of a character's language. From Shakespeare's Hamlet to August Wilson's Ma Rainey, a character expresses intentions, actions, objectives and super-objectives through language. When this language is fully explored for its expressive potential, both the character and the play are brought to life with a specificity and immediacy that engage the audience more fully in the theatrical experience. This book is about the expressive potential of language, and how you can develop the skills to release that potential.

We are born into a landscape of language, and from our very early years we are almost constantly engaged in some kind of linguistic communication: speaking, listening, reading, writing, signing or texting. Because we engage with verbal expression so constantly, we can easily take it for granted; it can become almost a reflex. In this book, we will ask you to take nothing about language for granted. Instead, we will invite you to explore every aspect of it to the full and, in so doing, to grow in your ability to use language with sensitivity, specificity and confidence.

This book will be of primary interest to students of drama. Most drama starts with language. Characters, intentions, conflicts etc. are all created through language. In Shakespeare's day, theatre patrons spoke of going to hear a play rather than going to see one – it was the words they heard rather than the images they saw that defined the experience for them. Of course, the work of getting underneath the language of the play – filling in back stories, defining tactics, creating stage pictures and so on – is a vital part of the rehearsal process, but the language sets the parameters. The better you understand how the language itself works, the easier it will be for you to understand and enter the world that the playwright has created.

It's important to note that understanding how language works isn't always something that happens in the head. It happens in the body, too. In drama, written language is merely a way of capturing spoken language, and spoken language works not only on the intellect but also on the senses. Your work as an actor or drama student is not to analyse the language from the outside, but to get it into your mouth and your imagination – to explore it actively and to feel how it stimulates you physically, emotionally and mentally. And to feel how it works on a listener or the other characters in a play, for we rarely speak without intending to provoke a response. You will then develop a full, rational, but also intuitive understanding of what exactly is dramatic about the dramatic text in front of you.

The Dramatic Text Workbook: An overview

The various elements that come together when language that moves or changes the listener is spoken are innumerable. There are, however, certain aspects of verbal expression that almost invariably come into play, and it is those which we will explore in this book.

The first is **sound**. Human language started with sounds. The alphabet came later as a way of capturing those sounds through symbols, but it was the shaping of sounds that first gave humans a way of communicating besides gesture. Even today, we use sounds that aren't yet formed into words to express ourselves. We make 'Shhhh' sounds to calm babies or to quiet noisy children. We release cries of 'Ow' or 'Ah' when we are in pain. We might dismiss someone who annoys us with an exasperated 'Uh' or encourage someone who interests us with a lively 'Mmm'. Arranging sound into patterns gives it even more expressive power. Rhyme and other repetitions of sound please the ear and stick in the memory – it's no co-incidence that they characterize the first pieces of heightened language most of us encounter: nursery rhymes. The first chapter gives you the opportunities to develop sensitivity to the qualities of speech sounds and learn how to use them more expressively.

The second chapter focuses on **image**. Creating images with language is a powerful means of transmitting one's inner landscape of thought, feeling and imagination to someone else. Images can be literal: descriptions of actual things or events; or they can be evocative: references that create associations between one thing and another. The greater the speaker's need to make the listener see what they see or understand what they experience, the more detailed, bold and energetic the image will be. This chapter will help you bring life and specificity to those images when you speak.

Clarity of image is important for many reasons, not the least of which is that it helps the listener understand what you are talking about. Chapter 3 looks at other things you can do to ensure that what you say makes **sense**. It will help you to identify the core thought you are trying to communicate and shape it so that your listeners can readily receive it. It will also help you to focus your energy on those words and phrases that convey what is most significant in a speech or scene.

The fourth chapter explores **rhythm**, which is one of the most powerful aspects of verbal expression. We all have experienced how rhythm in music can arouse and enliven, but one has only to listen to recordings of charismatic leaders from anywhere in the world to get a sense of how rhythm in spoken language can draw in listeners and unleash great emotional energy as well. Rhythm conveys feeling, reveals character and provokes response. This chapter examines how rhythm is created and used in both verse and prose.

The final aspect of verbal expression we look at is **argument**. We're using the word argument here not in the sense of a dispute, but in the sense of making a point. People generally speak to make points – points about how they are feeling, points about what they want, even points about the pointlessness of everything. In drama, you will find that some characters are much more successful at making their points than others, but there is usually something the speaker is driving towards and some structure or logic to how he or she is trying to get there. The better you understand that structure or logic, the better you will be able to speak the language with authentic energy.

Of course, there is a great deal of overlap between these areas – each argument will have its own rhythm; images are brought to life through sound; sense is communicated to the listener through all the others. Developing your understanding of and facility with these elements of language individually will build your confidence and skill, but eventually you will have to **put it all together** to deliver an effective performance. Chapter 6 describes how that process might work, using one classical and one more modern scene as examples.

In an appendix, we provide a couple of sample curricula which outline how a class or an individual might work through these chapters over various periods of time to achieve various goals.

On the whole, we would suggest exploring the chapters in sequence, as generally the early chapters cover fundamental principles and the later chapters more complex issues. If, however, you are working on a particular piece of text, you may want to start by looking at later chapters if they best address the demands of that piece. Or you may want to return to earlier exercises in the later stages of your work to help tie everything together. Verbal expression is a vast and sometimes messy subject, so use our structure to help you organize your learning, but don't feel bound by it.

Each of the first five chapters consists of several sections: *Framework, Exploration, Exercises, Follow-up, Suggested Texts* and *Further Reading*. In general, we directly address you, the reader, throughout the book; however, we also provide *Teaching Tips* which give specific notes for teachers and directors. What follows is a full account of each of the chapter sections and how they will help progress your learning.

Framework

Each chapter begins with a framework section which introduces the topic at hand. The most important learning you will do through this workbook will be practical – you will learn by doing – but having a little bit of background knowledge about the various areas of exploration can help to give you a context for your discoveries. Ideally, some intellectual understanding of the principles involved will enhance your experiential learning. The framework will also elaborate on how the work of that chapter contributes to your larger goals as an actor or a director.

In some instances, the framework section will give definitions of relevant terms. The terms themselves are of minimal practical importance; for example, knowing what the term 'iambic pentameter' means won't actually make you speak verse any more effectively; but it is important to create a shared vocabulary so that when there is an interesting point to be made about iambic pentameter, we have an efficient way to talk about it that everybody understands.

> *Teaching tip:* We recommend that you have your students read the *Framework* section of each chapter before beginning to do exercises from it.

Exploration

The exploration section of each chapter serves a couple of functions. In some instances, the exercises in it provide practical illustrations of principles that are discussed in the *Framework*. They can also provide a kind of warm-up for the more formal exercises, giving you a general feel for the topic before you get on your feet to start more in-depth work on text. Finally, they will help you build a habit of awareness. Much of your most important understanding about this subject will come as a result of paying close attention to speaking text as you do it. These exploratory exercises break the action of speaking down into discreet components and will help you to hone your powers of observation.

Exercises

Ultimately, the only way to learn how to speak text better is to speak text, so most of this book consists of practical exercises. They are designed to help you engage actively and creatively with language – specifically by focusing on sound, image, sense, rhythm and argument.

In doing many of these exercises, you may have an 'ah-ha' moment in which you first experience how giving your energy to a particular aspect of language helps you to be vivid and effective. Don't worry if that 'ah-ha' is stronger with some exercises than with others, or sometimes doesn't happen at all. Different exercises work for different people on different days with different pieces of text. In most instances, there will be at least a couple of exercises in every chapter that focus on the same general principle to help you find your own way in.

Most of the exercises bear repeating. Discoveries may not come in a rush for you with a given exercise, but if you come back to it, they may grow with time. And if you do have an 'ah-ha' moment with an exercise, there's still a journey to be made from that initial discovery of a powerful principle to its consistent application. As you move through the book, come back to earlier chapters regularly so that you can integrate what you've learned from them with the newer skills you are working on.

We use many dramatic texts in this book, and will often talk about acting issues like character and intention. It's important when you are doing the exercises that you imaginatively enter into the given circumstances of the texts and give them your full commitment. But remember too that they are exercises, not performances or even preparation for performances. Don't worry about whether or not you would actually 'do' the text in any given way – just look for what the exercises can reveal to you about the possibilities in the language. If you then take things to the next level of performance, the understanding you've developed of how the language works will greatly enrich your acting.

Many of the exercises are physically active – we believe that deep understanding happens in the body as well as the head – so we would advise you to wear clothing that is casual and easy to move in. If you know you are going to be doing a given exercise on a given day, read the text involved aloud several times in advance. It will help you to become familiar with the language – and, again, the more you speak text, the better you will get at speaking text.

Follow-up

We recommend that you keep a journal as you work through this book. It's startling how easily discoveries that seemed too vivid to ever be forgotten can slip away. The practice of reflecting back on the work you've done will also help you deepen your understanding of what you've experienced in doing the exercises. The questions in the *Follow-up* section of each chapter will help you to focus your reflections. This section may also offer suggestions of how you can apply the principles you've been investigating in the exercises to other work with language that you might do.

> *Teaching tip:* We would encourage you to make some time at the end of every class for a brief discussion of what the students have discovered in the course of the session in addition to making follow-up assignments.

Suggested texts

For some exercises, we work with a specific piece of text because it illustrates the principles we're exploring particularly well. That is not to imply, though, that the exercise will only work with that speech or scene, and we often suggest others that would work equally well. We would, furthermore, encourage you to adapt any exercise to any piece of text that you are interested in exploring. Certain exercises will bring some kinds of text to life more than others, but there's always value in experimenting.

For other exercises, we don't refer to any particular text, but give some options we feel might work well in the *Suggested Texts* section at the end of the chapter. These exercises in particular, though, will be applicable to any speech or scene you wish to work on.

The texts that we use in the exercises come from many different periods, styles and authors, but are largely drawn from plays that have been performed and studied for at least a couple of decades, if not centuries. We have chosen them because we hope that they will be easy to find and somewhat familiar to actors and drama students across the

English-speaking world. The authors we have chosen were also often innovators in the creative use of language and so laid foundations that later writers built on or responded to. Whether or not you ever choose to engage with the more 'classical' theatrical tradition in your life as an actor, we want you to feel that these works are accessible to you. At the same time, we strongly encourage you to seek out texts that are more contemporary and relevant to your own cultural environment, and in *Suggested Texts* we have tried to point you to a small sample of the many exciting newer works that have appeared in the last several decades as well as older works. We recognize, however, that we've really only been able to scratch the surface of all the rich and challenging dramatic literature the English-speaking world has produced.

You will find that there is one playwright who is represented more than any other in the exercises: William Shakespeare. There are those who argue that if you can 'do' Shakespeare, you can do anything. While this may be a bit of an over-generalization, it is true that when it comes to building language skills, working with the best makes you better and he is the best in our estimation. But we recognize that Shakespeare's vocabulary can be challenging to work with at first, and so we have supplied definitions of some of the less familiar words in these extracts. In his writing, you will find that all aspects of sound, image, sense, rhythm and argument are brought into play with boldness and inventiveness to illuminate a profound understanding of the human heart. Because Shakespeare is such a master in these areas, you can learn a tremendous amount about them through working on his texts. While some of the exercises that use Shakespearean texts address issues that are unique to verse (such as metre and line endings), the understanding they foster of how form and content work together in verbal expression is applicable to any piece of quality writing. We would, therefore, advise you not to skip them, even if you never see yourself being a Shakespearean actor.

A few of our exercises also focus on poetry. In our teaching, we use poetry for a number of reasons. Working with poetry is a very efficient way to expand your sensitivity to how heightened language in general operates. We also find that dramatic texts can set up the expectation that one needs to 'act', and it's good to step away from this from time to time. Poetry can encourage students to find a more personal voice. In the *Bibliography*, we provide a list of recommended single editions, anthologies and websites where you should be able to find the texts we suggest as well as other poems, plays and speeches.

Further reading

Dramatic language is a rich and vast subject, deserving of much deeper study than what we can provide in one volume, so we have included suggestions for further reading on every topic. Some of the works we recommend will be useful as references, some will offer you further practical work, and some will give you more background knowledge. We would encourage you to investigate what other authors have to offer; everyone responds to different vocabulary at different times. We believe that the more you read and experience, the more confident you will become in your own sense of verbal expressivity. We have been profoundly influenced by many teachers and colleagues, and, in *Appendix 5*, we give a more detailed account of those experiences and individuals who have shaped our approach to working with spoken language.

Video

> **VIDEO LINK**
>
> Introduction: https://vimeo.com/268960071

This book also comes with links to video footage where you can see us working with a group of young actors on five speeches ranging from the classical to the contemporary. We use two to three exercises from throughout the book in our exploration of each piece of text. In each chapter of the book, we indicate which exercises appear in the video. You can access them by following the links on p. 242. You may wish to watch each one separately to see how the individual exercise works in practice; watch all the exercises associated with one piece of text to see how a speech can be developed by work in a couple of areas; or watch the complete sequence in one sitting for a more immersive experience of the work.

This video footage is in no way meant to demonstrate the 'correct' way to teach or perform the exercises. Rather, it is intended to give you a sense of how the work might proceed and how this process can help you grow in confidence and clarity as you systematically explore various aspects of dramatic language. We hope the video will also encourage you to be creative in your exploration; you will see that when we are working with actors, we are constantly adapting to what is happening in the room. The underlying principles and structures remain constant, but the fact that no exercise ever develops the same way twice is the thing that makes this work so consistently valuable and engaging.

Working with *The Dramatic Text Workbook*

Before you begin any work on spoken language, we recommend that you get into the habit of doing some vocal and physical warming up first. When you are working on heightened text, it is essential – the situations which inspire heightened language are most likely impassioned, energetic and demanding. To throw yourself into this language without a proper warm-up is to risk vocal strain and may contribute to vocal damage. Furthermore, many of the exercises we employ involve some form of physical engagement with language – for example, we may ask you to physicalize a particular word or image. Your body will respond more actively and imaginatively if you have already warmed up with some stretches and swings. So please ensure that you have taken time to release your body from tension, that you can connect fully to breath and support, that you have woken up your voice's range and resonance, and that you are ready to engage in muscular articulation. If you are new to voice work, we recommend our book *Vocal Arts Workbook and Video*, where you will find many useful exercises. We have also provided a brief warm-up in *Appendix 1*.

Once you have warmed up, it is advisable to continue monitoring your vocal usage: in your excitement at engaging with dramatic text, it can be easy to get carried away and lose awareness of your vocal skill. Remembering to breathe, open your throat and connect to your

INTRODUCTION 11

support centre will not diminish your enjoyment – quite the opposite: you will be more likely to find the energy and emotional connection to language that comes with heightened experience.

If you are in a text class and feel temporarily unwell for any reason, let your teacher know. He or she may suggest that you sit out the work or ask you to engage with the work to the best of your ability at that time. Do not push yourself to extremes or undertake anything which feels unsafe in your weakened state. Your first responsibility is to preserve your own health – not to please the teacher!

If you suffer from asthma or have a physical disability, you may need to adapt an exercise appropriately. We have worked with a number of differently abled students, including partially sighted and deaf individuals, and have usually found that with consultation and ingenuity, exercises can be suitably tailored to their needs. If in doubt, however, do not engage in an exercise which might put you at risk of injury.

> *Teaching tip:* Always check with a new class whether any students have any health issues which may affect their ability to perform exercises. Talk with the students and become informed about how the issue affects them. Don't make assumptions about their abilities – ask them to take responsibility for telling you what they can or can't do.

At this point, we would like to address explicitly the needs of dyslexic readers. If you have been assessed as dyslexic, then you will know that dyslexia is a complex condition. Essentially, it consists of a number of symptomatic behaviours that are associated with language, usually in its written form. For example, you may experience words or alphabetic symbols swimming around on the page, getting reversed or confused, or you may misread one word for another, or mispronounce words. This can mean that reading a written text out loud presents certain challenges. However, the difficulty with written language may be complemented by a greater ease and facility with spoken language, or with dance or art.

We have worked with many dyslexic actors in drama schools and professional theatres. With the help of some support strategies, these individuals have been able to work very effectively with the core components of sound, image, sense, rhythm and argument that we teach. Furthermore, many of the exercises in this book are designed to break down written texts to make them more accessible and to enable any reader to feel confident with language. Dyslexia doesn't mean you will be limited in your ability to benefit from this work or to speak text expressively.

If you have been diagnosed as dyslexic, you may know that there are a number of strategies you can use to help overcome your difficulties with the text in front of you. Here are some that we have found particularly effective. You can ask your teacher to give you a copy of the text in advance of the next class so that you can familiarize yourself with it. You can ask for your copy to be printed on coloured paper, as this can reduce the effect of words or letters 'swimming' on the page, or you can get coloured transparent overlays to read through. You can ask for the font or font size to be in a more readable form. You can develop reading strategies which help you keep your eyes focused on the page, or which enable you to identify readable 'chunks' of text. Having someone else read the text aloud while you follow along the first time can also help. If these strategies are unfamiliar to you, you may benefit from consulting a dyslexia specialist who can advise you further on the most appropriate strategies to serve you.

Because dyslexia is such a complex condition, sometimes dyslexics progress all the way through the educational system without being diagnosed. The condition can affect one's perception of written or spoken language in many ways. For example, you may have a great love of words but sometimes get tongue-tied when speaking text or you may find it particularly difficult to memorize text. If, after reading this, you think you might be dyslexic but have never been tested, it is well worth having your abilities assessed. If you are diagnosed as having dyslexia, you may be eligible for a grant to purchase equipment. In addition, many educational institutions provide very good dyslexia support, and there is no need to feel self-conscious about using it.

INTRODUCTION

> *Teaching tip:* It is not uncommon for a disproportionately large number of drama students to be dyslexic, and we have found that our teaching has been greatly enriched by working with some outstanding dyslexia support staff. If you have any access to dyslexia training, we would urge you to take advantage of it. The related condition of dyspraxia largely affects physical coordination and sequencing skills but can affect speech. It can manifest itself in challenges with articulation, the sequencing of language and a student's ability to process verbal instructions into physical action. We strongly advocate for developing a greater awareness of these conditions and their impact on trainee actors among theatre arts professionals.

Finally, there are issues of personal, social and cultural sensitivity which we would like to address. The tradition of training that we come from grew out of European theatre practices and in many ways reflects the values of Western culture. However, we recognize that our own culture is rapidly evolving, and we consider the interaction between cultures to be one of the most exciting creative forces in the modern world. We also believe strongly in the need for sensitivity to personal and social boundaries as different cultures come together. We cannot anticipate all the cultural influences that may be at play within any given classroom, but would encourage teachers and students alike to be creative in finding ways to adapt our work so that it is inclusive of anyone who wishes to participate – for example, by modifying exercises that involve touch when appropriate.

In the exercises, we have mainly used texts originally written in English because we anticipate that this book will be used in countries where English is the primary language. Translations of works from other languages can be very nuanced and powerful, but they can also make it harder to find the author's original intent, particularly regarding sound and rhythm. In an intercultural classroom, however, you may find it useful to seek out good quality English translations of texts from other cultures, or of English texts in a language with which you or your students may be fluent, or to work in another language entirely. Language of all kinds gives us the opportunity to express ourselves – to build bridges between people so that we can share our disparate experiences.

Conclusion

While this book is concerned primarily with dramatic texts, it also explores the expressive potential of heightened language in general – that is, language which is elevated above the routine communication of our lives, language which characterizes those heightened moments of human experience when we are moved to express our thoughts, feelings, needs or desires as clearly, meaningfully and passionately as possible. Exploring the qualities of this language in drama and feeling it come alive as you speak it will enrich you, not only as an actor, but as an expressive being. We wish you well on your journey of discovering your potential as a verbal artist!

1
SOUND

Framework

When we speak, we use sounds to convey meaning. As soon as we feel the need to communicate, our brains unconsciously organize our thoughts into words and then programme our muscles to form the sounds needed to utter those words. The scope of what we communicate when we speak, however, is not limited to just the meaning of the words. The sounds that make up the words can themselves carry information about how the speaker feels and what her intentions are. Clipped vowels and tight consonants tell us a lot about a speaker, as do elongated vowels and dropped consonants. The individual vocal energy that goes into making speech sounds creates a musicality that affects the listener on an almost unconscious level. This is one reason why hearing a speech is so much more powerful than reading it. And this is why exploring speech sounds – getting to know the physical energy that goes into shaping them and the expressive energy that is latent in them – will enable you to convey more fully your character's inner world of thoughts, experiences and emotions through language. In this chapter, we're going to investigate those sounds in detail.

The speech sounds that we use in English divide into two categories: vowels and consonants. Vowels are the sounds that we make by using our vocal tracts to shape but not stop or otherwise interrupt the flow of vocal vibration that is produced by the larynx and passes out through the mouth. In writing, they are represented by the letters *a, e, i, o, u* (and sometimes *y*). Consonants, on the other hand, are made by disrupting the flow of breath in some way. It has often been said that in speech the vowels carry the emotion and the consonants carry the sense. It's true that the open nature of vowels means that they can be particularly expressive. Especially when uttered on their own, they can express excitement, tenderness, surprise, passion, delight, anger, disappointment, disgust etc. (see the first *Exploration* exercise for a more in-depth investigation of this). And it's also true that strong and precise consonants give definition to words. However, we would argue that vowel sounds that are flattened or not fully formed kill comprehension just as surely as weak consonants do. And consonants can convey feeling very powerfully – think of some popular English swear words and the energy and passion that can be expressed through the consonant sounds such as *f, sh, t, d* or *k*. All sound is expressive.

Speech sounds can become even more evocative when they appear in patterns. Repetition of sounds in various configurations, such as rhyme, can have a particular impact on the listener. They can delight and soothe or grate and unsettle. Patterns of sound get under the skin and stick in the memory – think about how nursery rhymes stay with us through our lives. This chapter will also look at how you can use the patterns of speech sounds that appear in your text to catch the ears and imaginations of your audience.

Before we get into the exercises, we want to note that not all sounds are used in every English accent. This is particularly true of vowels. For example, the *AW* sound that many British speakers use in words like *fawn* or *walk* is rarely, if ever, used by most Americans; they are more likely to use the *AH* sound (as in *father*) instead. The exercises we use will work in any accent, though, even if we sometimes talk about sounds that you don't normally use. You may want to spend some time studying accents, nevertheless; it is a useful discipline because it broadens your awareness of sound possibilities. You may discover qualities in words – darkness, openness, brightness, for example – that are not evident in your own accent. It can also be instructive, when working on text, to try speaking it in the writer's native accent. There are even scholars who have reconstructed how Shakespeare's accent might have sounded, and theatres that experiment with performing his plays in that accent, known as Original Pronunciation (or OP for short). See the *Further Reading* section for books that can help you explore different accents.

We'd also like to note that there is an excellent system of symbols for representing sounds called the International Phonetic Alphabet (IPA), and if you are at all serious about studying accents, please see *Further Reading* at the end of this chapter for books that you can pick up to learn about it. We're not going to use the IPA here because it's not familiar enough to many people, but studying it is a great tool for refining your sense of how speech sounds work. Alternatively, Edda Sharpe and Jan Haydn Rowles have an excellent book, *How to Do Accents*, which is a practical introduction to the subject that is designed to be accessible to readers unfamiliar with IPA (see *Further Reading*). The more precise and thorough your exploration of sound, the better you will be able to put it to use in service of your creativity and expressivity.

Exploration

I. Take a nursery rhyme or another simple poem you are familiar with, such as 'Humpty Dumpty', and speak it out loud very slowly, exaggerating each one of the sounds. Where do you feel the energy of different sounds in your mouth? Are some more lip-focused, or back towards the throat? Is the energy itself of a different quality from sound to sound? Do some sounds tickle? Pop? Droop? Are some more narrow? Others wider? Do the vowels feel different from the consonants? Note any observations.

II. Experiment with saying the vowel sound *OO* in your accent (as in *goose*). First of all, just say it quite neutrally, without any attempt at meaning. Then, as you repeat it, play with different images or emotions which the sound suggests to you – perhaps the image of something delicious, exciting or dangerous. Keep repeating it, but see if you can discover a new image, thought or feeling with each repetition. What happens if you vary the pitch more energetically?

Bring the *OO* sound to a rest and make a note of any thoughts, images or emotions that came to mind. Were there any common themes? What difference (if any) did the change in pitch make?

Try the same experiment with *OH, AH, EE* and *EYE* in your accent. What feelings or images do these evoke?

III. Experiment with saying the consonant sound *v*. First of all, just say it quite neutrally, without any attempt at meaning. Then, as you repeat it, play with different images or emotions which the sound suggests to you – perhaps the image of something sensuous, musical or threatening. Keep repeating it, but see if you can discover a new image, thought or feeling with each repetition. What happens if you vary the pitch more energetically?

Bring the *v* sound to a rest and make a note of any thoughts, images or emotions that came to mind. Were there any common themes? What difference (if any) did the change in pitch make?

Try the same experiment with the sounds *g, r, b* and *z*. What feelings or images do these evoke?

IV. Open your mouth wide enough to fit your thumb between your front teeth. Try making each of the sounds from *Explorations II* and *III* again, keeping that space between your teeth. You will probably have to use the muscles of your lips and tongue more than you usually do. What effect does this have on the sounds? Try it again with your mouth closed so that your back teeth are touching. What does this do to the sounds? Try going back and forth between an open mouth and a closed mouth on each sound. How does this change the sound quality? The energy of the sound?

V. Think of an object that starts with the letter *l* (as at the beginning of the word *letter*). Now string together as many words as you can that also start with the letter *l* that could describe that object. (If the letter were *h*, you might get a huge, horrible, hateful, hairy hat.) Speak your sequence of words leaning into the *l* sounds – drawing them out a bit and giving them lots of energy. Note the effect that creates. Speak it again giving the *l* sounds as little energy as possible. Note any changes to the overall energy of the image. Now give a full but not overstated energy to the *l* sounds and note what that does. Repeat with *m, r, t* and any other sounds you'd like to play with.

Exercises

> *Teaching tip:* The exercises in this chapter are divided into four sections: *Vowels, Consonants, Sound and Meaning* and *Sound Patterns*. Within each of these, the exercises tend to advance from basic exploration to more sophisticated application. You may, however, find it productive to move between headings fairly freely – for example, to do an early *Vowel* exercise and then an early *Sound and Meaning* exercise before coming back to more work on vowels.

The exercises in this chapter focus on the experience of creating and using speech sounds. You will be able to perform them most effectively if you take time to warm up a bit, shake out any 'holding patterns' in your muscles, let your breath settle into your lower torso and think about standing or sitting in a way that requires a minimum of effort (i.e. with a balanced and aligned posture). It will also help to think of the energy of your voice as coming from the middle of your body, where your breath happens, and not from your throat. You may have found in *Exploration IV* above that many consonant and vowel sounds have more energy and clarity when there is some space in the mouth, so work with a soft, not a clenched jaw, and feel free to yawn or flap your tongue in and out from time to time to keep a sense of openness in your mouth. The exercises set out in *Appendix 1* are a good preparation, as is all the work in our first book, *Vocal Arts Workbook and Video* (particularly from chapters 1, 2 and 5).

Vowels

As we've mentioned, vowel sounds are made by shaping but not obstructing the flow of sound created by the larynx and are often used to release emotion. This shaping is mainly achieved by movements of the tongue and lips and creates two main types of vowel: pure vowels (also known as monophthongs), in which the shape and sound of the vowel stays the same throughout, for example *AH*; and gliding vowels (also known as diphthongs), in which the shape and sound of the vowel changes as the lips and tongue move between two positions, for example *OW*. The variations that we hear among different accents are often a result of the different shapes and movements speakers use to pronounce these pure and gliding vowels. In some accents, vowels can also differ in length: for example, think about how long the vowel sound in *heed* feels versus the vowel sound in *hid*. Take a look at the following set of words, which was created by the phonetician J. C. Wells for his three-volume work *Accents of English* (see *Further Reading*), and speak them out loud in your own accent.

1. KIT	7. BATH	13. THOUGHT	19. NEAR
2. DRESS	8. CLOTH	14. GOAT	20. SQUARE
3. TRAP	9. NURSE	15. GOOSE	21. START
4. LOT	10. FLEECE	16. PRICE	22. NORTH
5. STRUT	11. FACE	17. CHOICE	23. FORCE
6. FOOT	12. PALM	18. MOUTH	24. CURE

Can you feel the different shapes, movements and lengths of the vowels? Try just saying the vowel in each word on its own. Not all accents make distinctions between all of these vowels, so don't be surprised if some of them sound the same in yours.

Work in your own accent when you do the following exercises.

Laban vowels (15–20 minutes after warm-up)

Take 10–15 minutes to warm up your body and your voice, and then find a place in the room where you can work without being too distracted by others.

Stand with feet just open from parallel and about hip-width apart, knees soft and arms relaxed by your side.

Close your eyes and focus your attention on your breathing.

Let your jaw drop open, and on your next out-breath, release a small *AH* sound.

Think of the sound as rising out of your body with a minimum of effort – it should be audible, but feel **light** and easy.

Over the next four or five breaths, let that *AH* grow in duration until you are **sustaining** it almost to the end of your breath (without pushing or squeezing).

Now, as you continue with the *AH*, imagine the sound vibrations coming not just out of your mouth, but from the back of your neck as well. Over the next few breaths, imagine the sound pouring from your body in **all directions (indirect)**.

Now, think about the word 'float'. On your next out-breath, start to move your body as if you were floating and think of the *AH* sound floating from you. Feel free to start moving through the room a bit. Repeat for three or four breath cycles.

Find a new place to stand still. Think about the word 'punch'. The energy of a punch moves in **one direction (direct)** only – it is **sudden** and **strong**. On your next out-breath, punch the air with your fist and think of punching with the *AH* sound as well. NOTE: keep your throat open and the energy of your voice centred in your lower torso to avoid vocal strain or injury. Repeat for three or four breath cycles.

Following the same steps, move through the following actions with the *AH* sound:

Pressing – so that the energy of your movement and voice is **direct, sustained** and **strong**.
Flicking – so that the energy of your movement and voice is **indirect, sudden** and **light**.
Wringing – so that the energy of your movement and voice is **indirect, sustained** and **strong**.
Dabbing – so that the energy of your movement and voice is **direct, sudden** and **light**.
Slashing – so that the energy of your movement and voice is **indirect, sudden** and **strong**.
Gliding – so that the energy of your movement and voice is **direct, sustained** and **light**.

Remember to keep your throat open and the energy of your voice centred in your lower torso to avoid vocal strain or injury.

Repeat the above in your own accent using the vowels from the following words: FLEECE, KIT, GOOSE, STRUT, GOAT, DRESS, PRICE, TRAP and FACE.

Discuss: When did you feel the sound and the movement really come together? What was that like? Were there moments when you felt that the sound and the movement were at odds with each other? What was that like? Did you make any sounds that surprised you? Did you make any movements that surprised you?

Teaching tip: This exercise and *Laban Consonants* (which comes later in this chapter) use Rudolf Laban's Effort Actions, which can be very effective for helping drama students to develop a repertoire of expressive movement. Laban's work can also help them to find variety and energy in vocal expression. Please see *Appendix 2* for more information and *Further Reading* for some useful references.

Students will probably need to be reminded to keep the effort of creating sound out of their throats when they are performing the stronger actions.

With groups that have already done this exercise once, or that are more self-directed, you may hang up a poster with the vowel sounds written on it, and another with the action words and their qualities, and have students mix and match actions and sounds at their own pace, as in *Laban Consonants* (see below). If they are working on a specific piece of text, you could hang up the poster with the action words, and have them try the various sounds of the text with each of the actions.

Secret song (15–20 minutes)

1. After you have warmed up your body and your voice, lie on the floor on your stomach.

Focus your attention on your breathing, and let it deepen until you feel that the breath is connected to your abdominal centre.

Let your jaw soften and your mouth drop open. Imagine that your throat is a big empty pipe. On your next out-breath, make a gentle GOOSE vowel (*OO*), imagining it floating up from the base of your torso, through your empty throat and out your open mouth.

Repeat on each out-breath, extending the *OO* sound until your breath naturally finishes, and then breathe in again. Focus your attention on the sensation of vibration that this creates in your body. Where do you feel this buzzing sensation most strongly?

For four or five breath cycles, try a different pitch on each *OO* until you have found the pitch that gives you the strongest sense of vibration in one area of your body – in your pelvis, your breastbone, your skull etc.

Repeat the above process with the GOAT vowel, the THOUGHT vowel and the PALM vowel. Then stretch, wiggle, roll over onto your back and repeat with the following vowels: DRESS, TRAP, KIT and FLEECE. Each one will probably give a feeling of vibration most strongly in a different part of your body; say, the back of the head or in your sinuses.

Stretch and wiggle when you finish; then pick up a copy of the first stanza of 'Spring' by Christina Rossetti (see below) and return to lying in supine or semi-supine.

> Frost-locked all the winter,
> Seeds, and roots, and stones of fruits,
> What shall make their sap ascend

SOUND

That they may put forth shoots?
Tips of tender green,
Leaf, or blade, or sheath;
Telling of the hidden life
That breaks forth underneath,
Life nursed in its grave by Death.

2. Identify the first vowel sound, which will be the CLOTH vowel sound in *frost*. Think of releasing this sound from your centre up through an empty throat and out your open mouth. Play with sustaining the sound for a few seconds on several different pitches until you find one that gives you a strong sense of buzz.

Move on to the next vowel sound in the poem and repeat.

Continue moving through the vowel sounds at your own pace, experimenting with each one until you find where it feels strongest and easiest. Note that some sounds may feel best when they are drawn out and others may be shorter. As you progress, you may find that you are able to find the buzziest note for each vowel more quickly and to move from sound to sound more fluidly.

Be aware of the other students working around you and the sounds that they are making.

Play with notes that join in to create a stronger sense of buzz in the room as well as in your own body.

3. When most of the class has worked through all the vowels in the stanza, stop, stretch and wiggle, and then gently come to standing.

Repeat the process that you went through on the floor of finding a note for each vowel sound that creates a strong sense of vibration in your body and in the room.

For some vowels sounds, you may have to play with a couple of notes until you find what fits; for others, you may hit just the right combination the first time.

Always work with an awareness of the other people in the room to build a buzzy soundscape together.

4. When most of the class has worked through all the vowel sounds, stop and shake out.

Next, you will add in the consonant sounds.

Continue, however, to draw out the vowels and move between pitches on each one. This will feel a bit like 'singing' the stanza – not in the sense of performing a song, but in the way that little kids sometimes 'sing' little stories to themselves.

Continue to be aware of the other voices in the room and work together to fill the space with vibrations.

Feel free to let your whole body move gently in response to the sounds of the words. Again, this is less like a proper dance than like a little kid easily turning and bopping and swaying.

5. Finally, stand still and simply speak the stanza, keeping an awareness of the melody that is built into the poem. You can do this as a group all at once or one at a time.

Discuss what you discovered. Where in your pitch range did you find the most resonance for different vowels? Where in your body did you feel the different vowels resonate most strongly?

> *Teaching tip:* You will need to prepare the text, preferably double-spaced, in a large, easy-to-read font, to hand out to the class.
> We have focused on the first stanza, but you might like to explore the whole poem. You could also try this exercise with other texts. As they work, encourage students to be responsive to the other sounds in the room and to the patterns of vowel sounds in the poem.

Consonants

Consonants differ from vowels in two important ways. First, as we noted earlier, vowels are all made with an open channel between the larynx and the lips, whereas most consonants are formed by the articulators (the tongue, lips and soft palate) creating some kind of obstruction in the vocal tract. Consonants come in all shapes and sizes in different languages and, by one measure, in more than fifty-seven varieties; but we will group them under three principal headings, with respect to how they are produced: **stops, nasals** and **continuants**.

A **stop** consonant is one where the passage of air from the lungs is stopped completely in the mouth so that there is a build-up of air pressure behind the obstruction; when this is quickly released, it creates an explosion of sound which we hear as a particular consonant. In English, the common stop sounds are *p, b, t, d, k, g*. You will also find these sounds referred to as 'plosives', because of the explosive sound they make.

A **nasal** consonant is one where the passage of air from the lungs, although it is stopped in the mouth, is allowed to pass freely out through the nose instead, creating an uninterrupted stream of sound. In English, the common nasal sounds are *m, n, ng* (as in the word *sing*).

A **continuant** consonant is one where there is only a partial obstruction of the passage of air through the mouth so that the sound can be made continuously. In English, the common continuant sounds are *w, f, v,* voiceless-*th* (as in *think*), voiced-*th* (as in *this*), *s, z, l, r, sh, zh* (as in the word *measure*), *y, h*.

In English, we also recognize two sounds which are formed by combining a stop with a continuant release – *ch* (as in *church*) and *j* (as in *judge*). These are known as **affricates**.

The second difference between vowels and consonants is that, while all vowels are made with vocal fold vibration in the larynx, some consonants are made with just breath. You can feel the difference: find your larynx by placing your thumb and forefinger lightly on either side of the middle of your throat and swallow; the little lump that goes up and down is your larynx. With your fingers lightly resting on either side of your larynx, make the following sounds: *EE, fff* and *vvv*. You should be able to feel a buzzing sensation as you say *EE* and *vvv*, but nothing as you say *fff*. The buzzing feeling is the result of your vocal folds vibrating. Experiment with the other consonants and make a list of which ones are **voiced** (use vibration in the larynx), and which are **voiceless** (just use breath). As you do the following exercises, be aware of the movements of the articulators that go into making the sounds.

Laban consonants (10–15 minutes)

After warming up your body and your voice, find a place in the room where you can work without being too distracted by others.

Stand with feet just open from parallel and about hip-width apart, knees soft and arms relaxed by your side.

Close your eyes and focus your attention on your breathing.

Let your jaw drop open slightly, and on your next out-breath, release a small *vvv* sound.

Keep the back of your neck and the area under your chin soft; think of the *vvv* energy coming up from your torso, not from your throat or your jaw.

Let the *vvv* sound become a bit longer for each of the next four to five breaths until you are **sustaining** it to the end of your breath without pushing or squeezing.

The sound should be audible, but **light** and easy.

Imagine the sound moving away from your body and **directly** to the wall in front of you.

Now, think about the word 'glide'. On your next out-breath, start moving your body as if you were gliding and think of the *vvv* sound gliding through space as well. Feel free to start moving through the room. Repeat for three or four breath cycles.

Find a new place to stand still. Think about the word 'wring'; wringing is also **sustained** (not sudden), but is **stronger** – you will need stronger muscular support for the sound in your torso. It is also **indirect**, so it will not focus solely to the front. On your next out-breath, make a wringing motion with your whole body and think of wringing with the *vvv* sound as well. NOTE: keep your throat open and the energy of your voice centred in your lower torso to avoid vocal strain or injury. Repeat for three or four breath cycles.

Next, look at the list of consonant sounds and choose one. Take a moment to practise making that sound with your throat open and the muscles of your lower torso engaged. Then pick an action from the Laban Effort Actions list and try putting the sound and the action together. Try three different actions with each sound, and then move on to a new sound and three new actions.

Continue until you have worked through at least two-thirds of the consonant sounds.

Discuss: when did you feel the sound and the movement really come together? What was that like? Were there moments when you felt that the sound and the movement were at odds with each other? What was that like? Did you make any sounds that surprised you? Did you make any movements that surprised you?

SOUND

> *Teaching tip:* Before beginning the exercise, write the Laban Effort Actions on a chalk board or a large poster and the consonant sounds on another and position them where the students will be able to see them easily.

The Effort Actions

Pressing – **direct, sustained** and **strong**
Flicking – **indirect, sudden** and **light**
Wringing – **indirect, sustained** and **strong**
Dabbing – **direct, sudden** and **light**
Slashing – **indirect, sudden** and **strong**
Gliding – **direct, sustained** and **light**
Punching – **direct, sudden** and **strong**
Floating – **indirect, sustained** and **light**

The consonant sounds are: *p, b, t, d, k, g, m, n, ng, w, f,* voiceless-*th,* voiced-*th, s, z, r, l, y, h, sh, zh, ch, j*.

Consonants and content (15–20 minutes)

1. After warming up your voice and body, find a place to stand where you have some room to move.

Take a moment to let your breath settle in your lower abdomen. Think of your throat being an empty pipe.

Everyone take up a copy of Leontes's speech from Shakespeare's *The Winter's Tale* Act I, Scene 2. In this passage, Leontes is convinced that his wife is having an affair with his best friend, which would make Leontes a cuckold – a cuckold is a man whose wife has cheated on him. He is considering that many other men have found themselves in the same situation. At the beginning of the speech he is also talking to his son and telling him to go play.

LEONTES
Inch-thick, knee-deep, o'er head and ears
  a forked* one!   *cuckolded*
Go, play, boy, play: thy mother plays, and I

Play too, but so disgraced a part, whose issue*   *outcome*
Will hiss me to my grave: contempt and clamour*   *outcry*
Will be my knell*. Go, play, boy, play. There have
    been,   *funeral bell*
Or I am much deceived, cuckolds ere now;
And many a man there is, even at this present,
Now while I speak this, holds his wife by the arm,
That little thinks she has been sluiced* in's absence   *rinsed out*
And his pond fished by his next neighbour, by
Sir Smile, his neighbour: nay, there's comfort in't
Whiles other men have gates and those gates opened,
As mine, against their will. Should all despair
That have revolted wives, the tenth of mankind
Would hang themselves. Physic* for't there is none;   *medicine*
It is a bawdy* planet, that will strike   *lewd, obscene*
Where 'tis predominant*; and 'tis powerful, think it,   *influential*
From east, west, north and south: be it concluded,
No barricado* for a belly; know't;   *barrier*
It will let in and out the enemy
With bag and baggage: many thousand on's
Have the disease, and feel't not. How now, boy!

Read the speech out loud together. Don't worry if it doesn't make complete sense straightaway.

2. After you have finished reading the passage, put the text down for a moment.

Focus again on your breath, and think of your jaw softening, letting it drop open far enough that you could easily fit your thumb between your teeth all the way around.

Using energy in your lips and breath, but not your throat, neck or jaw, make a strong *p* sound. Follow this with a strong *b* sound – remember to keep the throat open.

Using energy in your tongue tip and breath, make a strong *t* and then a strong *d*.

Using energy in the back of the tongue, the soft palate and the breath, make a strong *k* sound and then a strong *g*.

As in *Laban Consonants*, try connecting each of these plosive sounds (*p, b, t, d, k, g*) to several of the Laban Effort Actions (float, punch, press, flick, slash, dab, wring and glide). After a couple of minutes of experimentation, pick one action that you feel works best with the plosive sounds.

Pick up the text and hold it with one hand.

Everyone together will now read through the text very slowly. Every time you come to a plosive sound, perform your Laban action with your free hand as you say it. Go slowly enough that you can give your full energy to each action.

When you have finished, have a brief discussion about how the energy of your action and the energy of the speech did or did not complement each other. What discoveries did you make about Leontes's speech? Did this give you any insights into his state of mind?

Go through the same process with the sounds *s* and *z*. Find a Laban action that suits them and then perform the action every time you say those sounds as you read slowly through the speech. How does the energy of those sounds influence the energy of the text?

3. Now find a partner and stand at least three metres away from him or her.

Partner A will read the speech aloud to B without using any voice at all. Think of mouthing it rather than whispering, or you may end up pushing too much from your throat. Focus on taking the energy that you found in the Laban actions and putting it in your lips and tongue (not the back of your neck!).

Repeat with partner B mouthing the text.

Finally, partner A read the text out loud, using not only your voice but also the energy of the consonants to reach your partner.

Repeat with partner B reading the passage.

Discuss the relationship between the consonants, the energy you put into forming them, and the emotional content of the speech.

Sound and meaning

Sound and meaning are inescapably linked in all languages. The meaning of many words, in fact, is demonstrated in the very sounds that make up the words. Think of the word 'hiss', for example – the word sounds like what it is describing. **Onomatopoeia** is the term used for language which imitates the sound it describes. When we talk about the 'meow' of a cat or the 'woof' of a dog or use words like 'bang', 'hoot' and 'giggle', we are using onomatopoeia.

Although the relationship between sounds and meaning may not always be as vivid as when we speak onomatopoetically, all of us make conscious or unconscious use of the sound effects of speech, particularly in heightened moments of emotional intensity when we need to have an effect on our landscape. And good playwrights (and writers of all kinds) will make subtle or blatant use of such features to capture a feeling, an image or a character's psychological state in order to engage us more fully in the action of the drama. The following exercises will help you make that link between sound and meaning.

Sound and meaning (30–45 minutes)

1. Take 10–15 minutes to warm up your body and voice, and then lie on the floor in a supine (flat on your back) or semi-supine (on your back with your feet flat on the floor and knees pointing to the ceiling) position.

Focus your attention on your breathing, and let it deepen until you feel that the breath is connected to your abdominal centre.

Continue breathing from centre, and let your mind focus on some sense-experience you'd like to express with your breath: a feeling, a memory, a colour or an image. As you breathe in, let your mind form the intention to express this specific thing; as you breathe out, let the breath carry through this intention – your breath may become stronger, longer, softer, fall like a sigh, dart like a whistle etc., depending on what you're giving expression to. Explore the different qualities of this sense-experience and play with the different possibilities of connecting it to breath. Stay connected to centre.

2. When you feel ready to move on, start to release your breath on a long *sh* sound. Let your mind focus on some sense-experience you'd like to express with this *sh*: a different feeling, memory, colour, or image. As you breathe in, let your mind form this intention to express this specific thing; as you release your breath in the *sh* sound, let the sound realize this intention. Explore the different qualities of this sense-experience and play with the different possibilities of connecting it to *sh*. Stay connected to centre.

Stay with *sh* a little longer, but change the sense-experience and explore how the sound can express this new idea.

3. When you feel ready to move on, start to release your breath on a long *zh* sound (as in *measure*). This sound uses voiced vibrations – what

SOUND

new intentions suggest themselves to you? Try changing your intention with each new breath so that each time you breathe in, you focus on a new idea/experience/image you want to express; as you release your breath in the *zh* sound, the sound realizes this new intention. Stay connected to centre.

4. When you're ready to move on, explore expressing intentions with other sounds of your own choice: use a mix of vowels and consonants. Try expressing the same intention with different sounds – does this make you feel differently about the intention or the sound? And try expressing different intentions with the same sound – does this make you feel differently about the intention or the sound?

Does your body want to become involved in some way? Stay lying down for the time being, but explore using your body to support how your voice is expressing intention through sound – maybe with some wiggles, stretches or contractions.

5. Begin to combine sounds in short sequences – for example, *sh, OO, f, p* or *m, b, EE, k, l* – and give each sequence a meaning or intention. Keep changing your intention with each new breath so that each time you breathe in, your mind forms a fresh intention; and as you release your breath let a fresh sequence of sounds realize this new intention. Stay connected to centre, but allow your body to become more involved – you might want to move on to your knees or even stand up.

6. Choose one of these sound sequences that you like and explore it further. Try giving it different intentions – do some intentions seem to fit more appropriately than others? How does your body want to respond?

When you've finished, take some time to reflect on the sequence of work and what you've discovered about sound, meaning and language. For example, did different sounds suggest ideas more quickly than others? Where did your imagination take you, and did it make a difference to involve your body?

By the end, you were creating sound sequences which were like words or sentences. How strong was the connection between your intention and your word? Does your word mean something specific?

7. Finally, pick up a piece of text (a poem or dramatic speech) and read through it out loud. Look for opportunities to use the sounds to fulfil the intention of communicating an idea, experience or image.

The elements (30–45 minutes)

This exercise builds on *Sound and Meaning*.

1. Following a 10–15-minute physical and vocal warm-up, lie on the floor in supine or semi-supine and connect to your centred breath as described in *Sound and Meaning*.

Let your mind focus on something you'd like to express with your breath: a feeling, a memory, a colour, or an image. As you breathe in, let your mind form the intention to express this thing; as you breathe out, let the breath realize this intention.

When you feel ready, work through the following sequence of sounds, playing with the connection between sound and intention as you did in *Sound and Meaning*: f, s, v, m, AH, OO, EE, OW.

2. Once you feel that the connection between your intention and breath and sound is fully established, let your imagination begin to explore sounds and images associated with the element of *air*. You might start with the sound of a gentle breeze blowing through trees, or the image of an eagle soaring through the sky. Use the sounds you've been playing with (or any others) to express these ideas. Allow your imagination to suggest other airy ideas – spring gales, autumn leaves, howling winds – or imagine yourself flying over a landscape or a seascape. Let your voice express the images you are visualizing.

3. When you have fully explored *air*, bring yourself back down to the element of *earth*. Think of the feel of earth between your fingers, mud under your feet or sand between your toes. Imagine the different creatures that live underground: moles, worms, rabbits. Envisage the power of an earthquake, the grandeur of a mountain and the loneliness of moors. Take time to be specific and use vocal sounds to express these ideas. Let your imagination free-associate with other earthy ideas – let your voice express the images you are visualizing. Does your body want to become involved in some way? Stay lying down for the time being, but explore using your body to support how your voice is expressing intention through sound.

4. From *earth*, move on to the element of *fire*. Imagine the warmth of a living fire on a winter's night or the danger of a forest fire in summer. There's the exciting variety of fireworks, the calming glow of

a smouldering log; the violence of a volcano and the slow spread of molten lava; the beauty of starlight and the strength of the sun; the fire in your heart and the fire in your belly. Again, take time to be specific and use vocal sounds to express these ideas. Let your imagination free-associate with other images of fire – let your voice express the images you are seeing. Stay connected to centre, but allow your body to become more involved – you might want to move on to your knees or even stand up.

5. Finally, immerse yourself in *water*. Picture a rushing brook, a placid pond or wild waves out in the ocean. Feel the cold rush of a morning shower, the relaxing warmth of a bath; taste the purity of a mountain spring or the pungency of alcohol; hear the sound of surf, the crash of a torrent and the shudder of hail. Be specific in your sense-memories – let them affect your breath and feed them into your vocalization. Once again, let your imagination free-associate with other images of water, and let your voice express the images you are seeing. Stay connected to centre, and allow your body to be involved.

When you've finished, take some time to reflect on the sequence of work and what you've discovered about sound, meaning and language. For example, did different elements suggest ideas more quickly than others? Where did your imagination take you, and did it make a difference to involve your body?

6. Pick up the following extract from Wordsworth's 'The Prelude' and read through it out loud. If you're unsure of the meaning of any words, ask your teacher to explain them:

>   The immeasurable height
> Of woods decaying, never to be decayed,
> The stationary blasts of water-falls,
> And every where along the hollow rent
> Winds thwarting winds, bewildered and forlorn,
> The torrents shooting from the clear blue sky,
> The rocks that muttered close upon the ears,
> Black drizzling crags that spake by the way-side
> As if a voice were in them, the sick sight
> And giddy prospect of the raving stream,
> The unfettered clouds, and region of the Heavens,
> Tumult and peace, the darkness and the light

Were all like workings of one mind, the features
Of the same face, blossoms upon one tree,
Characters of the great Apocalypse,
The types and symbols of Eternity,
Of first and last, and midst, and without end.

Now read through the text again, looking for the words that are connected to the elements; explore using sound and movement to express that connection. Has your relationship to language changed as a result of your exploration?

> *Teaching tip:* You will need to prepare the text, preferably double-spaced, in a large, easy-to-read font, to hand out to the class. You could also try this exercise with other texts.

Verbal dynamics I (10–15 minutes)

This exercise was inspired by the work of Christabel Burniston and Jocelyn Bell, of the English Speaking Board, as described in their book *Into the Life of Things*.

    1. Begin by stretching your body in any way and direction that you feel like. Now, repeat the physical action, but as you do so, say the word *stretch* at the same time, fitting the word to the action. Explore stretching in different ways, each time letting your voice stretch out the word to fit the timing of the physical action. What happens to the word and how you express its meaning? Which parts of the word do you stretch out – the vowel, particular consonants, or all of it?

    Now, take the word *shrink*, and work with it in the same way: performing the physical action of shrinking and saying the word at the same time. What happened this time to the word and your vocal expression, to the vowel and the consonants?

    2. You're now going to use the same idea to explore some words of similar meaning. Start with the word *pull* – perform the action and

say the word at the same time. Imagine pulling a rope with a series of different-sized objects at the end of it: a sack of potatoes, a horse, a balloon, a toy car, a real car. How does the way you say the word reflect the action – what does the initial *p* give you? How does the vowel contribute to the action? And the final *l*? When you've fully explored *pull*, move on to the word/action *tug*, and work in a similar way: imagine tugging a series of different objects or people. How do the different ways of tugging affect the way you say the word? What is the difference between pulling and tugging? How is this reflected in the sounds of the two words? Compare these words/actions with *drag* or *haul*. What is the difference in meaning? How does this affect the way you use the sounds of the word?

You can substitute other groups of words of similar meaning. For example: *jump, hop, leap, bound*.

3. Here are some other words to explore: *float, glide, slide, stride, strut, skip, sneak, slink, twist, bulge, budge, nudge, shift, drift, drip, drizzle, freeze*. Take time to think about the similarities and differences between these words and their sounds and movements. For example, what is the difference between 'floating' and 'gliding' in meaning and how is this difference reflected in the sounds and the physical action?

4. Most of the words we've used so far have a clear physical action associated with them, but see what you can do with the following words: *dream, misty, cloud, soft, flood, swamp, crust, molten, tree, avalanche, thunder, calm*. As before, speak the word and perform a physical action suggested by the word at the same time. Don't think about it too much, just let your body respond to your imagination. How easy was it to find a physical action for these words? Was the action suggested by the meaning or by the sound of the word? How did the action affect the way you said the word?

5. Finally, explore the following more abstract words: *green, blue, wish, envy, power, force, ease, peace*. Which words took on more physical shape and energy? How far did this reflect the meaning? How did it affect the sounds of the words? How were words of similar meaning different?

What have you learnt about vowels and consonants, and their relationship to meaning? Do you think this could be applied to all language?

Verbal dynamics II (20–30 minutes)

VIDEO LINK

Verbal dynamics: https://vimeo.com/268972017

This exercise builds on the previous one and was also inspired by the work of Christabel Burniston and Jocelyn Bell, of the English Speaking Board, as described in their book *Into the Life of Things*.

1. Begin by stretching your body in any way and direction that you feel like. Now, repeat the physical action, but as you do so, say the word *stretch* at the same time, fitting the word to the action. Explore stretching in different ways, each time letting your voice stretch out the word to fit the timing of the physical action.

2. Here are some other words to explore: *tender, hidden, frost, roots, ascend, leaf, break, grave, life, tips, nurse, death*.

3. These words come from the Christina Rossetti poem 'Spring' that we worked with in the *Secret Song* exercise. Look at the first stanza of this poem again, and explore fitting each word to a physical action. Let all the sounds in the word inform the movement and discover the quality of the sounds through the movement. Take each word on its own and give yourself time to experiment with different possibilities of action and meaning, even with words like *all, or* and *of*.

4. When you have worked through each word on its own, go back to the beginning of the poem and start joining the words together, still speaking and physicalizing at the same time.

5. Finally, stand still and speak the whole stanza through, letting the memory of your physical actions be present in your voice.

> *Teaching tip:* See the exercise *Secret Song* for the passage. You might like to explore the whole poem if you have time. The exercise works well with other texts too.

SOUND

Onomatopoeia (10–15 minutes)

Dylan Thomas made extensive use of onomatopoeia in his play *Under Milk Wood*, which was originally written for radio and so was ideally suited to language which conjures meaning for the listener through its sound effects.

1. Speak this short extract from *Under Milk Wood* out loud, getting the feeling and sense of the language inside you. If you're unsure of the meaning of any words, ask your teacher to explain them:

> There's the clip clop of horses on the sunhoneyed cobbles of the humming streets, hammering of horseshoes, gobble quack and cackle, tomtit twitter from the bird-ounced boughs, braying on Donkey Down. Bread is baking, pigs are grunting, chop goes the butcher, milk-churns bell, tills ring, sheep cough, dogs shout, saws sing. Oh, the Spring whinny and morning moo from the clog dancing farms, the gulls' gab and rabble on the boat-bobbing river and sea and the cockles bubbling in the sand, scamper of sanderlings, curlew cry, crow caw, pigeon coo, clock strike, bull bellow, and the ragged gabble of the beargarden school as the women scratch and babble in Mrs Organ Morgan's general shop where everything is sold: custard, buckets, henna, rat-traps, shrimp-nets, sugar, stamps, confetti, paraffin, hatchets, whistles.

2. Now, find a partner and decide which of you is A and which B. While A speaks the text out loud, B is going to try to create the actual sounds that the onomatopoetic words are suggesting. Remember, onomatopoeia is the term used for language which imitates the sound it describes. So, for example, when A says 'the clip clop of horses', B will make the sound of horses' hooves striking the ground. You can use your body (stomping feet etc.) or your voice to make these sounds. Since there are a lot of such words in this passage, A may need to speak quite slowly.

3. Swap over. Now, while B speaks the text slowly, A imitates the sounds by repeating the onomatopoetic words or phrases themselves – for example by saying 'clip clop' in such a way that it sounds like the horse's hooves.

4. Individually now, speak the text through slowly, using the sounds in all the words to help evoke the thing being described. Can you feel how your lips and tongue are constantly moving? Speak it through again, and taste how all the words feel in your mouth. Close your eyes, and

listen to the patterns of vowel sounds, feel the clusters of consonants, and see all the different creatures and people which inhabit the town.

Sound patterns

A pattern usually implies some kind of repetition. One of the most familiar forms of sound repetition is **rhyme**. A rhyme happens when the final vowel sound and any following consonant sounds in two words are the same. So *go* and *slow; beast* and *least; stuff* and *enough* all rhyme. (Note that the words don't have to be spelt the same to rhyme.) Sometimes this principle can be extended so that the rhyme encompasses more than the final vowel and consonants; in *breezily* and *easily*, for example, all three syllables are included in the rhyme.

An important thing to note about rhymes in drama is that they are usually there for a reason. Closing couplets can be used to assert that a character has the final word by putting a sonic 'button' on a scene. Shared rhymes can suggest a growing closeness between characters. Extended rhyming can heighten the emotional stakes of a speech or a scene. Rhymes can give pleasure or irritate, move energy forward or bring energy to a stop. They always do something, and you, as an actor, need to commit to them, not run through them or throw them away.

Another familiar pattern of repetition occurs when we put words together that start with the same consonant sound or cluster of consonant sounds: *terrible twos; friendly fire; rock and roll.* This patterning of sounds is called **alliteration**. As in the last example, the words with matching sounds don't have to be next to each other for us to hear the alliteration; they just *need* to be *near* each other (there's another one).

Repetition of sounds can happen in the middle of words too. A pattern of reoccurring vowel sounds in the middle of words is known as **assonance** – for example, 'Have a great day'. The repetition of consonant sounds within words is called **consonance**, and it too can give texture and depth to the expression of a thought or feeling. Consider this passage from a speech in which Shakespeare's Macbeth is contemplating killing the king:

> If th'assassination
> Could trammel up* the consequence and catch   *tie up in a net*
> With his surcease*, success ...   *death*

Speak it out loud, leaning into the consonants just a bit. The rapid-fire reiteration of the *k* and *s* sounds expresses some of the urgency and tension that Macbeth is feeling – it's a kind of emotional onomatopoeia.

Subtler patterns of sound like this are not necessarily used by characters as consciously as a rhyme would be, but they do help characters to accomplish what they set out to do when they opened their mouths to speak. While they may not be planned, they are found in the moment because they suit the purpose. In the above example, Macbeth is probably not thinking, 'Hmmm, a sequence of *s* and *k* sounds would really capture how I feel about killing the king right now', but he *feels* it. As he chooses each word, he senses how the sound pattern gives momentum to his thought. The exercises that follow are partly about identifying these sound patterns, but mostly about discovering how they release the energy of an idea in the moment of speaking – how they serve the intention.

Rhyming partners (5–10 minutes)

Get together with a partner, and try to sustain a conversation that rhymes for as long as you can. Don't feel bound by the truth, incidentally – just make stuff up. Start with couplets, so that each group of two sentences or phrases rhyme: 'This weekend my cousin came to stay, so we went out to see a play. It really wasn't very good. The actors seemed to be made of wood.' See if you can share some rhymes between you, perhaps with questions and answers: 'What did you do last night?' 'I couldn't go out cos I was filled with fright.' 'What was it that scared you so?' 'A huge exam, don't you know?' If you're getting really good, try some rhymes that alternate: 'I just sat around with my cat. He really loves to eat. That's why he's getting so big and fat. But I love him cos he's sweet.' When you've finished, discuss how the rhyming influenced the tone and energy of the conversation.

Rap the rhyme (5–10 minutes depending on the length of the text)

This is a quick and fun exercise that works well with any rhyming text. You can try it with the Helena and Hermia dialogue used below in *Dramatic Patterns I*; Restoration prologues and epilogues are also good. See *Suggested Texts* for some ideas.

Take your text and find a space where you can work on your own.

Try speaking through the text with a rap rhythm. Rap music developed in inner-city African American and Latinx communities in the United States during the 1960s and 1970s and is characterized by chanted lyrics over a steady beat, a strong landing on down beats and strong lifting of rhyming words. (Its most notable use in theatre is in the award-winning musical *Hamilton*.) Experiment with using this type of rhythm on any of the suggested texts, putting it into your body as well as your voice.

When you've finished, read through the text again without the rap rhythm but keeping the sense of lifting, almost showing off the rhyming words.

Poetic patterns (20–30 minutes)

VIDEO LINK

Poetic patterns: https://vimeo.com/268961230

Gerard Manley Hopkins was a Victorian poet who pushed the use of sound patterns to the extreme. Take a look at the first stanza of his poem 'Spring':

> Nothing is so beautiful as spring –
> When weeds, in wheels, shoot long and lovely and lush;
> Thrush's eggs look little low heavens, and thrush
> Through the echoing timber does so rinse and wring
> The ear, it strikes like lightnings to hear him sing:
> The glassy peartree leaves and blooms, they brush
> The descending blue; that blue is all in a rush
> With richness; the racing lambs too have fair their fling.

Read it out loud. How many sound patterns can you recognize?

SOUND

We'd like you to be quite methodical at this stage. So, first, look at the end of each line and notice the rhymes. How many different rhymes does Hopkins use in this stanza, and how does he arrange them?

A common method of identifying rhyme is to assign a different letter of the alphabet to each new set of rhyming words: (A) represents the first set of rhymes; (B) the second; (C) the third; and so on. Hopkins uses just two sets of rhyming words in this stanza: -*ing* words and -*ush* words; and he arranges them as ABBA, ABBA.

Speak the text through again, and really dwell in those rhyming words. What does it feel like to repeat those sounds? And in that order? Where else does Hopkins use -*ing* and -*ush* sounds in this stanza? What does this add to the feeling of the poem?

Now, notice any alliteration at the beginning of words. What are the particular consonant sounds that Hopkins uses for alliteration? You might like to underline them with different coloured pencils. (We told you Hopkins liked to push things to the extreme.) Work with these sounds individually, exploring the feeling of them in your mouth and body. Imagine the sights, sounds and smells of springtime as you do so.

Speak the text through again, and really enjoy the alliteration – it will probably feel way over the top, but relish it and see how it makes you feel about the words. Notice how Hopkins uses some of the same consonant sounds in clusters with each other. Are there particular consonant sounds that occur throughout the stanza? What does this add to the feeling of the poem?

Now, look at the patterns of vowels in the poem and notice any assonance running through it. Are there particular vowel sounds which Hopkins returns to? You might like to underline them with different coloured pencils. Work with these sounds individually, exploring the feeling of them in your mouth and body. Imagine the sights, sounds and smells of springtime as you do so.

Get a partner. Partner A, read the poem to B, giving particular energy to the *rhyming* sounds.

B, read the poem to A, giving particular energy to the *alliterative* sounds.

A, read the poem to B, giving particular energy to the *assonant* sounds.

B, read the poem to A, not leaning into any sounds in particular, but with an awareness of all the sound patterns you've discovered, letting the sights, sounds and smells of springtime resonate in you as you do so.

> *Teaching tip:* As an antidote to Hopkins's lush use of sound, you might like to look at some of the verse of William McGonagall. McGonagall, a Scotsman, was a weaver, an amateur actor and a poet. His poem, 'The Tay Bridge Disaster', is often described as the best bad poem ever written. He was a contemporary of Hopkins, and it's fun to compare the two for their different approaches to poetry.

Dramatic patterns

Just as Hopkins is a good example of a writer who uses sound patterns for a poetic intent, Shakespeare is a great example of a playwright who uses them for dramatic purpose. We looked earlier at a short example of Shakespeare's use of sound patterns in Macbeth's speech which begins 'If it were done when 'tis done'. Now, we're going to explore some examples from Shakespeare's plays *A Midsummer Night's Dream* and *Richard III* to look in more detail at how he uses rhyme, alliteration and other patterns for dramatic effect.

I. *(15–20 minutes)*
Look at the first of the extracts, from Act I, Scene 1 of the *Dream*. This is a section from an extended sequence in rhyming couplets between Hermia, Lysander and Helena, three young Athenians. Hermia and Lysander are deeply in love. Helena loves Demetrius, another young Athenian, but he only has eyes for Hermia. Helena wants Hermia to teach her how to make Demetrius fall in love with her.

HELENA
    O, teach me how you look, and with what art
    You sway the motion of Demetrius' heart.

HERMIA
I frown upon him, yet he loves me still.
HELENA
O that your frowns would teach my smiles such skill!
HERMIA
I give him curses, yet he gives me love.
HELENA
O that my prayers could such affection move!
HERMIA
The more I hate, the more he follows me.
HELENA
The more I love, the more he hateth me.
HERMIA
His folly, Helena, is no fault of mine.
HELENA
None, but your beauty: would that fault were mine!
HERMIA
Take comfort: he no more shall see my face;
Lysander and myself will fly this place.

Get into pairs and decide who is to be Helena and Hermia, and then speak the passage through a couple of times to get the sense of the dialogue.

Speak it through again, but now explore the rhymes. (Note: although 'love' and 'move' are only half-rhymes for us, they would have originally rhymed for Shakespeare.) First, speak it as if your character is unaware that there is any rhyme.

Next, speak it and emphasize both rhyming words – make an appropriate gesture at the same time as speaking the rhyming word, as this helps to put energy in the language.

Finally, speak it with an awareness of the rhyme, but only gesture on the second rhyming word.

Discuss with your partner the dramatic effect of each choice. What did you discover about the energy of the rhyming words? Some of the rhymes are simply repetitions of the word at the end of the previous line. Is this Shakespeare being lazy, or does it suggest something shifts between the characters?

You might like to look now at the whole scene (Act I, Scene 1, lines 128–251) and explore how the rhyming couplets (which begin at line 171) help shape its emotional development.

II. *(15–20 minutes)*
Now, look at the second of the extracts, from Act V, Scene 1 of the *Dream*. This is taken from the comical Pyramus and Thisbe scene near the end of the play. In it, Pyramus discovers the bloody cloak of his love, Thisbe, and assumes that she is dead. He is so distraught that he decides to kill himself. Shakespeare infuses this tragic moment with comedy partly through his use of rhyme and alliteration.

PYRAMUS
    Sweet Moon, I thank thee for thy sunny beams;
    I thank thee, Moon, for shining now so bright;
    For, by thy gracious, golden, glittering gleams,
    I trust to take of truest Thisbe sight.
    But stay, O spite!
    But mark, poor knight,
    What dreadful dole* is here!   *sorrow*
    Eyes, do you see?
    How can it be?
    O dainty duck! O dear!
    Thy mantle* good,   *cloak*
    What, stained with blood!
    Approach, ye Furies fell*!   *cruel*
    O Fates, come, come,
    Cut thread and thrum*;   *tufted end of thread*
    Quail, crush, conclude, and quell!

    Speak the text through a couple of times to get the sense of it.
    Speak it through again, and notice the amount of alliteration in the speech. Repeat, and really indulge in the alliteration. Feel free to have fun and go over the top.
    Speak it through again, but now explore the rhymes. (Note: although 'good' and 'blood' are only half-rhymes for us, they would have originally rhymed for Shakespeare.)
    How many different rhymes does Shakespeare use in this speech, and how does he arrange them? Mark up your text with (A), (B), (C) etc.

just to be clear. Why do you think Shakespeare chose this particular arrangement of rhymes? What dramatic purpose might it serve?

Now, as you speak the speech through again, make a very melodramatic gesture or action as you say each rhyming word. Again, feel free to go over the top.

Finally, say the text with a full sense of both the alliteration and the rhyme. Can you feel how much of the comic potential of the language is in the sounds?

III. (*30–40 minutes*)
Take a look at the extract from Gloucester's opening soliloquy in *Richard III*. This speech is fascinating for many reasons, but here we'd like to explore how Shakespeare uses sound patterns to sharpen Gloucester's expression of cynicism. Richard of Gloucester and his brothers of the House of York have just defeated the followers of the House of Lancaster in a vicious civil war. Gloucester's eldest brother, Edward, has been proclaimed king, but Richard sees no place for himself in peacetime. His physical deformities don't make him a natural courtier, and so he'd rather be a villain than a lover.

GLOUCESTER

Now is the winter of our discontent	
Made glorious summer by this sun of York;	
And all the clouds that loured* upon our house	*frowned*
In the deep bosom of the ocean buried.	
Now are our brows bound with victorious wreaths;	
Our bruisèd arms hung up for monuments;	
Our stern alarums* changed to merry meetings,	*battle cries*
Our dreadful marches to delightful measures*.	*dances*
Grim-visaged war hath smoothed his wrinkled front*;	*face*
And now, instead of mounting barbèd steeds*	*armoured horses*
To fright the souls of fearful adversaries,	
He capers nimbly in a lady's chamber	
To the lascivious pleasing of a lute.	
But I, that am not shaped for sportive* tricks,	*amorous*
Nor made to court an amorous looking-glass;	
I, that am rudely stamped*, and want love's majesty	*roughly formed*

To strut before a wanton* ambling nymph;	*lascivious, lustful*
I, that am curtailed of this fair proportion,	
Cheated of feature by dissembling* nature,	*false*
Deformed, unfinished, sent before my time	
Into this breathing world, scarce half made up,	
And that so lamely and unfashionable	
That dogs bark at me as I halt* by them;	*limp*
Why, I, in this weak piping time of peace,	
Have no delight to pass away the time,	
Unless to spy my shadow in the sun	
And descant on* mine own deformity:	*comment on*
And therefore, since I cannot prove a lover,	
To entertain these fair well-spoken days,	
I am determined to prove a villain	
And hate the idle pleasures of these days.	

We've divided the speech into two parts. Begin by looking at the first. Speak it through a couple of times to get the feel of the language in your mouth. If you need to check on the meaning or pronunciation of any words, that's fine. Ask your teacher or look them up in a dictionary or online.

Now, speak it through again, giving a strong energy to all the consonant sounds. You might like to try whispering it as well, as this helps to focus more energy in the consonants. What patterns of alliteration and consonance can you feel? What sounds and clusters of sounds does Gloucester use most often? Does the balance of sounds shift at any point?

Speak it through again, relishing the patterns of sounds you've discovered. What does this tell you about how Gloucester is feeling?

Now, speak it again, really giving energy to all the vowel sounds. Perhaps speak the vowel sounds on their own, as this can bring out the patterns more vividly, but make sure you pronounce them as they sound in the fully articulated words. What patterns of assonance can you feel? What vowel sounds does Gloucester use most often? Does the balance of sounds shift at any point?

Speak the passage through again, relishing the patterns of sounds you've discovered. What does this tell you about how Gloucester is feeling?

Repeat the same process with the second part of the speech.

The first part of the speech focuses on Gloucester's experience of the world – the world of the house of York. The second part of the speech focuses on Gloucester's experience of himself – the experience of disability. Put the two parts together now, and speak the whole text through. Feel the vowel and consonant patterns in your mouth. What do you discover about Gloucester as a character from this exploration?

Follow-up

Reflective practice questions:

- Think about words that you use to express enthusiasm – e.g. 'cool' or 'brilliant'. What are the sounds in those words that you emphasize, and how do you emphasize them? By making them longer? Louder? Changing pitch? Think about words that you use to express dismay or frustrations – e.g. 'shoot' or 'darn' (or something stronger if applicable). How do you use the sounds in those words to convey your feelings?
- When you did the exercises, were there any particular sounds that you especially enjoyed working with? Were there any physical sensations that went along with the exploration of those sounds, such as openness or buzzing? Lightness or heaviness? Warmth or coolness?
- Did you find yourself associating any sounds with colours? Emotions? Genders? For example, was EE red, or envious, or masculine?
- Did you find that your lips or tongue or jaw became tired during any of the exercises? If so, do you think you habitually underuse your muscles of articulation? Or might you overuse them?
- When doing the exercises, did you have to create more space than usual in your mouth to fully explore the sounds? If so, try speaking with this amount of openness in every day conversation.

Suggested texts

Consonants

Consonants and content

Howard Barker, *Gertrude – The Cry*, Scene 3, Hamlet: 'I expected to be more moved'
Ben Jonson, *Volpone or The Fox*, Act III Scene 1, Mosca: 'I fear I shall begin to grow in love'
Eugene O'Neill, *The Iceman Cometh*, Act III, Larry: 'I'm afraid to live'
Rajiv Joseph, *Guards at the Taj*, Scene 3, Babur: 'Tumbling, tumbling'

Sound and meaning

Verbal dynamics II

Eisa Davis, *Bulrusher*, Act I, Bulrusher: 'I float in a basket'
Tony Kushner, *Homebody/Kabul*, Act I Scene 1, Homebody: from 'A party needs hats' through 'synchitic expegeses'
Jose Rivera, *Cloud Tectonics*, Celestina: 'How do you know what "time" feels like'
Paula Vogel, *How I Learned to Drive*, Female Greek Chorus: 'A Mother's Guide to Social Drinking'

Sound patterns

Rap the rhyme

Aphra Behn, *The Lucky Chance*, Prologue
Caryl Churchill, *Serious Money*, Act I, Corman: 'Right you all know the position'
William Congreve, *The Way of the World*, Prologue
William Shakespeare, *Love's Labours Lost*, Act V Scene 2, Berowne: 'This fellow pecks up wit'

Poetic patterns

Lewis Carroll, 'Jabberwocky'
Imtiaz Dhaker, 'This Room'
Langston Hughes, 'Jazzonia'
Philip Levine, 'They Feed They Lion'
Sylvia Plath, 'You're'
Anne Stevenson, 'Stasis' from 'Sonnets for Five Seasons'
Derek Walcott, 'In late-afternoon'

Dramatic patterns

Samuel Beckett, *Endgame*, Nagg: 'Let me tell it again'
Caryl Churchill, *The Skriker*, Skriker: 'Josie went futher and murther'
Toni Morrison, *The Bluest Eye*, Act II Scene 2, Soaphead Church: 'Only a musician'
Dylan Thomas, *Under Milk Wood*, first voice: 'And the shrill girls giggle'

Further reading

Adrian, Barbara, *Actor Training the Laban Way*, Allworth Press, New York, 2008.
Ashby, Patricia, *Speech Sounds* (2nd edition), Routledge, London, 2005.
Berry, Cicely, *The Actor and the Text* (revised edition), Virgin Books, London, 1993. Chapter 6: Substance of the Text, pp. 143–156.
Berry, Cicely, *Text in Action*, Virgin Book, London, 2003. 'Vowel and Consonant Length', pp. 164–166.
Burniston, Christabel and Jocelyn Bell, *Into the Life of Things*, English Speaking Board, Southport, Lancashire, 1972.
Carey, David and Rebecca Clark Carey, *The Shakespeare Workbook and Video*, Bloomsbury Methuen Drama, London, 2015. Chapter 2: Language in Action, pp. 85–94.
Carr, Philip, *English Phonetics and Phonology*, Blackwell Publishers, Oxford, 1999.
Colaianni, Louis, *The Joy of Phonetics and Accents*, Drama Book Publishers, New York, 1994.
Houseman, Barbara, *Tackling Text*, Nick Hern Books, London, 2008. 'Connecting with the Vowels', pp. 48–54; 'Connecting with the Consonants', pp. 55–58; 'Rhyme', pp. 116–119.

Lessac, Arthur, *The Use and Training of the Human Voice* (3rd edition), Mayfield Publishing, Mountview, CA, 1997. Chapter 5: The Dynamics of Consonant NRG, pp. 61–121; Chapter 7: The Dynamics of Structural NRG: The Music of the Vowels, pp. 160–184.

Linklater, Kristin, *Freeing Shakespeare's Voice*, Theatre Communications Group, Inc., New York, 1992. Chapter 1: Vowels and Consonants, pp. 11–29; Chapter 7: Rhyme, pp. 141–152.

Newlove, Jean, *Laban for Actors and Dancers*, Nick Hern Books, London, 2001.

Rodenburg, Patsy, *The Actor Speaks*, Methuen, London, 1997. 'Speech Work with the Text', pp. 183–187.

Rodenburg, Patsy, *Speaking Shakespeare*, Methuen, London, 2002. 'Alliteration, Assonance, Onomatopoeia', pp. 78–83; 'Rhyme', pp. 126–154.

Sharpe, Edda and Jan Haydn Rowles, *How to Do Accents* (revised edition), Oberon Books, London, 2009.

Wells, J. C., *Accents of English* (3 volumes), Cambridge University Press, Cambridge, 1982.

2
IMAGE

Framework

One of the most remarkable things about language is how it can awaken our senses and imaginations and help us to perceive things that aren't there. Places we've never visited can seem unforgettable to us if they are described well. We can feel we know characters from favourite novels better than we know our neighbours. A fictional mystery story can give us very real chills. Language creates pictures and sensations in the mind that we respond to as if they were real.

The job of an actor is similar to the job of a writer – to use language to help make real for people things that aren't there. A good writer and a good speaker will use the same tools – detail, energy, inventiveness, variety, bold strokes and subtle shades. As they activate and exercise their own imaginations (through hard work we might add), they activate and exercise the imaginations of their audiences.

For those who wish to use language in this way, it's important not to take words for granted. Language is a very efficient tool. If every time we wanted to communicate something about a flower we had to find one and point to it, very little communication about flowers would take place. It's wonderful that over the centuries of developing the English language we've all agreed that we can just put together the sounds *f, l, OW, ə* and every one will think about those lovely, colourful things with petals that grow on plants. In fact, while still children, we usually become so fluent in this process that when we say or hear those sounds *f, l, OW, ə*, we barely think about the colours, textures, scents of actual flowers at all. That's fine for most casual communication, but if you want to have a deeper impact on your audience, you need to make the things you're talking about real in your own imagination.

For an actor, in particular, it's easy to be so eager to start affecting the audience or one's scene partner that one doesn't take the time to connect to the images imbedded in the language. When the image is not vivid for you, though, it will not be vivid for anyone. The audience will receive a general idea of what you're talking about, but they won't really engage with it – it won't be real for them. The work in this chapter on **literal images** is to help you with this key step – connecting language with sensory perceptions so that the images in your text will be clear and concrete for you and your listeners.

As well as helping us to perceive things that aren't there, language can also convey feelings. It can help us to share what is hidden – build bridges between hearts and minds. In order to communicate our inner world of thoughts and feelings to each other, sometimes we use words that refer to the outer world in non-literal ways. For example, the primary and most concrete meaning of the word 'cold' refers to the sensual experience of a low temperature. Somewhere in the evolution of language, though, people started using it to describe what it feels like when someone is socially unresponsive: 'He was so cold to me.' While the actual temperature in the room doesn't change when someone is aloof, we make associations between the way it makes us feel in our souls and the way we feel in our bodies when it's chilly. This power of association – the way that one word can link two very different phenomena – is one of the most exciting and interesting aspects of language.

There are many examples of how we've come to use 'outside-world' words to express 'inside-world' experiences. One mark of a good writer is that he or she will do this in ways that are fresh and particularly apt. You may never have thought of a soul extending itself into space like a body does, but when deeply in love, many people will read Elizabeth Barrett Browning's line 'I love thee to the depth and breadth and height my soul can reach', and think, 'Yes, that's exactly it'. She has enabled us to make a connection between what we are experiencing and what she has experienced by creating an image – not an image the eye ever has seen or ever will see, but an image that evokes a feeling through the associative power of language. The exercises on **evocative images** will help you to engage with this kind of language and speak it with authenticity and authority, arousing the imaginations of those who hear you.

Exploration

> *Teaching tip:* Many of these explorations could be done in class in groups or with partners.

I. Find a picture – an interesting photograph or a painting (but avoid advertisements or glossy pictures from magazines, as these tend to focus on surface rather than detail). Take 5–10 minutes to write a description of it in your journal. You can then read this description to a friend or classmate and ask him or her to draw a picture based on your description. How well did you communicate the most important features of the picture? How many of the details did your friend get?

II. Look through the library or your book collection for a passage that describes a scene or an object. There are some selections in the *Suggested Texts* section that are good for this, or many novels begin with descriptive paragraphs. Read the passage once, and then try to draw what it portrays. The drawing can be very sketchy – just try to get in all the facts. Go back and read it again to see if you missed any details. Adjust your drawing, and then read the passage out loud.

III. Look around the room and find something blue. Just look at that blue for about 30 seconds, then start to notice if the colour affects you. Is it calming? Depressing? Uplifting? Have any of your muscles tightened as you looked at it? Have any relaxed? Is your breathing any different? Say the word 'blue' – don't think about it too hard, just do it. Find a different shade of blue to look at and repeat the process. Find something red and, again, look at it for 30 seconds, and then reflect on how you've responded to it. Finish by speaking the word, 'red'. You can try this with many different shades of different colours.

IV. Think of a moment yesterday when you experienced a particularly strong emotion – maybe intense frustration in traffic or a rush of affection when a friend did something nice for you. Reflect on that moment – the circumstances, how you felt physically, how you felt inside. Now look around the room. Try to create a comparison to your emotion using something in the room. For example, 'When he came in and kissed me, it was like someone suddenly flipped on a light switch.' Or, 'Sitting in that traffic jam was like trying to push a sofa up the side of a mountain.' Speak your image out loud and see if it expresses the feeling.

V. Think of someone you love. Think about food you like. Find a way to describe the person using food. 'She is a cup of hot cocoa on a cold winter morning.' 'He is the chilli pepper in my curry.' Try to be very precise about lining up the special qualities of your loved one with the right food. Speak your sentence out loud and see if it captures what you'd like to say about that person.

Exercises

> *Teaching tip:* The exercises in this chapter are organized into two sections: *Literal Images* and *Evocative Images*. We would suggest working through the first before moving on to the second.

As with any work on speaking text, it's a good idea to start your sessions with a warm-up. Do some exercises that help you to relax, align your body, feel connected to your breath and give you a sense of ease and openness when using your voice. The exercises set out in *Appendix 1* are a good preparation, as is all the work in our first book, *Vocal Arts Workbook and Video* (particularly from chapters 1, 2 and 5).

Literal images

The following exercises are designed to help you find a vivid and specific connection to your imagination and the descriptive imagery that you meet in any text.

Scene building (10–15 minutes)

As a group, get into a comfortable circle and close your eyes. You are going to create and describe an imaginary scene, taking it in turns to add an element or detail. Decide who is going to begin: this is person A; the person on their left is B and so on round the circle.

When everyone is relaxed and focused, person A begins by saying 'There is …' and describing a visual element of a scene they have begun to imagine. Perhaps they say, 'There is a snow-capped mountain.'

Person B, after taking time to imagine this, then says, 'There is a snow-capped mountain' and adds another element to the scene, perhaps 'and the sun rising behind it'.

Person C takes time to see this scene, and then adds a further element: 'There is a snow-capped mountain and the sun rising behind it. In the foreground is a log cabin.' And so on round the circle. Depending on the size and creativity of the group, the exercise can continue for several turns. Once the scene is complete, individuals can draw a picture of it or write a story about the characters or events portrayed.

Teaching tip: Visualization doesn't come naturally to every student, and so it may be useful to widen the scope of the exercise to include the option to hear or feel elements of the scene that is being described. So, for example, the first student may say 'I hear birds singing in a valley' or 'I feel the cold of a snowy morning'.

The exercise works best in groups of 10–16. It can work with smaller groups. If you have a larger group, you may want to work in two separate circles.

It is useful to remind the group that this is a collaborative exercise which requires focus and sensitivity. Or, you could run the exercise once and, if it doesn't go so well, elicit from the group the need for focus and sensitivity and collaboration.

It is also helpful if students add just a single detail at a time. Person C might have said, 'In the foreground is a log cabin with smoke coming from the chimney. There is a man with a shotgun sitting on the ground – he's skinning a rabbit.' This would have been

> too much information in one go, as it closes down possibilities and inhibits collaboration.
>
> It is important to ensure that students repeat what they have just heard. It encourages listening and collaboration. Of course, as the description gets fuller and more detailed, it becomes more difficult to remember the exact order of the different elements in the scene. However, the point is not to remember everything in the right order but to engage the imagination in a detailed description, and to connect that with language.

Descriptions

Characters in drama are often drawn to describe people, places and landscapes. The following exercises are particularly useful for working with descriptive texts of any kind.

I. Line painting one (*5–10 minutes*)

VIDEO LINK

Line painting: https://vimeo.com/268971556

After a brief warm-up to shake out tensions and wake up your voice, sit comfortably on the floor or in a chair, holding your text in one hand. Read it out loud to the class.

Now, as you read it out loud again, you are going to pretend to paint each thing you talk about. Your painting will be very simple – think of those pictures which use just a few brush strokes to create a portrait or a landscape.

As an example, we're going to use Enobarbus's speech about Cleopatra arriving on a barge from Act II, Scene 2 of Shakespeare's *Antony and Cleopatra*. So, as you read the words 'The barge she sat in, like a burnished throne, burned on the water,' sketch a few lines in the air with your free hand to create a splendid boat on a river. If it takes you a bit longer to sketch something than to speak the words, it's fine to pause. This exercise will slow down your reading considerably, which is part of its purpose.

When you come to things that are more abstract (e.g. 'so perfumèd that the winds were love-sick with them'), you can paint shapes to convey the idea – maybe soft flowing lines to suggest the perfume and the wind's love for it. Don't worry too much about getting it right – just let the images flow through your hand in a simple way.

ENOBARBUS

The barge she sat in, like a burnished throne,
Burned on the water: the poop* was beaten gold; *the rear part of a ship*
Purple the sails, and so perfumèd that
The winds were love-sick with them; the oars were silver,
Which to the tune of flutes kept stroke, and made
The water which they beat to follow faster,
As amorous of their strokes. For her own person,
It beggared all description: she did lie
In her pavilion*–cloth-of-gold of tissue– *tent*
O'er-picturing* that Venus where we see *surpassing*
The fancy* outwork nature: on each side her *imagination*
Stood pretty dimpled boys, like smiling Cupids,
With divers-coloured* fans, whose wind did seem *variously-coloured*
To glow the delicate cheeks which they did cool,
And what they undid did.
Her gentlewomen, like the Nereides*, *sea-nymphs*
So many mermaids, tended her i' the eyes,
And made their bends* adornings: at the helm *glances*
A seeming mermaid steers: the silken tackle* *ropes*
Swell with the touches of those flower-soft hands,
That yarely* frame the office. From the barge *nimbly*
A strange invisible perfume hits the sense
Of the adjacent wharfs. The city cast
Her people out upon her; and Antony,
Enthroned i' the market-place, did sit alone,

Whistling to the air; which, but for vacancy,
Had gone to gaze on Cleopatra too,
And made a gap in nature.

When you've finished, read the speech out loud again.

Discuss what changed for you from the first reading to the last and what changed for the listeners.

> *Teaching tip:* In this exercise and the one below, you may want to have the students all find a place in the room where they can work on their own simultaneously – e.g. all of them doing their line paintings at the same time. When they come together, either all of them or a few volunteers can do a final reading of their pieces for the group. While it takes more time, it can also be very useful for the students to watch one another work through the process. You may want to have all the students do the exercise in front of each other, one after another, or, again, you could ask a few volunteers to try the entire exercise in front of the group and then send the others off to work on their own simultaneously. You can also have the students each work with a different text.

II. Breathe the image (*7–10 minutes*)

Find a piece of text that uses a good deal of imagery for this exercise. (See *Suggested Texts* for some ideas.)

After a brief warm-up of stretching and centring your breath, find a comfortable stance with soft knees, soft shoulders and jaw, and a long neck.

Hold your text up in front of your face with one hand.

Read the first sentence silently to yourself.

Lower the paper and breathe in fully but quietly as you simply think about that first sentence and picture what it's talking about – a person, a place etc. If the sentence is complex, feel free to take more than one breath to consider all the elements in it.

When you have a clear picture in your mind (and have taken a full in-breath), raise the paper in front of your face again and whisper that first sentence – just breath, no voice at all.

Let your breath fill again, and then speak the sentence out loud.

Repeat until you have worked your way through the text one sentence at a time, and then simply read the entire text out loud.

You can do this exercise with a partner: stand facing your partner and whisper then speak each line to him or her then switch.

Narratives (10–20 minutes per student)

Many dramatic situations involve people telling stories. From Greek tragedies to soap operas, characters describe events that have happened offstage, using vivid narrative images. The following exercises are useful for working with any text that involves narrative imagery: folk tales, children's stories, as well as dramatic storytelling. In our teaching, we often introduce these techniques through work on fairy stories, folk tales and children's literature, moving on at a later stage to Shakespearean monologues, Greek messenger speeches or Restoration prologues, as well as contemporary dramatic material. We set out the exercises here as if you are working on a folk tale or fairy story, but as a next step you could apply them to a passage from a play where a character is telling a story. See *Suggested Texts* for some other pieces to work with.

Each person in the class should bring in a fairy story or folk tale. If your story takes longer than 3–4 minutes to read out loud, you can use an excerpt. There are many good collections available in libraries and on the internet. Look for something traditional and relatively simple from any storytelling tradition that speaks to you.

After a 10–15-minute vocal warm-up, one person at a time stands in front of the class and reads their story out loud. Then each student tries one of the following:

I. Sculptures

Five or six members of the class need to volunteer to be 'clay'.

Read the first sentence or two of your story out loud and then, gently and respectfully, move your 'clay' into sculptures that will illustrate what you have just described. If your story starts in a forest, you may want to start by moulding a couple of people into trees – lifting their arms into branches, for example.

If you want your clay to have a specific facial expression, you can model what you want and let the 'clay' copy it rather than trying to mould faces.

Go back to your story and read another sentence or two out loud. Every time something significant happens, stop reading and make the appropriate changes to your sculpture. You may need to do this every sentence or two, which may slow you down considerably, but that's fine. (Just make sure you don't let any of your 'clay' get stuck in an uncomfortable position for very long.)

Continue until you have worked your way through the first few major events of the story – about 8–10 minutes. Then let your 'clay' sit down and read the story again.

Discuss what changed for you from the first reading to the last and what changed for the listeners.

II. Actors

Members of the class need to volunteer to be actors in your narrative.

Begin to speak your narrative out loud, and then, as you mention any characters or creatures in your story, allocate the part to your actors. Now it is their job to act out their characters' parts of the story. You should continue telling the story, but your actors will act it out in front of you. You'll need to take your time and be clear and specific in shaping the events of the narrative so that your actors understand their parts and how they can best act.

Continue until you have worked your way through the first few major events of the story – about 5 or 6 minutes. Then, ask your actors if there were any episodes in the story which were unclear. Repeat the exercise, focusing on those particular episodes until your actors are able to fully play their part, and then let them sit down.

Read the story again by yourself. Discuss what changed for you from the first reading to the last and what changed for the listeners.

III. All the parts

In this exercise, you get to play all the parts.

Glance through your story and identify all the places that are mentioned – a cottage in the woods, a castle, a gingerbread house, a stream etc. Decide where in the room you want each of these places to be and put a chair in each one.

Read the first part of your story out loud. Whenever you come to a new character, you must physically transform yourself into that character – be it a wolf, an old woman, a princess etc. – and stand in the space where that character is (the castle, the cottage etc.). You must also speak as each character whenever they say anything. Whenever a character goes from one place to another, you must travel through the room from one chair to another. Be aware that the narrator is separate from the other characters. You may need to read a bit out loud and then stop reading while you perform the appropriate action or switch from one character to another – that's fine.

Work this way for about 5 or 6 minutes or until you've finished the story.

Once you've finished playing the parts, simply stand in front of the group and read the story again.

Discuss what changed for you from the first reading to the last and what changed for the listeners.

IV. Sandbox

VIDEO LINK

Sandbox: https://vimeo.com/268962778

Get a variety of objects from the room or your bag (a book, a pencil case, an umbrella, a shoe etc.) and place them in front of you on the floor – you'll probably need about a dozen things.

Sit down like a kid in a sandbox and begin to read your story out loud. As you do, use the objects to illustrate what you're talking about. So, if you are talking about a boy and girl walking through the woods, you might take a pencil case and an umbrella and move them together across the space in front of you. If they get in a fight, you might make them hop up and down with anger as they 'speak' – think of how little kids tell stories with their toys.

For each new element of the story, pick up a new object – if you don't have enough hands to keep all the relevant 'figures' in play, you may need to leave one or two on the ground when they are not the most active. This will slow you down considerably, and you may need to take a bit of time to find your place on the page when you look away from it – that's fine.

Work this way for about 7 or 8 minutes or until you have finished the story.

Finally, stand back up and read the story again.

Discuss what changed for you from the first reading to the last and what changed for the listeners.

V. Take a walk

Get a partner and take him or her by the arm.

Holding your story in the other hand, start to read it fairly slowly. Every time something new happens in the story, take your partner for a little walk to a different part of the room so they can 'see' what is happening there. You may need to turn them around so they can see the prince ride by or take them to one side of the room to look at the great mountain where the dragon lives. You may need to crouch down together to get a good look at the golden egg in the nest. Feel free to stop talking long enough to physically point out what you're talking about, and check in to make sure your partner is really seeing it as clearly as you are.

Work this way for about 7 or 8 minutes or until you have finished the story.

Finally, let your partner re-join the rest of the class and simply stand and read the story again.

Discuss what changed for you from the first reading to the last and what changed for the listeners.

Cameraman (20–30 minutes)

For this exercise, we're going to use the Chorus speech from Act III of Shakespeare's *Henry V*. In this text, Shakespeare uses language to create a dramatic visual narrative to engage his audience because his Elizabethan theatre lacked the resources to stage such an epic event. The Chorus jokes about this throughout the play, in fact. Modern theatre and, in particular, film have much greater resources. What Shakespeare achieves with language, a film director today would achieve with camera movements and editing. This exercise is designed to reveal the dynamic potential of verbal imagery through a connection with the visual imagery of the movies.

CHORUS

Thus with imagined wing our swift scene flies
In motion of no less celerity* *speed*
Than that of thought. Suppose that you have seen
The well-appointed* king at Hampton pier *well-equipped*
Embark his royalty; and his brave fleet
With silken streamers the young Phoebus* fanning: *sun god*
Play with your fancies, and in them behold
Upon the hempen tackle* ship-boys climbing; *ropes*
Hear the shrill whistle which doth order give
To sounds confused; behold the threaden*
   sails, *canvas*
Borne with the invisible and creeping wind,
Draw the huge bottoms through the furrowed sea,
Breasting the lofty surge: O, do but think
You stand upon the rivage* and behold *shore*
A city on the inconstant billows* dancing; *waves*
For so appears this fleet majestical,
Holding due course to Harfleur. Follow, follow:
Grapple your minds to sternage of this
   navy*, *sterns of the whole fleet*
And leave your England, as dead midnight still,
Guarded with grandsires, babies and old women,
Either past or not arrived to pith and
   puissance*; *strength and power*
For who is he, whose chin is but enriched
With one appearing hair, that will not follow
These culled* and choice-drawn cavaliers to France? *selected*
Work, work your thoughts, and therein see a siege;
Behold the ordnance* on their carriages, *cannon*
With fatal mouths gaping on girded* Harfleur. *besieged*
Suppose the ambassador from the French comes back;
Tells Harry that the king doth offer him
Katharine his daughter, and with her, to dowry,
Some petty and unprofitable dukedoms.
The offer likes not: and the nimble gunner
With linstock* now the devilish cannon touches,
   stick holding a lighted match

And down goes all before them. Still be kind,
And eke out* our performance with your mind.   *add to*

1. Begin by walking round the room muttering the text to yourself just to feel the words in your mouth and on your tongue.

Don't worry about making complete sense of it at this point. However, if there are words that you don't recognize or know the meaning of, take a moment or two to check your understanding and pronunciation of them in a dictionary or with your teacher.

2. Now, speak the text out loud as you move around the room. As you do so, physicalize each of the images in the text as you speak it – perhaps you might embody it, or act it out, or just use your hands and arms to describe it in some way. Take your time to really imagine each detail of the scene and to be specific in your physicalization as you speak the words.

Again, don't worry about making complete sense of the speech; your focus is on the individual images. However, you may find that you need to clarify the meaning of other words in the text once you've finished. That's fine. Again, take a moment or two to check your understanding and pronunciation of these words in a dictionary or with your teacher.

When you are ready, speak and physicalize the text again but allow the images to flow into each other more smoothly.

What have you discovered about the images in this text? Are they all of the same kind or size? Are they all visual? Are they static or dynamic? What are some of the most vivid images? How is Shakespeare using language to create these images? How is this similar to the movements of a film camera?

3. You are now going to imagine that you are a film cameraman who is filming this scene. (You might like to imagine you are holding a camera in your hand.) Shakespeare's text is the film script and, as you speak it through, you are going to record the events using a range of camera movements and edits. You might need to review the most common camera effects before you begin: for example, long shot, close-up, aerial shot, pan, tracking shot, cut, montage.

Work through the text a couple of times, speaking the text while you imagine that you are filming the scene in front of you. The first time through, take time to imagine the point of view of each moment: Where does the language suggest that the camera is situated? Is it in the air,

IMAGE

on the English shore, on a ship? Is it tilted up or down? Does it move or cut from image to image? Speak the language and see the scene unfold before you from that point of view.

The second time through, speak and film the text again but allow the images to flow into each other more smoothly.

4. Finish the exercise by speaking the text through once more, without either physicalizing or filming, but keeping your visual imagination engaged in the language as you say it.

Reflect on the journey that you've been on with this text. What have you learnt about imagery in language? What have you learnt about acting with this kind of language?

> *Teaching tip:* In this exercise, you may want to have the students all find a place in the room where they can work on their own simultaneously. They can then come together and either all of them or a few volunteers can take part in a final reading of their pieces for the group. While this takes more time, it can also be very useful for the students to watch one another work through the process.

Evocative images

Where literal images help us to understand what another person sees, evocative images help us to understand what another person feels. A particularly potent way to make the connection between the world outside, which we sense, and the world inside, which we feel, is to say that something is 'like' something else. When Robert Burns famously wrote that 'My love is like a red, red rose that's newly sprung in June', he was comparing the feelings he had for his beloved with his sensual experience (the colour, texture, smell, shape, freshness) of a freshly blooming rose, and in this way expressed a tenderness which still speaks to us today. This kind of comparison is called a **simile**. Similes are usually easy to spot because they use the word 'like', or sometimes the word 'as', to link things together. If you haven't already, go back and try *Exploration IV* for some work on creating similes.

Even more compelling than saying that something is like something else is saying that it *is* something else. When John Donne wrote that 'She's all states, and all princes, I', he captured the intensity of his passion for his beloved by boldly announcing that she was all countries and he all monarchs – that's how huge and important their love was to him. This calling one thing something else ('Juliet is the sun') is known as **metaphor**. Metaphors break boundaries. They can use language to take us places we'd never imagined. If you haven't already, go back and try *Exploration V* for some work on creating metaphors.

Another way that we use images to make connections is by employing them as **symbols**. There are very specific Greek terms for different kinds of symbols, which we will not refer to here; instead we will use the general term 'symbol' to talk about an image of one thing representing something else. For example, in show business, it's common for creative artists (actors, directors, writers etc.) to refer to administrators (producers, accountants, network executives) as the 'suits'. The actual suits become a symbol for the people who wear them. In the hands of a good writer, symbols can become quite complex and evocative. When T. S. Eliot writes, in 'The Love Song of J. Alfred Prufrock', 'I have measured out my life with coffee spoons', the image symbolizes the whole experience of spending all one's time on the mild stimulation of trivial social encounters. Eliot uses something from the outside world to symbolize an internal feeling of futility.

The following exercises will help you develop your sensitivity to evocative imagery. The more precision and care you bring to similes, metaphors and symbols, the better you will be able to use them to express a great deal with a minimum of effort.

Line painting two (10–15 minutes)

This exercise was inspired by the work of Sue Cowen.

Instead of working on your own, find a partner to share the painting with.

After a brief warm-up to shake out tensions and wake up your voice, read your text out loud to your partner (see *Suggested Texts* for some ideas).

IMAGE

This time, as you read the text out loud again, stand next to your partner and take one of her hands in your free hand and guide it to create a line painting of the images. So, if you were doing Romeo's speech comparing Juliet to an angel, as you read the words 'As is a wingèd messenger of heaven', you would help your partner to sketch a few lines in the air with her hand to create an angel with wings.

If it takes you a bit longer to sketch something than to speak the words, it's fine to pause. The important thing to remember is that you are speaking the text while physically guiding your partner to paint the images. Don't worry too much about getting it right – just let the images flow through you into your partner's hand in a simple way.

When you've finished, read the speech out loud again.

Swap over, so that you become the painter for your partner's text.

Discuss what changed for you from the first reading to the last and what changed for your partner.

Sensual imagery (20–30 minutes)

> *Teaching tip:* Before beginning the language-based work in *Sensual Imagery*, you may find it useful to explore the exercise *The Elements* from Chapter 1 (*Sound*).

1. Lie on the floor in supine or semi-supine and connect to your centred breath. Take a moment to recall a moment of intense emotion: joy, fear, anger, sadness, passion. Remember the feelings it generated in you – how would you describe those feelings to someone, what images would you use? Think of comparisons of height, depth, breadth, length; of other physical sensations such as taste, sight, hearing, smell; of another creature; and of the elements of earth, water, fire and air.

2. Find a partner and take it in turns to use those images to describe the feelings in language (you don't have to narrate the event itself). For example, 'It was like a hurricane. It was immense, like a mountain. I just

wanted the earth to open and swallow me up. I could hear it roaring in my ears, like a lion. It was a snake coiling inside my stomach.'

Focus on partner A's description. Partner B, as A speaks, you should listen and allow the images to resonate inside your body and imagination.

As A continues to describe their feelings (or repeats the earlier images), B should physicalize the description – perhaps embody it, or act it out, or just use your hands and arms to describe it in some way. Let the words affect you.

Repeat, with the focus on B's description.

3. Now, return to working individually. Pick up an appropriate text – we're going to use some text from Act III, Scene 3 of Shakespeare's *Othello*. Othello is so tormented by conflicting feelings of rage, jealousy and love that he has to express himself with a number of evocative images:

OTHELLO
    Look here, Iago;
    All my fond* love thus do I blow to heaven.   *foolish*
    'Tis gone.
    Arise, black vengeance, from thy hollow cell!
    Yield up, O love, thy crown and hearted throne
    To tyrannous hate! Swell, bosom, with thy fraught*,   *load*
    For 'tis of aspics'* tongues! ...   *venomous snakes*
    Like to the Pontic sea*,   *the Black Sea*
    Whose icy current and compulsive* course   *forceful*
    Ne'er feels retiring ebb, but keeps due on
    To the Propontic* and the Hellespont,   *the Sea of Marmora*
    Even so my bloody thoughts, with violent pace,
    Shall ne'er look back, ne'er ebb to humble love,
    Till that a capable and wide revenge
    Swallow them up.

Once you have read through the text for sense, speak it out loud and let the images resonate inside your body and imagination.

As you continue speaking the text, start to physicalize the imagery in some way, as above. How does the language affect you emotionally? Can you feel the power of Othello's passion that is driving this language?

IMAGE

Extended imagery (20–30 minutes)

As we pointed out earlier, metaphors and similes are two of the most compelling types of evocative imagery. And when a character feels the need to be particularly potent or persuasive in expressing himself or herself, or feels desperate or impelled, he or she is likely to make use of multiple metaphors or similes.

To explore this, we are going to use some text from Act V, Scene 2 of Shakespeare's *Antony and Cleopatra*. Following Antony's death, Cleopatra is captured by the Romans under Octavius Caesar. In reckless defiance of their power, she recounts a dream of Antony:

CLEOPATRA
I dreamed there was an Emperor Antony:
O, such another sleep, that I might see
But such another man!
His face was as the heavens; and therein stuck
A sun and moon, which kept their course,
and lighted the little O, the earth.
His legs bestrid* the ocean: his reared arm   *stretched over*
Crested the world: his voice was
    propertied*   *had the same qualities*
As all the tunèd spheres*, and that to friends;
                                                  musical orbits of the stars
But when he meant to quail and shake the orb*,   *planet*
He was as rattling thunder. For his bounty*,   *generosity*
There was no winter in't; an autumn 'twas
That grew the more by reaping: his delights
Were dolphin-like; they showed his back above
The element they livèd in: in his livery*   *servant's uniform*
Walked crowns and crownets; realms and islands were
As plates dropped from his pocket.

1. You will need to memorize the speech for this exercise.
Begin by working individually. Lie on the floor in a relaxed position – either supine or semi-supine. Close your eyes and speak the text out loud a couple of times, letting the images resonate inside your body and imagination.

Now, stand up and, keeping your eyes closed, start to embody the imagery in some way as you continue to speak the text out loud. You may create shapes with your body that correspond to the images, or use your arms and hands to describe them, or move in a way suggested by the images.

How does speaking and moving with the language affect you emotionally? Can you feel how Cleopatra's love is reflected in the size of the images?

2. Now, find a partner and explore each of the similes/metaphors that Cleopatra uses. First, A will speak and B will move A's arms and body to create shapes that embody the imagery. A, take the language quite slowly to give B time to 'sculpt' you; give yourself up to the experience of both the words and the physical positions. B, try to be as specific as possible with the physical sculpture. Some of the images are quite humorous – it's alright to find them funny, but don't make fun of Cleopatra. Repeat, with B as the speaker.

3. Now, get into groups of five or six. Each of you will take it in terms to work in the following way:

Choose one of you to be the speaker, who will stand in the middle of a small circle formed by the others.

Speaker, close your eyes and allow yourself to relax as much as possible.

With the circle as small as possible, the others should begin to move the speaker gently around between them, building up a sense of trust among you all. Try to avoid moving the speaker around mechanically in the same direction all the time.

Speaker, when you feel ready, begin to speak the text as your partners continue to pass you around the circle. Give yourself up to the experience of being out of control of your body, and let the language and the imagery flow through you freely.

If the speaker feels comfortable and relaxed, try widening the circle slightly, so that you move him or her around more freely. Again, when the speaker feels ready, he or she should speak the text as he or she is being moved around.

4. Once the whole group has finished the task, discuss the effect of all these similes on both speaker and listeners. What happened as your partners kept you moving between them? The physical work is intended to mirror how the character is feeling emotionally. Could you feel how carried away Cleopatra feels, or wants to feel?

IMAGE

> *Teaching tip:* This work on *Extended Imagery* will work best if students have memorized the text beforehand. This may require you to do some preliminary work on sense and context.
>
> The exercise also requires trust and sensitivity on the part of students, and so should not be used with a group who have not already built up a degree of trust with each other. It is also important to monitor the groups carefully. Students should not be subjected to peer-pressure to undertake the wider circle experience if they do not feel comfortable with it.

One word at a time I (about 15–20 minutes)

This and the following exercise were inspired by Kristin Linklater's 'Dropping In' exercise from *Freeing Shakespeare's Voice* (see *Further Reading*).

Use the first section of 'Song of the Open Road' by Walt Whitman, which follows, or another text of similar length and richness of imagery:

A
Afoot and light-hearted I take to the open road,
Healthy, free, the world before me,
The long brown path before me leading wherever I choose.

Henceforth I ask not good-fortune, I myself am good-fortune,
Henceforth I whimper no more, postpone no more, need nothing,
Done with indoor complaints, libraries, querulous criticisms,
Strong and content I travel the open road.

B
The earth, that is sufficient,
I do not want the constellations any nearer,
I know they are very well where they are,
I know they suffice for those who belong to them.

(Still here I carry my old delicious burdens,
I carry them, men and women, I carry them with me wherever I go,

I swear it is impossible for me to get rid of them,
I am filled with them, and I will fill them in return.)

1. Find a partner and a place to sit comfortably together, not too close to any other pair. Pick one partner to be A and one to be B.

B, take a copy of the text and fold it or cover it so that you can only see *part A*.

B, read the first word to A, as neutrally as possible – just giving the information but not colouring it in any way.

A, take 5–10 seconds to think about that word. Find a memory, a picture, a person, a sensation that, for you, is connected to the meaning of the word. If the word were 'mountain', for example, you might think about a particular mountain you have visited. Take the time to recall details and remember what being there and looking at the mountain felt like. When you feel that you have a connection to the word (and it will take some focused concentration to get there), speak the word back to your partner. Don't feel that you have to use your voice to illustrate what the word is like or how it makes you feel; just trust that your connection to the word will be present in your speaking of it.

Go through the rest of part A one word at a time, B reading the word and A listening, connecting and speaking it back.

NOTE: Some words don't carry much meaning on their own, so don't feel that you have to spend a lot of time trying to find a deep connection to words like 'the' and 'a'. You can repeat them back to partner B fairly quickly. Don't, however, rush past a word just because it's small. For example, the word 'if' represents a moment of possibility, or 'up' represents a wide variety of physical and emotional experiences, so take the time to think about what small words mean to you.

Once you have worked your way through part A, take a couple of minutes to discuss what the experience was like, both for partner B and for partner A, until the whole class is finished and ready to move on.

2. A, take the paper and fold it over or cover it so you can see *only part B*. You will then repeat the process with this part of the poem – A reading one word at a time and B listening, connecting and speaking it back.

3. A and B each now 'own' the lines that they 'received' from their partner and repeated back. Unfold your copy, and take a moment to identify the lines that are 'yours', consulting with your partner to avoid confusion.

IMAGE

Everyone should now stand up, move around the room and find a new partner. Stand facing your new partner and clasp right hands, as if you were shaking hands. Silently agree which one of you will go first.

The first partner will read *his or her first line* to the other, one word at a time (this may or may not be the first line of the poem). It should not take you as long to find a connection to each word as it did before, since you've already done it once, but do make sure that you establish in your mind what it was that you thought of that made that word vivid and real for you before you speak it.

The second partner will then read *his or her first line* to the other in the same way. NOTE – if both are A's, they will both be reading the same line; if one is an A and one a B, they will be reading different lines.

Once you have both read your first lines, release hands and walk around the room until you find a new partner. With the new partner, you will repeat the process with *your second line*. You will then find a new partner for each of the following lines. NOTE – it's okay if some people go more quickly than others, so you may be doing your third line with someone who is doing his fourth.

4. You're now going to go through the same process of finding a new partner, holding hands and speaking your text one line at a time. This time, however, trust that your connection to each word is now strong enough that you don't have to stop on every one – you can start to put them together and think about communicating the meaning of the line as a whole to your partner. Don't, however, feel that you have to illustrate the meaning or entertain in any way.

5. When all have finished, everybody jog around the room for a minute to refresh your energy, and then return to your original partner and take hands. You will now read 'your' lines of your poem to each other – partner A taking part A, partner B taking part B.

Again, trust that you have found meaning in the words, and think now about sharing that meaning, very simply, with your partner as you speak.

6. Everyone have a seat and discuss the process. Were some words harder to connect to than others? What did it feel like when you spoke a word for which you had a very strong association? How would it have been different if you had read through the poem first? In the last stages, did you start to feel the need to 'perform'? What did you observe in other people's work that you found effective?

> *Teaching tip:* It will help if you prepare the copies of the text in a large, easy-to-read font on paper that can be folded.
>
> During the first two steps, it can be very distracting to hear other teams doing the same word at the same time. It will help if you stagger the starting times of the various pairs. Throughout the exercise, encourage students to keep things simple and focused on the language.

One word at a time II (20–25 minutes)

Patsy Rodenburg describes working in a similar fashion in her section on 'Anchoring the Text' in *Speaking Shakespeare* (see *Further Reading*).

Pick about six to eight lines of a speech from a play that you know well. It's important that you understand the character's background and circumstances.

1. Get a partner and sit comfortably facing each other in chairs or on the floor.

As in the exercise above, have your partner read the first word of your text to you and take 5–6 seconds to find a memory, a picture, a person, a sensation that, for you personally, embodies the meaning of the word. At this point, work from your own experiences; don't worry about the character's circumstances. When you feel that you have a connection to the word, speak it back to your partner without worrying about illustrating your connection in any way – just trust that it's there. You can move fairly quickly through words that lack significance on their own, such as 'and' or 'the'. Proceed in the same way until you have worked all the way through the selection.

2. Switch partners, so that you will feed your partner the words from his or her text one at a time. It works best if the two partners have different texts.

3. Switch back and repeat the exercise, but this time instead of thinking about your own experience of each word, think about your character's experience. If the word were 'war', for example, the first time through you might have connected to images you've seen of a recent conflict. But this time, if your character lives in the fifteenth

IMAGE

century, you will focus on images of hacking with broadswords and being pierced by arrows. For some words, your experience and your character's may overlap, which is fine, but stay actively involved in imagining your character's world and experiences as they relate to each individual word.

Repeat this process for your partner.

4. When you've finished, stand facing your partner. Read your text to her, taking the time to remember the associations you had with each word from both your character's and your own perspectives. Your partner will do the same.

5. Finally, stand back about two metres from your partner and speak your text, focusing on bringing her into the images and the story, trusting that your own connection to the words will stay firm. Your partner will do the same.

Discuss: Were there any words for which your experience and your character's experience were sharply divergent? Were there words where the experiences overlapped? Did you find anything in your text that you hadn't noticed before? What was it like speaking the text at the end of the exercise? What was it like listening to your partner?

Follow-up

Reflective practice questions:

- Which exercises helped you to perceive the images in the text most clearly?
- Did you connect more readily with literal images or evocative images? Why do you think this is?
- Did connecting with the images change the way you spoke the language – e.g. did you feel more or less comfortable? Did your voice have more or less energy? Did your tempo change? What about your pitch range? And your articulation?
- Does your breathing change when you are strongly connected to the images in your text?
- What tends to distract you from the image when you read or perform text?

- As a listener, when did you receive the text being spoken most clearly? What did the speaker do that helped you to see the images?

Suggested texts

Literal images

Line painting one

Brian Friel, *Faith Healer*, Part Four, Frank: from 'It was a September morning'
Lynn Nottage, *Ruined*, Act II Scene 2, Salima: 'Do you know what I was doing'
Rajiv Joseph, *Guards at the Taj*, Scene 2, Humayun: 'But I was wondering'
August Wilson, *The Piano Lesson*, Act I Scene 1, Avery: 'Well, it come to me in a dream'

Breathe the image

Caryl Churchill, *Top Girls*, Act I, Gret: 'A bridge and houses'
Toni Morrison, *The Bluest Eye*, Act I Scene 3, Pecola: 'Amen. If I squeeze my eyes shut'
Lynn Nottage, *Sweat*, Act I Scene 5, Tracey: 'Yeah? Well my family's been here since the 20s'
Harold Pinter, *Old Times*, Act I, Anna: 'Queuing all night'

Narratives

Nilo Cruz, *Anna in the Tropics*, Act I Scene 5, Conchita: 'I knew a fellow from New London'
Brian Friel, *Faith Healer*, Part Three, Teddy: from 'There was one night in particular' through 'And they all went out'
Susan Glaspell, *Alison's House*, Act III Scene 3, Eben: 'Her brown hair is parted in the middle'
Lisa Loomer, *The Waiting Room*, Wanda: ' … But Snow White's wicked old stepmother' (see *American Theatre Book of Monologues for Women*)

Conor McPherson, *The Weir*, Jack: from 'And Maura used to say that one Saturday' skipping Finbar's line
Sam Shepard, *A Lie of the Mind*, Act I Scene 1, Sally: 'Maybe. Maybe you can't' (skip Lorainne's lines)
Robert Schenkkan, *The Kentucky Cycle*, 'Tall Tales' Scene 2, JT from 'Now, the Capulets had a daughter'

Cameraman

Stephen Adly Guirgis, *Jesus Hopped the 'A' Train*, Act II Scene 2, Angel: 'We usta, me and Joey'
Lorraine Hansberry, *A Raisin in the Sun*, Act II Scene 2, Walter: 'You wouldn't understand yet'
Quiara Alegría Hudes, *The Happiest Song Plays Last*, Scene 10, Agustin: from 'I was stuck in Puerto Rico' through 'the bull he loved the most who died'
Lynn Nottage, *Sweat*, Act I Scene 1, Chris: 'And then there's Jason'

Evocative images

Line painting two

Phillip Kan Gotanda, *Ballad of Yachiyo*, Yachiyo: 'His skin was smooth' (see *American Theatre Book of Monologues for Women*)
Lauren Gunderson, *The Book of Will*, Act II Scene 1, Henry: 'Then we'll both starve'
Tony Kushner, *Angels in America Part Two: Perestroika*, Act V Scene 10, Harper: 'Night flight to San Francisco'
Jose Rivera, *Marisol*, Marisol: 'I'm killed instantly'

Sensual imagery

James Baldwin, *Blues for Mister Charlie*, Act I, Richard: 'Not for me'
Howard Barker, *Gertrude – The Cry*, Scene 21, Gertrude: 'Two weeks in a warm climate'
Anne Devlin, *Ourselves Alone*, Act II Scene 1, Donna: 'The devil's back'
August Wilson, *Joe Turner's Come and Gone*, Act II Scene 3, Bynum: 'I can tell from looking at you'

Extended imagery

Nilo Cruz, *Anna in the Tropics*, Act II Scene 1, Cheche: 'Well, then there's Mildred'
Robert Schenkkan, *The Kentucky Cycle*, 'Tall Tales' Prologue, Adult Mary Anne: 'Spring usta explode'
Dylan Thomas, *Under Mild Wood*, Mr Edwards: 'I am a draper mad with love'
August Wilson, *Joe Turner's Come and Gone*, Act I Scene 3, Bynum: 'Alright. Let's try it this way.'

One word at a time I

Maya Angelou, 'A Plagued Journey'
Carol Ann Duffy, 'Havisham'
T. S. Eliot, 'Preludes'
Robert Frost, 'Birches'
Edwin Muir, 'The Horses'
Sylvia Plath, 'Blackberrying'
Sarah Kane, *4.48 Psychosis*, from 'to achieve goals and ambitions' through 'to be free'
Tony Kushner, *Angels in America Part One: Millennium Approaches*, Act II Scene 7, Joe: 'Yesterday was Sunday', skipping Louis's 'Creepy'
Toni Morrison, *The Bluest Eye*, Act I Scene 2, Claudia: 'Mama meant well'
William Shakespeare, *King John*, Act III Scene 4, Constance: 'Grief fills the room up of my absent child'

One word at a time II

Frances Ya-Chu Cowhig, *Snow in Midsummer*, Act I Scene 5, Dou Yi: 'Fog locked, cloud buried'
Ben Jonson, *Volpone or The Fox*, Act IV Scene 5, Volpone: 'Then know, most honoured fathers'
Rajiv Joseph, *Guards at the Taj*, Scene 2, Babur: 'I fell into a trance'
Paula Vogel, *Desdemona: A Play about a Handkerchief*, Scene 27, Emilia: 'When I was married in the Church'

Further reading

Berry, Cicely, *From Word to Play*, Oberon Books, London, 2008. 'Where the Image Lies', pp. 95–99.

Carey, David and Rebecca Clark Carey, *The Shakespeare Workbook and Video*, Bloomsbury Methuen Drama, 2015. Chapter 2: Language in Action, pp. 71–85, 94–109.

Houseman, Barbara, *Tackling Text*, Nick Hern Books, London, 2008. 'Connecting with the Words and Images', pp. 58–64, 120–124; 'Internal Geography', pp. 66–68, 125–127.

Kaiser, Scott, *Mastering Shakespeare*, Allworth Press, New York, 2003. Scene 3: Images, pp. 65–96.

Linklater, Kristin, *Freeing Shakespeare's Voice*, Theatre Communications Group, Inc., New York, 1992. Chapter 2: Words and Images, pp. 30–44.

Rodenburg, Patsy, *The Need for Words*, Methuen, London, 1993. 'Simple Storytelling', pp. 98–102.

Rodenburg, Patsy, *The Actor Speaks*, Methuen, London, 1997. Stage Three: Voice and Speech Meet Word and Text, pp. 204–221.

Rodenburg, Patsy, *Speaking Shakespeare*, Methuen, London, 2002. Part 3: The Imaginative.

3
SENSE

Framework

When you get up to perform as an actor, your number one job is to make sense. This may seem like a very obvious point, but it is easily overlooked. Actors have so many balls to juggle – character, intention, obstacles, emotion – that something as prosaic as making sense can seem not at all artistic or important. But the fact remains that if your audience can't understand you, you have failed in your job.

Of course, there are some qualifications to that statement. Sometimes, particularly in classical texts, you may come across passages that are extremely dense: the syntax is confused; the references are obscure; and the vocabulary may be centuries out of date. In these cases, the audience may never understand the precise meaning of every word you say; they will, however, be able to sense whether or not you know exactly what you are a talking about. If you yourself are not crystal clear about the meaning of your text and committed to getting the sense across, you will be vague in your actions and intentions; you might rush; your articulation is likely to be muddy; and you will probably be under-energized or have a falsely bombastic energy. In other words, *you won't inhabit the language fully*, and the audience will be able to tell. They may not consciously think, 'Hmm, that actor didn't seem to know what the key word was in that sentence', but they won't be able to follow your argument, and they will lose interest in you very quickly. If, however, you are very clear about the meaning of what you are saying, you will shape the ideas, bring out the most important words, carry the energy of the thought to its conclusion and, most importantly, you will speak with confidence. You will *own* the language. The audience will then grasp the sense of what you are saying, even if a few details escape them.

Establishing the overall meaning of a speech or a scene takes time and work – it is often what the first few days of rehearsal are about. In the process, you will find that the meaning of any language has several layers and is influenced by a number of factors: the context in which it is spoken, the personality of the speakers, their attitudes, feelings and intentions, and the literal sense of the words they use. There are, however, a few simple things you can do to help along this procedure of finding the meaning of your text. First and foremost, look up words you don't know in a dictionary or ask somebody. This may seem like an obvious point, but you'd be surprised at the number of times that we have stopped a student or an actor in the middle of a speech to ask what their understanding of a particular word was, and found that they could only make a generalized guess. If you're working with Shakespeare or any other classical text, we would suggest that you get an edition that has notes on the same page so you can find the meaning of words quickly (see *Further Reading*).

Don't stop at looking up words that are completely alien, either. 'Kind of' knowing what a word means isn't enough. There may be multiple definitions or shades of meaning to words that you 'kind of' know that will open up a whole world of acting possibilities to you.

And you may simply be wrong if you think you know what an unfamiliar word means. 'Wherefore', for example, doesn't mean 'where', as many people assume it does. It means 'why'. So when Juliet is on her balcony saying, 'O Romeo, Romeo, wherefore art thou Romeo', she's not asking where Romeo is; she's asking *why* he has to be *Romeo* – why it had to be a Montague who stole her heart. That's a very different opening beat for the scene. If you speak the line as if the word means 'where', you're just a girl with a crush wondering where that cute boy is; if you speak the line with the meaning that Shakespeare intended, you're a girl who has a very specific and scary dilemma – much more interesting for you and your audience.

You also need to look up any allusions to places, people or stories that you are not familiar with. Later in the play, Juliet says, 'Gallop apace you fiery-footed steeds towards Phoebus' lodging.' There's a wonderful Greek myth about the sun god, Phoebus, who drives the sun across the sky in his chariot every day. If you don't know that story (and about what happens to his son, Phaeton, whom she mentions in the next line), you're not going to be able to make full sense of the speech.

Once you're sure that you know what all your words mean, you can start to explore and deepen your understanding of the larger meaning of your text, which is what the exercises that follow will help you to do. They involve looking at individual sentences to find how they are shaped. Where's the key information? Where is the thought going? They also involve looking at speeches and scenes to find how all the pieces fit together and give meaning to each other.

You will find that the discoveries that you make as you do this work will enable you not only to communicate more clearly, but also to be more specific in your acting choices. In his book *Year of the King* (1985: 181), Antony Sher talks about a session he had with David at the Royal Shakespeare Company to work on the opening speech of *Richard III*. In that session, he became conscious that in his mind he had been putting a full stop after 'Now is the winter of our discontent'. It's such a famous image, he just stopped with it. In the context of the speech, however, it doesn't make sense on its own, and it's hard to really commit to something that doesn't make sense. In working on it with David, Sher realized that the thought continues into the next line of verse: 'Now is the winter of our discontent//Made glorious summer by this son of York.' The sense of the sentence is 'winter is made summer'. Sher comments that once he had made this discovery, the line became much easier to speak. Ultimately, making sense of your text isn't just something you do for you audience; it's something you do for yourself. With clarity comes conviction, and with conviction comes power.

Exploration

Teaching tip: Some of these exercises can be done in class in groups or pairs. The second one takes a fair bit of time and effort, but is very worth doing to develop a feel for how one extracts sense from difficult texts. Parts could be assigned as homework and the rest done in class.

I. Write out what you think each of the following words means, then get a good college dictionary or Shakespeare glossary (see *Further Reading*) and find out how close you came:

Fain
Lief
Surcease
Bodkin
Fardels
Breach
Choler
Palmer
Doff
Interred
Lour
Maidenhood
Skulk
Sluice

II. Pick one of the following sonnets by William Shakespeare: 12, 17, 18, 23, 27, 29, 57, 61, 90, 130, or another that you like. (Most collected works of Shakespeare will include the sonnets, or you can find them on the internet.) Read the sonnet through once and write down what mood the sonnet expresses – is it sad, hopeful, loving, angry etc.? Read through the sonnet again and find one sentence or phrase that you think sums up the main point of the sonnet – e.g. 'Love is not love which alters when it alteration finds'. Write out the same idea with different words – e.g. 'Love isn't really love if it changes when it sees the beloved has changed'. Read the sonnet again looking for how the different phrases and sentences relate to that main idea. Now look up any words you don't know and write down their meanings. Read the sonnet again, referring back to your list of definitions. Read the sonnet one more time, and then try to write three or four sentences that sum up what the whole sonnet says. Now read the sonnet aloud to a friend and ask them to tell you what they thought it meant.

III. Grab a newspaper you haven't read yet. Cut out a dozen or so articles without reading them. DO NOT cut out the headlines above the articles – leave those in the paper, and try not to pay too much attention to them as you're cutting. Read your headline-less articles and write a headline for each one which states who did what (and to whom if applicable). For example: 'Russia Tested Missiles' or 'Famous Author Died'.

Exercises

> *Teaching tip:* The exercises in this chapter are divided into two sections: *Thoughts* and *Themes*. In general, we would start with the first section, which helps students to be specific about the meaning of sentences, and then move on to the second, which is about sustaining an arc of meaning through a speech or scene. In some instances, however, working on uncovering the theme of a whole piece first may make it easier to then unpick the sense of individual thoughts within it.

As with other chapters, many of the exercises that follow are physical, so you will want to wear loose clothes and take some time to stretch, warm up your body, connect to your breathing and open your voice before you begin. Some of the exercises will also require you to have a pencil to hand.

Thoughts

In order to make sense of a text when you speak it, you need to understand the thoughts it is expressing. In some cases, they may be quite easy to grasp and communicate; but in much of the world's great dramatic literature the language is particularly rich and dense. The thoughts may be long and complex, and it may take a bit of work not only to understand them intellectually, but also to feel comfortable enough with them that you can convey them with fluidity and clarity.

The exercises in this section will help you to identify the thoughts in your text and understand how they are put together. Although the elements we will be looking at include punctuation and parts of speech, rest assured that there are no grammar tests involved! In the back of the book (*Appendix 3*), we've included definitions of terms you may find useful to review, and we'll mention a few here as preparation for the work. But the only test involved is the practical investigation of how to make the most out of the language you speak.

While people tend to think that punctuation is concerned mostly with rules of grammar, actually it exists to help capture in writing what we naturally do with our voices when we speak. For example, when we curse another motorist for cutting us up, we are likely to exclaim with some force – the exclamation mark is one way of showing that force on paper. So, when it comes to reading a piece of written text out loud, punctuation marks can be your friend, because they point up things that are important for speaking. Where does a thought begin? Where does it end? Are there changes of direction along the way? Are some parts of the sentence more important than others? There's a complete list of the punctuation marks we'll refer to in the appendix, but it's worth noting now that we'll be using the British term 'full stop' to refer to what Americans call a 'period'. See *Appendix 3* also for a note about punctuation in modern editions of Shakespeare's plays.

Parts of speech are useful to know about because they can help identify the core information in a sentence: **who is doing what to whom**. The **subject** is the 'who' – the person or thing that is doing the action. The **verb phrase** is the 'doing' word or words. The **object** is the 'whom' – the person or thing being affected by the action. So in the sentence 'Joan picked the rose', we would say that 'Joan' is the subject, 'picked' is the verb phrase, and 'the rose' is the object. But note that not all sentences have objects: in the sentence 'John was sleeping', there is just the subject 'John' and the verb phrase 'was sleeping'. And sometimes verbs – like 'am' or 'is' – can be 'being' words, in which case you have to identify *what* the subject *is*. In the sentence 'John is happy', for example, 'happy' is what John *is*. You may also know that some sentences can contain both a direct object and an indirect object. For our work, the difference between a direct object and an indirect object is usually not vital. What's important is being able to identify who or what is affected by the action of a verb. So, in the sentence 'Joan gave the rose to John', we would say that 'John' (the indirect object) and 'the rose' (the direct object) are both affected by the action of giving. We use all of these terms fairly loosely because our purpose is not to give a detailed grammatical analysis of sentences, but to uncover and energize the thoughts within them.

More complex sentence structures might include further information about these basic elements, making full use of adjectives, adverbs, prepositions and conjunctions, which we talk about in the appendix; but the subject, verb phrase and object are the building blocks of a sentence. The exercises in this section will help you to identify them and focus your energy on them. They are the essence of the thought and the heart of your argument: somebody is doing something. Everything else is extra – it gives you more detail about when or where or why etc. That extra information may be very important, but you never want to lose sight of the basics.

Twitter (10–15 minutes)

This exercise goes back to Rebecca's secondary school days, when we used to call it 'Telegram'.

Find a partner to work on a speech or short scene with.

Partner A, read the first sentence (to a full stop) out loud to partner B.

Partner B, repeat back the two to four words that caught your ear most strongly – that seem to you to be particularly important. A, circle those words.

Now, A give the text to B, who will read the next sentence with A repeating back the important words. Go back and forth in this manner until you have worked through the entire text.

Now look together at the text. You job is to create a tweet (internet posting of 280 characters or fewer) which conveys the most important points. Looking at the words you have circled will help you get an idea of what you might want to include.

As an example, Hamlet's famous 'To be or not to be' soliloquy might become: 'Question: to live or die? Dread of what might happen after death makes us bear awful lives'.

When everyone has finished, share your tweet with other pairs.

> *Teaching tip:* This exercise is, admittedly, reductionist, and we would never claim that it alone will lead students to understand the text in a meaningful way. Nonetheless, it can be a great place to start, giving students a point of orientation from which they can move into other exercises.

Question time (10–12 minutes per partner)

VIDEO LINK

Question time: https://vimeo.com/268973346

This exercise has been described and used by many, many teachers. It's a classic, and very good for helping to sharpen the sense of a text, so we're including our version here.

Find a partner.

Partner A, speak your entire text for partner B (see *Suggested Texts* for some ideas).

Then, A, speak your first sentence and pause. B, ask A a question about the verb, or action in that sentence. For example, if the sentence were 'But soft, what light through yonder window breaks?', you could ask, 'What is the light doing?' A, repeat the entire sentence as a response to the question: 'What light through yonder window **breaks**?'

Next, B, ask about the person or thing doing the action, for example, 'What's breaking through the window?' A, repeat the sentence as a response to that question.

B, if it's appropriate, ask another question about where, when, or how the action is taking place: 'Where is the light breaking?' A, answer.

If it's a particularly rich sentence, B can ask another question about any of the elements, such as 'Where's the window?'

SENSE

A, as you answer each question, let each element of the sentence become more and more specific. You don't have to stress every word every time, but do let the questions push you to make the whole picture more detailed and vivid.

Continue working through at least the first third of A's text. A, then speak your entire text again, working to be so clear in your thoughts that no one could be left with any questions.

NOTE: the purpose of the exercise is not to make your speech over-emphatic, but to help your thinking be clear.

Swap over and work with B's text.

> *Teaching tip:* Depending on the size and makeup of your class, you might want to do the questioning yourself, working with one student at a time while the others watch. It can be a very compelling exercise to watch.

Who's doing what? (about 20 minutes)

We're going to use a Mark Antony speech from Shakespeare's *Julius Caesar* here, but the exercise is good for finding your way through any complex piece of text.

We give glosses for many of the less familiar words or phrases in this one – if you have chosen another text, go through it and find definitions for any words you don't understand. In this speech, Antony is standing over the body of the murdered Caesar. He believes this murder will bring great destruction to all of Rome.

MARK ANTONY

Over thy wounds now do I prophesy,–	
Which, like dumb mouths, do ope* their ruby lips,	*open*
To beg the voice and utterance* of my tongue–	*speech*
A curse shall light upon* the limbs of men;	*land on*
Domestic fury and fierce civil strife	
Shall cumber* all the parts of Italy;	*afflict*

Blood and destruction shall be so in use*	*common*
And dreadful objects so familiar	
That mothers shall but smile when they behold	
Their infants quartered* with the hands	
of war;	*torn in four pieces*
All pity choked with custom of fell* deeds:	*cruel*
And Caesar's spirit, ranging for* revenge,	*travelling in search of*
With Ate* by his side come hot from	
hell,	*goddess of chaos (**Ah-tay**)*
Shall in these confines* with a monarch's voice	*regions*
Cry 'Havoc,' and let slip the dogs of war;	
That this foul deed shall smell above the earth	
With carrion* men, groaning for burial.	*rotting flesh*

Read the text out loud once just to get a feel for it.

Now, read it out loud until you come to a verb phrase – those are **action** words or sometimes **being** words. Circle the verb phrase.

Next, identify who or what is doing that action – this is the subject. Some may be pretty obvious, but some may take a while to track down. When you've found the subject, underline it and draw a line between it and the verb.

So, to go through our example, the first verb phrase we come to is 'do prophesy'. The person who is doing the prophesying is 'I' (Mark Antony). The next verb phrase is 'do ope'; you have to go back a bit to find what is opening – it's the wounds from the first line. Note that a subject can connect to more than one action and a verb phrase can have more than one subject. In this instance, the wounds not only 'ope', they 'ope … to beg'.

Continue through the speech, circling all the verb phrases and connecting them to their subjects.

Each person in the group take one of the verb–subject pairings. Spend a minute or two creating a bold physical embodiment of the verb or verbs. A verb phrase like 'to beg' offers you the literal option of kneeling and holding your hands out in supplication. An action like 'prophesy' is a little more abstract; maybe you would open your arms out to the heavens to call down your inspiration.

Line up in order of verbs – so the person with the first verb ('do prophesy') goes first.

SENSE

Each of you, in turn, speak your verb–subject pairing and perform your physicalization. ('I do prophesy' followed by 'wounds do ope to beg' etc.)

Now, go back to the text and underline all the words around your pair that relate directly to it – that tell when, how, where, or to what the action is being done. For 'I do prophesy', you would underline 'Over thy wounds now do I prophesy'. For 'wounds do ope', you would underline 'thy wounds which, like dumb mouths, do ope their ruby lips to beg the voice and utterance of my tongue'. Don't worry if there's some overlap with other people.

Finally, line up once again in order and read what you have underlined, physicalizing each verb as you come to it.

Discuss any discoveries about the text that you made.

For bonus points: you will notice that there is only one full stop in this speech, so technically it's all one sentence. If you had to identify one verb that everything else in the sentence relates to, what would it be?

Teaching tip: You may have students with a more sophisticated understanding of grammar who will ask questions about infinitives, participles etc. Let them know that for the purposes of this exercise we refer to all action words as verbs because our goal is to find and embody the action energy within the text. It's okay if students make some grammatical 'mistakes' in doing the exercise as long as the work is taking them deeper into the meaning of the text.

If you have a large group, it can be fun to divide it in two so they can show each other their work at the end. If you have a small group, individuals may need to double up on subject–verb pairs.

Subordinate cuckoo clock (20–30 minutes)

In some texts, the core information can be buried particularly deep. This exercise will help you bring it to the foreground.

We're going to work with a speech from *'Tis Pity She's a Whore* by John Ford, but it's useful for any text with long, complex sentences. In this speech from Act IV, Scene 2, Richardetto is talking to his niece, Philotis (whom he addresses several times). Richardetto begins by talking about his wife, who had been involved in some nefarious plotting and died as a result. Soranzo has also plotted against Richardetto and has not yet suffered any consequences, but Richardetto perceives that there is trouble between Soranzo and his wife and decides to let that run its course rather than take revenge on Soranzo directly. In the end, he advises his niece to get out of town and away from all the plotting.

We've divided the speech into three sections, which you don't need to worry about for now. We've also included some definitions of obscure words.

RICHARDETTO
  1. My wretched wife, more wretched in her shame
  Than in her wrongs to me, hath paid too soon
  The forfeit* of her modesty and life.   *penalty*
  And I am sure, my niece, though vengeance hover,
  Keeping aloof* yet from Soranzo's fall,   *at a distance*
  Yet he will fall, and sink with his own weight.
  2. I need not now (my heart persuades me so)
  To further his confusion; there is One
  Above begins to work; for, as I hear,
  Debates* already 'twixt his wife and him   *quarrels*
  Thicken and run to head; she, as 'tis said,
  Slightens* his love, and he abandons hers: *treats as worthless*
  Much talk I hear. 3. Since things go thus, my niece,
  In tender love and pity of your youth,
  My counsel is, that you should free your years
  From hazard of these woes, by flying hence
  To fair Cremona, there to vow your soul
  In holiness, a holy votaress*;   *woman who has taken a vow*
  Leave me to see the end of these extremes*.   *sufferings*

1. As a class, read the text out loud once in unison. There was probably quite a bit that you didn't understand, which is fine. Talk about what you did get out of it.

SENSE

Read it again, this time going round the circle with each person reading until he gets to a punctuation mark (including any parentheses). Did that help make it any clearer?

2. Divide the class into three teams. Each team take one of the sections of the speech.

With your team, read through the first sentence in your section going round the circle, each person speaking until they get to a punctuation mark, at which point a new reader begins. (It may be that not everyone gets to read, which is okay at this point.)

Read the sentence again, but this time skip the first person and the bit they read – so you will start with the second person reading the bit between the first and second punctuation marks. For example, if you were doing section 1, you would leave out the first person saying 'My wretched wife', and the second person in the circle would start by reading, 'more wretched in her shame than in her wrongs to me'. From there you would continue around the circle to the end of the sentence.

Discuss whether or not the sentence still makes sense without that first bit (in this case, it doesn't). If the sentence **doesn't** make sense without the bit you skipped, **underline that bit**.

Next try skipping the second person. So the first person reads 'My wretched wife'; the second person and his bit are skipped; the third person reads, 'that paid too soon / the forfeit of her modesty and life', and so forth.

Discuss whether or not the sentence makes sense without that second bit. As before, if the sentence **doesn't** make sense without the bit you skipped, **underline it**.

Continue until you've tried leaving out each bit between punctuation marks in each of your sentences, underlining those that are necessary for the sentence to make sense.

When you've finished, read just the underlined bits out loud. Discuss what you've learnt about what your section means.

3. Stand up with your group. Make sure that everyone has a bit of text between punctuation marks. If you have a small group, some of you may need to take two bits and move around between them. If you have a large group, a couple of you can double up and speak a bit together.

Those of you who have bits that are underlined, stand next to each other about a metre apart.

Those of you who have bits that are not underlined, stand just behind whoever has the bit before you (if you have the first bit and it's not underlined, you won't have anyone to stand behind, so just stand to the side).

Read through your section. If you are standing behind someone, when it's your turn to speak, lean out to the side so you can be seen and return to standing upright when you're done. The effect is something like popping out of a cuckoo clock. Practice this once and then perform it for your other classmates.

Discuss: Could you understand the other sections better this way? Why do you think that was? How did having those people with the essential information stand in front help? What about having the others 'cuckoo clock' in and out? If one person were reading this, how do you think they could bring the important bits to the foreground?

Try reading the section once yourself, sitting in a chair for the bits that are underlined and standing for the bits that are not.

> *Teaching tip:* This exercise can take some time to set up, but it rolls along once students get into it. It's very useful for getting a feel for the relative energy subordinate clauses require. While it's important that students recognize which bits of the sentence cannot be left out, if they fail to recognize that a piece of information is not actually vital, it's not as big a problem.
>
> If you prefer to have students work on their own, they can work with a chair as above or designate one spot on the floor as the point of delivery for key information and move away from it for the subordinate clauses.

Fill in the blanks (about 10–15 minutes)

In some texts, you will have trouble finding the subjects and verbs because they are implied. This happens often when people are giving commands. Think about Henry V's famous cry: 'Once more unto the breach, dear friends, once more!' Where's the verb? It's implied: '*Charge* once more unto the breach.' Later on, he says, 'Then imitate the action of a tiger.' Where's the subject? It's implied: '*All you soldiers,* then imitate the action.' At other times playwrights may leave out words to help capture the fragmented nature of a character's thought process or difficulty in speaking in the given circumstances. You need to be able to fill in the blanks for yourself, so that you understand the sense of the thought.

Take this text from *The Life and Adventures of Nicholas Nickleby,* adapted from Dickens by David Edgar. Brooker is talking to Ralph Nickleby about Nickleby's dishonourable behaviour in his marriage.

BROOKER
> But, of course, it had to be a secret, from the father. He was rich. And if he'd known, the daughter would have lost a great inheritance. And that would never do. Oh, would it. So, a secret wedding. And a little secret son. Put out to nurse. A long way off. So not to interfere. (Pause) And then, as time went on, began to see her less and less. Stayed up in London, making money. And your wife, a young girl, alone, in a dull old country house. And eventually, she couldn't bear it any more, could she?

Find a partner and go through the speech sentence by sentence together. Whenever you find a sentence without a subject and/or without a verb, write in what you think the missing words should be. For example, for 'So, a secret wedding', you would write something like, 'So *you had* a secret wedding'.

Now one partner read the words from the speech, leaving room for the other partner to read in the words you've written.

Take your time with this to get a sense of how those things that are left unsaid are nevertheless present in the mind of the speaker.

Switch partners, and then each of you try reading the speech as it was written. Don't pause where the missing words are, but be aware that there are parts of the thought that you're not speaking.

> *Teaching tip:* This exercise can work well with some of the more elliptical Beckett and Pinter plays, as well as many others that use sentence fragments. It also works well in particularly convoluted Shakespeare passages.

Carry the bag (12–15 minutes)

VIDEO LINK

Carry the bag: https://vimeo.com/268972242

If you have any arm or shoulder injuries, you may want to use shoes instead of bags.

This exercise works well with any text.

1. Everyone in the class, grab your bags (backpacks, handbags, bookbags, briefcases – the heavier the better), zip them up so nothing can fall out, and place them on the floor around the room so they are more or less evenly spaced.

Take your text and read through it once out loud – everyone together. Then go and stand in front of a bag – it doesn't have to be yours.

Hold your text in front of you with one hand, and, on the instructor's cue, reach down, grab a bag with the other hand, and lift it in the air above your head **as you speak the first word of your speech**. Everyone in the class should begin at the same time. It's important that you are grabbing and lifting the bag **at the same time** as you are speaking the first word, not before or after. If the first word is short, you may get out a few words before the bag is lifted all the way over your head, which is fine; what's important is that the talking and the lifting begin at the same moment.

Start walking around the room (with purpose and energy) with the bag held over your head as you continue reading out loud until you come to a full stop (or question mark or exclamation point).

As you speak the last word of the sentence, stop walking and place the bag back on the floor. Again, it's important that you land the bag on the floor **at the same time** as you speak the last word, not before or after. Don't slam or drop the bag, but do put it down with a sense of purpose; don't just let it dribble to the floor.

Walk over to another bag and begin the process again with the next sentence. Continue lifting a new bag on the first word of every sentence, walking with the bag **over** your head (don't let it slump) for the length of the sentence, and landing it on the floor on the last word through to the end of the speech.

Take a moment to discuss the exercise. Did you have a tendency to start lifting the bag after you'd started speaking or to want to put it down before you finished? What did it feel like to fight that tendency? Did it change your feel for the energy of the text? What did it feel like to have to carry the bag all the way through very long sentences? When the sentences were short, what did it feel like to have to stop and find a new bag frequently?

2. Repeat the exercise, lifting and putting down bags at the beginnings and ends of sentences as before; only this time, as you walk, change directions every time you come to a punctuation mark that is not a full stop. The change of direction doesn't need to be huge, but you should make a clear pivot on every comma, semicolon, dash etc.

3. Clear the bags to the side of the room. This time, you will continue to walk and change direction at every punctuation mark that is not a full stop. But instead of picking up a bag at the start of every sentence, you will take a strong in-breath before you start speaking and a decisive step forward on the first word. On the last word of every sentence, you will stop walking and lightly stomp your foot on the floor.

Take a moment to discuss. Could you still feel that energy of lifting at the beginning of sentences and landing at the end without the bags? Could you still keep the energy up through long thoughts without physically having to keep your arm up?

> *Teaching tip:* This is a great exercise to help students get a feel for the energy required to carry long thoughts and to overcome the tendency many people have to let their energy fade before sentences finish. You can have all the students work with the same text, or they can each work a different piece. Many students will need to be reminded as they do the exercise to keep the bag held high, to walk with energy and purposefulness, and not to start dropping the bag before the final word of the sentence. It's worth insisting on all these things, as the students won't really get the benefits of the exercise if they don't do them. If you have a large group and can't monitor everyone at once, you could do the exercise in half groups – it's an interesting one for the students to watch. Or, if the students have good rapport with each other, you could assign students a buddy to follow them and make sure they're not flagging.

Punctuation play

This exercise is useful for texts that use a wide variety of punctuations marks (see *Suggested Texts* for some ideas). The timing depends on the length of the text and the number of variations you use.

Do as many of the following as apply to your text.

Start by doing the first step of *Carry the Bag*.

Repeat, but this time, in addition to putting down the bag on each full stop, come to a stop without putting the bag down at every colon (:). Start walking again on the next word.

Repeat, but also rise up on your toes on each semicolon (;), coming down on the next word.

Repeat, but also change direction on every comma.

If you have any dashes, carry the bag to the full stops, but also kick an imaginary ball on every dash.

If you have any ellipses (...), carry the bag to the full stops and take three little hops on the ellipses (note, sometimes an ellipsis may be followed by a full stop).

If you have any parentheses, carry the bag to the full stops and take a big sliding step to the side on both the opening and closing parenthesis.

Working without a bag, jump on every exclamation point. Turn in a circle on every question mark.

> *Teaching tip:* You can mix and match as many of the above as makes sense for the text you are working on. Note, though, that it can be hard for students to keep track of more than three actions at once, so you might find it useful to hang up a poster with the punctuation marks set out on it and another with the movement choices and have students mix and match actions and punctuation marks at their own pace. You may notice that this exercise bears a resemblance to some of the work in the *Rhythm* chapter, and at this point it can be worth talking about how the punctuation can give the text a rhythm as well as shaping the thoughts.

Turning words (timing depends on the length of the speech; generally about 5–10 minutes)

'Turning words' are any words that might mean the speaker is qualifying what he's said or is about to say – that is, he's taking his thought in a different direction. Some common ones are: **but, though, although, however, nevertheless, nay, or else** etc. Some words don't change direction so much as take things up a notch: **so, therefore, thus, for, in addition, and** etc. In some speeches and scenes, you will not find many turning words, but in some speeches you will find them frequently. (We've found that many Restoration prologues are packed with them, for example.) Whenever they do appear, they're important.

Go through your text and look for any turning words. Circle any of the above that you find or any others that seem to serve this function.

Read your speech aloud walking around the room and each time you come to one of the circled words, change direction.

Experiment with how sharp your change of direction is. Do some words seem to pull you all the way around? Do others knock you off course just a little?

Try always going to the left on qualifying words and always going to the right on words that take things to the next level.

Stand still to read the speech one last time. Can you still feel the thought take on a new energy when you come to those turning words?

Themes

When characters start to speak for an extended period of time, it is usually because they have something important that they wish to talk about. That 'something important' is their theme. They may not know precisely what they're going to say when they start speaking, but they know what their theme is, and it often reveals itself in their first few words, as in a news headline. For example, when Henry V cries to his soldiers, 'Once more unto the breach dear friends', it's clear that his theme is getting back to the battle. In *Julius Caesar,* Cassius declares to Brutus, 'Well, honour is the subject of my story' and proceeds to talk at some length about honour.

Sometimes, however, characters are not so forthcoming. It may take them awhile to find a way to express their theme, or they may put off revealing it in order to have a particular effect on their listeners. They may be shy or coy or subtle or manipulative about divulging their theme. Sometimes they may never state it overtly at all, but you as the actor need to have a firm sense of what that theme is. Identifying what the focus of your speech is will help you to understand what action your character is trying to achieve or what problem he or she is trying to solve, and you will then be able to use the language effectively to that end. The same is true in dialogues – knowing the focus of the conversation will help you move the scene forward with energy and clarity. The exercises in this section will help you to identify themes and use them to bring purpose and drive to your acting of speeches and scenes. We were first introduced to this way of working by Cicely Berry (see *Further Reading*).

Spot the theme (15–20 minutes for each exercise)

Themes are made up of words, ideas or images which are repeated throughout a speech or scene. For this exercise, we use a speech of Adriana's from Shakespeare's *The Comedy of Errors*, Act II, Scene 2. She believes that her husband has been unfaithful to her and is now confronting him.

ADRIANA
>How comes it now, my husband, O, how comes it,
>That thou art thus estrangèd* from thyself?   *alienated*
>Thyself I call it, being strange to me,
>That, undividable, incorporate*,   *made of one body*
>Am better than thy dear self's better part.
>Ah, do not tear away thyself from me!
>For know, my love, as easy mayest thou fall*   *drop*
>A drop of water in the breaking gulf*,   *whirlpool*
>And take unmingled that same drop again,
>Without addition or diminishing,
>As take from me thyself and not me too.
>How dearly would it touch thee to the quick*,   *living flesh*
>Shouldst thou but hear I were licentious*   *lustful*
>And that this body, consecrate* to thee,   *devoted*
>By ruffian lust should be contaminate!
>Wouldst thou not spit at me and spurn at* me   *kick at*
>And hurl the name of husband in my face
>And tear the stained skin off my harlot-brow
>And from my false hand cut the wedding-ring
>And break it with a deep-divorcing vow?
>I know thou canst; and therefore see thou do it.
>I am possessed with an adulterate* blot;   *unfaithful*
>My blood is mingled with the crime of lust:
>For if we two be one and thou play false,
>I do digest the poison of thy flesh,
>Being strumpeted* by thy contagion.   *made a prostitute*
>Keep then fair league and truce with thy true bed;
>I live unstained, thou undishonourèd.

Read through the text as a class, and clarify any words or phrases which you are unsure of.

Read through the speech in unison again, starting to imagine yourself in Adriana's circumstances. As you read, stomp your foot on any words you feel you want to emphasize. Don't worry if not everyone stomps at the same time.

When you've finished, talk about which words seem to get the most stomps. How do these words relate to Adriana's circumstances? Do these words have anything in common?

You've probably found a lot of words that have to do with joining together (as in a marriage) and a lot that have to do with division and coming apart (as in a divorce).

Get a partner. Start by standing a couple of metres away from each other. Read the speech out loud together, fairly slowly. Every time that you come to a word that has to do with coming together, get physically closer to each other. Every time you come to a word that has to do with separating, move away from each other.

Some words will pretty obviously move you in one direction or another; be mindful of words that might suggest union or disunion more subtly, such as 'bed' (a possible place of joining) or 'unmingled' (not mixed together). Don't worry if you don't always move on the same words.

Discuss what you've discovered about the point Adriana is trying to make to her husband and how she is making it. What have you discovered about her state of mind?

Now, partner A be Adriana and partner B be her husband. A, speak the speech and on all the joining words, try to get closer to B; B, try to avoid her.

Next, partner B be Adriana and A be her husband. B, speak the speech. This time, A will try to get close to you and you should use all the separating words to get away.

What have you discovered about themes in this exercise? How does Adriana use the theme in this speech to affect her husband?

II. In Mark Antony's speech to the Roman plebeians (*Julius Caesar* Act III, Scene 2), we find a character who uses his theme to even subtler effect:

ANTONY

Friends, Romans, countrymen, lend me your ears;	
I come to bury Caesar, not to praise him.	
The evil that men do lives after them;	
The good is oft interrèd* with their bones;	*buried*
So let it be with Caesar. The noble Brutus	
Hath told you Caesar was ambitious:	
If it were so, it was a grievous* fault,	*painful*
And grievously hath Caesar answered it.	
Here, under leave* of Brutus and the rest–	*permission*

> For Brutus is an honourable man;
> So are they all, all honourable men—
> Come I to speak in Caesar's funeral.
> He was my friend, faithful and just to me:
> But Brutus says he was ambitious;
> And Brutus is an honourable man.
> He hath brought many captives home to Rome
> Whose ransoms did the general coffers* fill: *chests of money*
> Did this in Caesar seem ambitious?
> When that the poor have cried, Caesar hath wept:
> Ambition should be made of sterner stuff:
> Yet Brutus says he was ambitious;
> And Brutus is an honourable man.
> You all did see that on the Lupercal*   *a Roman festival*
> I thrice presented him a kingly crown,
> Which he did thrice refuse: was this ambition?
> Yet Brutus says he was ambitious;
> And, sure, he is an honourable man.
> I speak not to disprove what Brutus spoke,
> But here I am to speak what I do know.
> You all did love him once, not without cause:
> What cause withholds* you then, to mourn for him?   *prevents*
> O judgement! thou art fled to brutish beasts,
> And men have lost their reason. Bear with me;
> My heart is in the coffin there with Caesar,
> And I must pause till it come back to me.

1. Read through the text as a group, and clarify any words or phrases that you're unsure of. Antony says his intention in speaking to the plebeians is to 'bury Caesar not to praise him'. So, the burial of Caesar is his stated theme.

Now, get a partner and read through the text together, making a note of any words or ideas related to the burial of Caesar. For example, 'Caesar's funeral', or 'mourn for him'.

Antony explicitly says that he hasn't come to praise Caesar. However, read through the text again, this time making a note of any words or ideas related to the praise of Caesar. For example, you might note Caesar 'was a faithful and just friend', 'refused the crown'.

Now, Partner A, speak the text as Antony and, as you do so, Partner B will make some kind of mournful sound (a sob or moan, for example) in response to any of the words or ideas related to the burial of Caesar. Then, swap over, and as B speaks the text, A will cheer in response to any of the words or ideas related to praise of Caesar. What discoveries did you make about Antony's use of these themes in the context of this speech? What is Antony's real purpose/intention/action in this speech?

2. Although Antony says that he isn't speaking to disprove what Brutus said, that is nonetheless what he is trying to achieve. His theme may be Caesar, but his purpose is to disprove Brutus.

To explore this relationship between theme and intention further, choose one person from the group to be Antony. Now, divide the rest into four groups: one group will be the Caesars, mourning or cheering anything related to the themes you've already explored; another will be the Brutuses, cheering his name every time it is mentioned; a third will be the Ambitious, echoing or repeating the words 'ambitious' and 'ambition' every time they are spoken by Antony; and the last group will be the Honourable, echoing or repeating the word 'honourable' whenever it is spoken.

The idea is not to compete with each other or try to drown out Antony, but to really listen to the text and respond appropriately whenever you hear your theme or words.

Discuss how the themes and repetitions of names and words work in this speech. What does this tell you about Antony as a character? What does it tell you about how Antony is thinking and feeling at this point? And what did the person playing Antony discover about the energy of the language?

> *Teaching tip:* Depending on the size of the group, stage 2 of the exercise could be done in smaller groups (of five or more), with each group having its own Antony. Alternatively, you could repeat the exercise with a different Antony each time, exploring the potential for irony in Antony's use of 'ambitious' and 'honourable'.

Themed dialogues (15–20 minutes each exercise)

Looking for the repetition of words or ideas is a very useful way to discover the theme, and can be applied to conversations too. One character can initiate a theme, which another will develop or change.

I. Look at this excerpt from Act I Scene 8 of *Our Country's Good* by Timberlake Wertenbaker. Dabby and Mary are two female convicts in eighteenth-century Australia. They have become involved in a project to put on a play for the other convicts:

MARY
Are you remembering your lines, Dabby?

DABBY
What lines? No. I was remembering Devon. I was on my way back to Bigbury Bay.

MARY
You promised Lieutenant Clark you'd learn your lines.

DABBY
I want to go back. I want to see a wall of stone. I want to hear the Atlantic breaking into the estuary. I can bring a boat into any harbour, in any weather. I can do it as well as the Governor.

MARY
Dabby, what about your lines?

DABBY
I'm not spending the rest of my life in this flat, brittle burnt-out country. Oh, give me some English rain.

MARY
It rains here.

DABBY
It's not the same. I could recognise English rain anywhere. And Devon rain, Mary, Devon rain is the softest in England. As soft as your breasts, as soft as Lieutenant Clark's dimpled cheeks.

MARY
Dabby, don't!

DABBY
You're wasting your time, girl, he's ripe for plucking. You can always tell with men, they begin to walk sideways. And if you don't –

MARY
  Don't start. I listened to you once before.
DABBY
  What would you have done without that lanky sailor drooling over you?
MARY
  I would have been less of a whore.
DABBY
  Listen, my darling, you're only a virgin once. You can't go to a man and say, I'm a virgin except for this one lover I had. After that, it doesn't matter how many men go through you.
MARY
  I'll never wash the sin away.

Read through the text as a class, and clarify any words or phrases which you are unsure of. Then, get a partner and read the text through together, underlining any words (other than 'and', 'is', 'to' or other connecting words) which are repeated.

Now, speak it as the characters, but when you get to any word that you've underlined, tap your partner on the arm.

Discuss what you've discovered about each character's theme, and how these themes interact. What does this tell you about the characters and their relationship to each other?

You probably noticed that the repetitions were less frequent in the second half of the dialogue. This is because the theme changes to a variety of words and images about sex. Read through the text again, this time circling any words or images connected to sex.

Now, speak it as the characters again, but when you get to any words that you've circled, nudge your partner on the arm.

Discuss what you've learnt about each character's attitude to sex. While their conversation shares this theme, their different attitudes create tension and energy between them. Does this give you new information about the characters and their relationship?

II. Sex is one of several themes which tend to occur again and again in dramatic dialogues (death/violence is another common theme), but not always as explicitly as in the previous example. For example, look at this opening scene between Theseus and Hyppolita from *A Midsummer Night's Dream* Act I, Scene 1.

THESEUS

Now, fair Hippolyta, our nuptial hour*	*wedding hour*
Draws on apace*; four happy days bring in	*quickly*
Another moon: but, O, methinks, how slow	
This old moon wanes! she lingers* my desires,	*draws out*
Like to a step-dame or a dowager*	*rich widow*
Long withering out a young man's revenue*.	*income*

HIPPOLYTA

Four days will quickly steep* themselves in night;	*dip*
Four nights will quickly dream away the time;	
And then the moon, like to a silver bow	
New-bent in heaven, shall behold the night	
Of our solemnities*.	*wedding ceremonies*

THESEUS

Go, Philostrate,	
Stir up the Athenian youth to merriments;	
Awake the pert* and nimble spirit of mirth;	*lively*
Turn melancholy forth to funerals;	
The pale companion is not for our pomp*.	*festival procession*
Hippolyta, I wooed thee with my sword,	
And won thy love, doing thee injuries;	
But I will wed thee in another key,	
With pomp, with triumph and with revelling.	

Sit in chairs or on the floor in a circle and rest the text in your lap. Split the group into two halves. One half of the circle take one character, the second half the other character. Read the text out loud and review any bits that are difficult to understand. Establish what the characters are talking about.

Read the text out loud again, and every time you come to a word that could possibly have or suggest a sexual meaning, clap your hands. Some words, like 'wooed' might be very obvious, but try to stay open to any possibility of sexual connotation – for example in a word like 'withering' or 'revelling'.

It's fine if not everybody is clapping on the same words – this isn't an exercise about getting the right answer but about opening your imagination to levels of meaning.

Were there more or fewer sexual words than you had anticipated? Does the number of sexual words seem appropriate to the topic of conversation? What purpose could they serve?

Read through the text again and every time you get to one of the words with a possible sexual meaning, raise the pitch of your voice. How does that change the feel of the text? Try it again lowering your pitch on the sexual words.

Read through the text one more time without doing anything in particular with the sexual words beyond staying aware of their presence. How does this theme give energy to the scene? What does it tell us about the characters and their relationship?

See Cicely Berry's *The Actor and the Text* for a more detailed exploration of this dialogue and its themes.

> *Teaching tip:* The sexual component of these exercises will clearly not be appropriate for some groups. The exercise can also be done tracking words that imply a threat or violence in speeches like Henry's in *Henry V* Act II, Scene 1, beginning at line 259 or Antony in *Julius Caesar* Act III, Scene 1, beginning at line 184. In some texts, like the one suggested in the exercise, it can be interesting to explore the mix of sex and violence by clapping on one type of word and stomping on the other.

III. As a final example of a themed dialogue, let's look at this edited version of a longer scene between Brutus and Cassius from *Julius Caesar* Act IV, Scenes 2 and 3.

CASSIUS
Most noble brother, you have done me wrong.
BRUTUS
Judge me, you gods! wrong I mine enemies?
And, if not so, how should I wrong a brother?

CASSIUS
Brutus, this sober* form of yours hides wrongs;   *serious, dignified*
And when you do them–
BRUTUS
Cassius, be content.
Speak your griefs softly: I do know you well.
Before the eyes of both our armies here,
Which should perceive nothing but love from us,
Let us not wrangle*: bid them move away;   *fight*
Then in my tent, Cassius, enlarge your griefs*,   *explain your grievances*
And I will give you audience.
...
CASSIUS
That you have wronged me doth appear in this:
You have condemned and noted* Lucius Pella   *dishonoured*
For taking bribes here of the Sardians;
Wherein my letters, praying on his side,
Because I knew the man, were slighted off*.   *dismissed as insignificant*
BRUTUS
You wronged yourself to write in such a case.
CASSIUS
In such a time as this it is not meet*   *proper*
That every nice* offence should bear his comment.   *insignificant*
BRUTUS
Let me tell you, Cassius, you yourself
Are much condemned to have an itching palm*   *be greedy for bribes*
To sell and mart* your offices for gold   *trade*
To undeservers.
CASSIUS
I an itching palm!
You know that you are Brutus that speak this,
Or, by the gods, this speech were else your last.

BRUTUS
> The name of Cassius honours this corruption,
> And chastisement* doth therefore hide his
> > head.   *punishment*

Split the group into two halves, with everyone sitting in chairs or on the floor in a circle and resting the text in their laps. One half of the circle, take one character, the second half the other character. Read the text out loud and review any bits that are difficult to understand. Establish what the characters are talking about.

By now, you don't need telling that the theme is 'wrong': the repetition of the word is very noticeable. Read the text out loud again, and every time you come to the word 'wrong', stomp your foot.

You probably noticed that the repetitions got fewer in the second half of the dialogue. Is this because the theme changes or for some other reason? To explore this, get a partner and read the text through together, underlining the word 'wrong' and circling any other words that have any connotations of 'wrong'. Some words, like 'corruption' might be very obvious, but try to stay open to any possibility of wrongful connotation – for example, in a word like 'griefs' or 'slighted'.

Now, stand up and move to opposite sides of the room. Speak the text as the characters, and stomp your foot whenever you say 'wrong' or 'wronged'; but, in addition, when you get to any word that you've circled, take a step towards your partner.

What does this tell you about the characters and their relationship to each other?

Repeat this exercise, but now play with how forcefully you stomp your foot and how big a step you take towards each other. Let the energy of your movement reflect the emotional energy of the language.

Follow-up

Reflective practice questions:

- What discoveries have you made about language through the work of this chapter?

- Which exercises helped you most in getting a deeper understanding of your texts?
- Look at a text that you have found difficult to understand. What makes it so challenging? Could the author have expressed the ideas more simply? Why do you think he or she chose not to? Does the difficulty reveal something about the character or the situation? Or could the dense language be intended to have a particular effect on the listener? What effect would that be?
- On your next visit to the theatre, listen to how well the actors make sense of the author's language. Notice where characters develop themes. Write a brief report in your reflective journal.

Suggested texts

Thoughts

Question time

Luis Alfaro, *Oedipus El Rey*, Scene 19, Tiresias: 'You think your father is made of blood'
Frances Ya-Chu Cowhig, *Snow in Midsummer*, Prologue 1, Woman: 'This exhausted body'
Hannah Cowley, *The Belle's Stratagem*, Act I Scene 3, Doricourt: 'Ay, but that was at eighteen'
Eisa Davis, *Bulrusher*, Act I, Madame: 'His tree just fell on my property'
Ben Jonson, *The Alchemist*, Act III Scene 1, Tribulation: 'Not always necessary'

Who's doing what

Aphra Behn, *The Lucky Chance*, Act II Scene 1, Landlady: 'My Husband!'
John Ford, *'Tis Pity She's a Whore*, Act IV Scene 3, Annabella: 'Pleasures, farewell'

Kate Hennig, *The Last Wife*, Act I Scene 8, 'His Highness most prudently and wisely considering'

Tony Kushner, *Angels in America Part Two: Perestroika*, Act I Scene 1, Prelapsarianov: from 'An Theory'

Subordinate cuckoo clock

David Edgar, *Pentecost*, Act II Scene 5, Leo: 'And thus doubtless won't need telling'

Christopher Marlowe, *Doctor Faustus*, Act I, Chorus: 'Not marching'

William Shakespeare, *Henry IV Part Two*, Prologue (Rumour): 'Open your ears'

Oscar Wilde, *An Ideal Husband*, Act II, Lady Markby: 'And a very good thing too'

Fill in the blanks

Suzan-Lori Parks, *Imperceptible Mutabilities in the Third Kingdom*, Part 4A, Mr Smith: 'I'll have four'

Conor McPherson, *Dublin Carol*, Part 1, John: 'You'd want to die'

William Shakespeare, *Cymbeline*, Act I Scene 6, Iachimo: 'Had I this cheek'

Bernard Shaw, *Heartbreak House*, Act I, Lady Utterword: 'I know what you must feel'

Carry the bag

James Baldwin, *Blues for Mister Charlie*, Act I, Lorenzo: 'Yeah. Well, I wish to God I was in an arsenal'

Eisa Davis, *Bulrusher*, Act I, Madame: 'The river tells you everything'

Suzan-Lori Parks, *Topdog/Underdog*, Scene 5, Lincoln: 'I think there was something out there'

Tom Stoppard, *Salvage: The Coast of Utopia Part III*, Act I, February 1853, Herzen: 'It's true – I haven't entered into English life'

Punctuation play

Edward Albee, *The Zoo Story*, Peter: from 'It's just … it's just that' through 'Just that, a dog'

SENSE

Kwame Kwei-Armah, *Statement of Regret*, Act II Scene 4, Junior: 'Alright, you wanna bring this down'
David Mamet, *Glengarry Glen Ross*, Act I Scene 3, Roma: 'I don't know'
Paula Vogel, *Desdemona: A Play About a Handkerchief*, Scene 13, Emilia: '- then she's gullin' you'

Turning words

William Congreve, *The Way of the World*, Epilogue
Tony Kushner, *Homebody/Kabul*, Act I Scene 1, Homebody: from 'Oh I love the world' through 'it's very hard, I know'
William Shakespeare, *Henry IV Part 2*, Act I Scene 2, Falstaff: 'Men of all sorts'
John Webster, *The Duchess of Malfi*, Act III Scene 2, Ferdinand: 'The howling of a wolf'

Themes

Spot the theme I–II (either of these exercises can be adapted for use with any of the texts below)

Lauren Gunderson, *The Book of Will*, Act II Scene 1, Henry: 'I said to feel again'
Quiara Alegría Hudes, *Elliot, A Soldier's Fugue*, 4/Prelude, Ginny: 'Gardening is like boxing'
Christopher Marlowe, *Dido Queen of Carthage*, Act IV Scene 4, Dido: 'Are these the sails'
Bernard Shaw, *Saint Joan*, Scene 5, Joan: 'Where would you all be now'

Themed dialogues I–III (any of these three exercises can be adapted for use with any of the texts below)

Frances Ya-Chu Cowhig, *Snow in Midsummer*, Act 1 Scene 1, from Madam Wong: 'No messy mishaps tonight' through Madam Wong: 'Madam Wong intends to survive'
Yasmina Reza, *Art*, Marc and Yvan from Marc: 'And what about Serge' through Yvan: As long as it's not doing harm to anyone else'

William Shakespeare, *Twelfth Night*, Act I Scene 5, Viola and Olivia from
   Viola: 'Good madam let me see you face' through Olivia: 'How does
   he love me'
Paula Vogel, *How I Learned to Drive*, Peck and Li'l Bit from Peck: 'I want
   you to know your automobile' through Li'l Bit: 'If I put my hands on
   the wheel – how do I defend myself'

Further reading

Berry, Cicely, *The Actor and the Text* (revised edition), Virgin Books, London,
   1993. 'Energy through the Text', pp. 82–90.
Crystal, David and Ben Crystal, *Shakespeare's Words: A Glossary and
   Language Companion*, Penguin Books, London, 2004.
Houseman, Barbara, *Tackling Text*, Nick Hern Books, London, 2008.
   'Exploring Structures and Rhythms', pp. 37–46, 84–95; 'Handling Complex
   Sentences', pp. 136–138.
Kaiser, Scott, *Mastering Shakespeare*, Allworth Press, New York, 2003. Scene
   1: The Art of Orchestration, pp. 1–32.
Onions, C. T., *A Shakespeare Glossary* (revised by Robert D. Eagleson), Oxford
   University Press, Oxford, 1986.
Rodenburg, Patsy, *The Actor Speaks*, Methuen, London, 1997. 'The Length of
   Thought', pp. 193–198.
Rodenburg, Patsy, *Speaking Shakespeare*, Methuen, London, 2002. 'The
   Word', pp. 72–77.
Schmidt, Alexander, *Shakespeare Lexicon and Quotation Dictionary* (in 2
   volumes, revised by Gregor Sarrazin), Dover Publications, New York, 1971.
Shewmaker, Eugene F., *Shakespeare's Language: A Glossary of Unfamiliar
   Words in His Plays* (2nd edition), Checkmark Books, New York, 2008.
Usher, George, *Shakespeare A–Z: Understanding Shakespeare's Words*,
   Bloomsbury Publishing, London, 2005.

4
RHYTHM

Framework

Periodically, we have the opportunity to teach workshops or short courses. Our time with the students on those courses is limited and usually devoted to helping them make the most of one particular piece of (often prose) text. When we do this kind of short, intensive work, we've found that the element of language that we focus on most is rhythm. Character, emotional state, intensity, intention are all manifest through rhythm – if you can get the rhythm, it opens the door for you to do work that is both transformational and truthful.

Rhythm is energy, it is the blood in our veins, a tapping toe, a jabbing finger; it's there in the way we walk, skip, run, waltz or boogie; and it's in the way we speak. Rhythm in speech arises from the physical roots of language. Indeed, our very first experience of any rhythm is likely to be physical: in the womb, the baby is exposed to the sensation of the mother's heartbeat, her breathing, her walking – all activities of the body which are repeated in a regular way. And it is the regular repetition of an activity – a movement, a beat, a clapping sound – which constitutes rhythm. We enjoy the rhythms of dance, of music, of skipping rhymes and of football chants because rhythm is infectious; it affects us physically, emotionally and mentally, changing the way we think and feel. Rhythm can be hypnotic, sexual, dramatic, soporific, soothing, rousing and even aggravating. See *Exploration I* for an investigation of this.

Although it might not be as strong or infectious as the rhythms of rock music or salsa, spoken language also uses a beat which has an underlying regularity and can change the way we think and feel. This beat is created in different ways in the languages of the world but all will use some combination of pitch, loudness and tempo. English does it by the regular occurrence of **stressed** (or **strong**) syllables – stress being the term that phoneticians use to describe how some syllables in a word or sentence sound more prominent than others. For this reason, English is often described as a stress-timed language. Some other languages are also said to be stress-timed (Russian, for example), while others are said to use a syllable-timed rhythm, in which it is the syllables which occur at regular intervals (French, for example), creating a machine-gun like effect in speech. Yet other languages may make use of pitch placement as the important element in creating rhythm (e.g. many languages of South and East Asia). If you are not a speaker of a stress-timed language, you may find work on English rhythm challenging, particularly if you are unfamiliar with the English language's use of **unstressed** (or **weak**) syllables in contrast to the stressed (or strong) ones. Unstressed syllables tend to be quieter, shorter and often lower in pitch than stressed ones.

For example, in the three-syllable word un**like**ly, the second syllable would normally be stressed, that is, the **like** part of the word would be made to stand out more. On the other hand, in the three-syllable word **beau**tiful, a speaker would normally stress the first syllable, whereas in the word enter**tain** it is the **tain** part of the word which normally stands out most. To get a feel for how stressing usually works, it can help to explore unconventional stressing. Try saying *unlikely, beautiful* and *entertain* with the stress on a different syllable – for example, say **un** with more emphasis than *like*. Did you find that you needed to accompany your choice with a small movement of your head to assist you in breaking the normal pattern? Or perhaps you raised the pitch of your voice, or changed your facial expression. Stressing a syllable means we give more physical energy to it, which tends to make stressed syllables louder, longer and often higher in pitch in contrast to the unstressed ones.

Patterns of stressed and unstressed sounds don't just occur within words, they also form the rhythmic component of the sentences we speak. When native English speakers put words together in a sentence, they give the greatest emphasis to the stressed syllables in those words which carry most importance for them. This has the effect of making those words more prominent for the listener and can help shape the meaning of the sentence.

To get a sense of this, speak the following sentence: '*I'm unlikely ever to entertain a beautiful millionaire.*' Repeat it several times and see if you can identify the stressed syllables. To help you identify these, you can tap along to the sentence with your foot – you will probably stress and tap at the same time. Now speak the sentence as if you were answering the question: 'How often will you entertain a beautiful millionaire?' You probably gave an extra strong stress to the **ev** in **ev**er, which helped to shape the meaning of what you were saying. Now speak the sentence as if you were answering the question: 'What kind of millionaire are you unlikely to entertain?' This time the extra strong stress probably went to the **beau** in **beau**tiful. Note (and this will become a very important point later) that not all the stressed syllables in a sentence have to be equally strong.

Now go back to speaking the sentence as you did when you weren't answering any particular question, and tap out the stresses with your finger or foot as you say it. If you are speaking the sentence fluently, you will probably notice that the stresses occur in a fairly regular pattern. You will probably also notice that the weaker syllables get squashed together in order to maintain this pattern, so that it takes roughly the same time to say the four unstressed syllables between **ev** and **tain** ('*er to enter*') as it does to say the one unstressed syllable between **tain** and **beau** ('*a*'). This is the basis of speech rhythm in the English language: stressed syllables tend to occur at roughly equal intervals, while unstressed syllables are contracted to accommodate this.

When we are on a roll – feeling really fluent and committed to expressing ourselves – this rhythmic feature of language becomes more evident. When it is regularized and formalized in a written pattern, we call it **verse**, which we find in most poetry and some plays, such as those of Shakespeare. **Prose**, on the other hand, is the term usually given to written language which does not display such a formalized pattern. But this does not mean that it lacks rhythm. We can still feel a heightened sense of rhythm emerge in prose when the intention to affect the reader is particularly strong. The same is true of speech. A good public speaker instinctively speaks in a rhythmic and fluent way; a poor speaker may be too nervous or incoherent in his thoughts to establish a strong rhythm.

In fact, part of what makes us think of a speaker as 'good' is his or her ability to speak with a sense of rhythm. As listeners, we respond physically to the rhythmic element of language; we resonate with it, are uplifted and carried along by it. If it falters or becomes disjointed, we lose interest. Many politicians employ professional speech writers for this very reason – see *Exploration IV* to get a feel for this.

But if we were always to speak in the same rhythm, it would get monotonous and our listeners would again lose interest. As any good jazz musician will tell you, the main reason to establish a rhythm is so that you can then riff on it, playing variations on the established pattern to create emotional, physical and mental changes in the players and listeners. As a drama student or professional actor, you will be able to capture the power of bold, passionate speech or embody the inner turmoil of halting, broken speech by getting the beat in your belly and working with the rhythm of both prose and verse texts.

Exploration

I. Begin either sitting or standing, and notice how you are breathing and feeling. Start to rock gently from side to side. Establish an easy rhythm to this movement. How does it make you feel? Play with the tempo of your rocking – you could make it quicker or slower. Does this change how you feel? Does it change how you think? What happens if you change the scale of your rocking by making the movement larger or smaller?

Let the side-to-side motion come to an end and notice how you are breathing. Now start to rock backward and forward. Again, establish an easy rhythm to this movement. How does it make you feel? Play with the tempo of your rocking by making it quicker or slower. Does this change how you feel? Does it change how you think? What happens if you change the scale of your rocking by making the movement larger or smaller? After a short while, come to a rest. How are you breathing and feeling? Has your heartbeat altered at all?

II. Find an interview in a foreign language on the internet or stream a foreign film. Listen to a few minutes of it with your eyes closed. What do you notice about the speakers' rhythms? Would you say they're quick, slow, steady, broken, sustained, choppy? What do these rhythms suggest to you about the speakers' age, status, emotional state, relationship to the listeners?

III. Read over the following extract from Robert Louis Stevenson's novel *Kidnapped*. When you feel you understand it, speak it out loud a couple of times. Then speak it aloud a third time, paying more attention to which words you are stressing. Try tapping with your foot or conducting with your hand while you speak it.

> The sun began to shine upon the summit of the hills as I went down the road; and by the time I had come as far as the manse, the blackbirds were whistling in the garden lilacs, and the mist that hung around the valley in the time of the dawn was beginning to arise and die away.

Do you feel any rhythmic pattern to the stresses? Does that shift at any point? Does this complement any emotional effect of the language? We've taken the liberty of doing a bit of re-writing:

> The sun started to shine on the tops of the hills as I went down the road; and by the time I got to the manse, the birds were whistling in the lilacs, and the morning mist was starting to lift from the valley and die away.

Try speaking this version aloud a couple of times, and then speak it with a focus on the words you are stressing. Have we changed the rhythm of how you speak it? If so, has this changed the emotional effect of the narrative?

We suggest that there is a quicker rhythm in our version, and that this contributes to it feeling more factual and less lyrical, less evocative. The way Stevenson sets up patterns of stressed and unstressed syllable seems to lend this passage a sense of hope and optimism.

IV. Find a famous speech. The speeches of Martin Luther King Jr., John F. Kennedy, Winston Churchill, Margaret Thatcher and others are all widely available on the internet. Read the speech to yourself, and when you feel you understand it, speak it out loud a couple of times. Then speak it aloud a third time, paying more attention to which words you are stressing. Try tapping with your foot or conducting with your hand while you speak it. Does it have a rhythm?

V. If you can, find an audio or video clip of the speech you used in *Exploration IV* and listen to it, or pick a more contemporary figure such as Barack Obama or Harriet Harman. Try tapping your foot or conducting with your hand as you listen to identify the rhythm. Are there any characteristics of the rhythm that seem to get a response from the listener (like regular pauses or a pattern of stressing certain words)?

Exercises

> *Teaching tip:* The exercises in this chapter are divided into four sections: *Prose: Finding the Rhythm, Verse: Finding the Rhythm, Verse: Breaking the Rhythm* and *Verse: The Energy of the Line.* You can start with (or limit yourself to) either the prose work or the verse work; the verse work is best done in sequence, though.

As in other chapters, many of the exercises that follow are physical, so you will want to wear loose clothes and warm up your body and voice before you begin. Stretching and shaking out would be a good start. Some of the exercises will also require you to have a pencil to hand.

Prose: Finding the rhythm

When you are working with verse, there is usually one regular rhythmic pattern that you can identify early on. In prose, however, rhythms can be a little more difficult to distinguish. They are no less important, however, in creating the specific energy of a passage. If you haven't already done so, try *Exploration III* or *IV* above to get a feel for this.

There are several elements that can create a prose rhythm: a pattern of alternating stressed and unstressed syllables; repetition of words or types of words; use of pauses; shifts of tempo; uniformity or variety of sentence length. Go back to *Exploration IV* and try to identify which of these the speaker you've picked is using. All of these techniques give prose speeches and scenes momentum; the rhythms can hook us and carry us along, and before we know it we might be nodding our heads in time with something we may not agree with at all.

In the exercises that follow, you will learn to get a feel for the rhythms of prose and use them to bring energy and specificity to your text work.

Riffing on repetition (10–15 minutes for each piece of text)

Riffing on the repetition of words, phrases and even whole sentences is a great source of rhythm for prose writers.

I. Look at the following extract from Bernard Shaw's play *Man and Superman*. The Devil is engaged in a debate with another character about the merits of human life, and has this to say as part of his argument:

> This marvellous force of Life of which you boast is a force of Death: Man measures his strength by his destructiveness. What is his religion? An excuse for hating me. What is his law? An excuse for hanging you. What is his morality? Gentility! An excuse for consuming without producing. What is his art? An excuse for gloating over pictures of slaughter. What are his politics? Either the worship of a despot because a despot can kill, or parliamentary cock-fighting.

Read through the text out loud once to get a feel for it. Review any words or sections that are hard to understand.

Get a partner and decide which is A and B. You are both going to be the Devil, but A will ask the questions and B will answer them (split the first sentence between you as well, with A reading to the colon).

Speak the text through in this way a couple of times until you feel you are in sync with each other.

Speak it through again, but now, as you do so, tap your foot or click your fingers along with the words that you are stressing. What do you notice about your own rhythm? What do you notice about each other's rhythm?

Speak it through once more, but this time wag your finger at your partner in time to your rhythm, as if you're scoring points off each other in a debate. Count the number of times your partner wags his or her finger.

Discuss what repetitions and variations Shaw has used to create these rhythmic effects. Where and how does he break the rhythm? What effect does this have?

II. Shaw's Devil is in a serious debate with another character; Shakespeare's Benedict is in a comic debate with himself in the following speech from *Much Ado about Nothing*, Act II, Scene 3. He is considering what it would take for him to give up his freedom as a bachelor:

One woman is fair, yet I am well; another is wise, yet I am well; another virtuous, yet I am well; but till all graces be in one woman, one woman shall not come in my grace. Rich she shall be, that's certain; wise, or I'll none; virtuous, or I'll never cheapen her; fair, or I'll never look on her; mild, or come not near me; noble, or not I for an angel; of good discourse, an excellent musician, and her hair shall be of what colour it please God.

Read through the text out loud once or twice to get a feel for it. Review any words or sections that are hard to understand.

Get a chair and stand facing it to begin with. Speak the text through, but every time you come to a comma turn away from the chair in one direction or another and every time you come to a semicolon or full stop turn back to face it again.

Repeat this stage of the exercise, but now imagine that sitting in the chair is the succession of women that Benedict is considering. So, every time you turn back to the chair a different aspect of womanhood is sitting there.

Repeat again, but now add appropriate gestures and explore Benedict's reactions to these women.

Now, explore the rhythm of the text more fully by moving rhythmically towards and away from the chair in time to the phrases.

Discuss what repetitions and variations of stress and language Shakespeare has used to create these rhythmic effects. Where and how does he break the rhythm? What effect does this have?

Length of thought (10–15 minutes)

You can use either of the texts from the *Riffing on Repetition* exercises or one from *Suggested Texts*.

Read your text out loud a couple of times if you're not familiar with it.

Walk alongside a wall as you read your text out loud. Every time you come to a full stop (or question mark or exclamation mark that ends the sentence), slap the wall with the hand closest to it. Slap with a strong energy, but not so hard that you hurt your hand.

In addition, every time you come to a punctuation mark other than a full stop (or other sentence-ender), turn around and walk alongside the wall in the opposite direction.

RHYTHM

If you get to the end of the wall before you come to a direction-changing punctuation mark, you can change direction – just try not to let it interrupt your flow.

What did you discover about the rhythm of the speech? Is there any pattern of longer or shorter sentences? Longer or shorter phrases within those sentences?

> *Teaching tip:* With four clear walls, you can have four students do this exercise at once; if there is more than one to a wall, however, they risk running into each other as they change direction.

Syllabic variations (10–15 minutes)

How a writer uses words with different numbers of syllables can have a big influence on the rhythm and tempo of a text, not only in prose but also in verse. Look at this extract from *Serious Money* by Caryl Churchill. Jacinta is a Peruvian businesswoman reflecting on the financial crisis of the 1980s. Money is her theme:

JACINTA
Father got his hands on enough of it but what happened, massive inflation, lucky he'd put the money somewhere safe, the Swiss mountains so white from the air like our mountains but the people rich with cattle and clocks and secrets, the American plains yellow with wheat, the green English fields where lords still live in grey stone, all with such safe banks and good bonds and exciting gambles, so as soon as any dollars or pounds come, don't let them go into our mines or our coffee or look for a sea of oil under the jungle, no get it out quickly to the western banks (a little money in cocaine, that's different).

Read the text out loud once or twice to get a feel for it.

Speak it through again, but now as you do so, tap your foot or wag your finger along with the words (or, actually, the syllables) that you are stressing. Repeat this, if necessary, so that you feel a strong sense of the stressed syllables.

Speak it again, this time moving round the room as you do so. Let your body move in time to the stresses.

Get a pencil and underline all the words which have only one syllable. Put another line under any of these words that you have been stressing.

Speak the text once more, again moving around the room as you do so. But this time only move your body on the words you have underlined twice. What do you notice about your rhythm and tempo this time? What does this tell you about the speaker and her attitude?

Discuss what you've discovered about rhythm and tempo in relation to the stressed syllables, and particularly Caryl Churchill's use of monosyllables.

Dialogue – sharing rhythm (10–15 minutes for each piece of text)

A playwright can also play with rhythms in dialogue.

I. Choose a scene from the *Suggested Texts* for this exercise or another extract of dialogue that involves characters alternating lines of similar length.

Get a partner and familiarize yourselves with the text.

Now, with each of you taking one of the characters, speak the text quite fluently but conversationally.

Speak it again, perhaps swapping roles, and listen for the stressed syllables in each line.

Speak it a third time, conducting the stresses in your line with your hand, but avoid leaving any pauses between each other's lines so that the dialogue becomes continuous. Feel how the rhythm changes through the text.

When the line length or the pattern of stressed and unstressed syllables changes, what effect does it have on the emotional energy of the scene?

II. Choose a scene from the *Suggested Texts* for this exercise or another scene that involves two or more characters and requires a driving pace.

Get into groups of as many students as there are speaking characters in the scene. Read the text round the group a couple of times to familiarize yourselves with it. You don't have to allocate parts at this stage – just change speaker when the character changes so that everybody has a roughly equal go at it.

Read it through again in the same way but with pace and picking up cues promptly. Since you aren't necessarily speaking in character, this gives you a chance to feel just the rhythm and tempo of the language on its own.

What have you discovered about this bit of dialogue? Are there any repetitions of words, phrases or patterns? How do the repetitions contribute to the overall rhythm?

Now, allocate parts and play the scene again. At first, take your time, so that you can discover the interplay between the characters; but then, as you become more confident, build up a sense of pace. What happens if anyone misses a beat or slows the tempo down too much?

Verse: Finding the rhythm

In its earliest forms, poetry is strongly associated with regular rhythms: the rhythms of ritual, the rhythms of song and of dance, the rhythms of physical work (hoeing, hauling, hacking) and the rhythms of play (skipping, chanting). The rhythmic nature of poetry helps make it memorable and, before the age of written histories, people remembered the key events of their tribe or clan through stories in rhythmic verse, as in Homeric epics and Norse sagas.

The first Western plays that we have records of are in rhythmic verse, and grew out of the rituals associated with the festival of the Greek god Dionysus. Greek verse has given us the names for many different rhythmic patterns, and if you're interested in learning more about these terms you'll find some good texts in the *Further Reading* section of this chapter. We're not going to go into a lot of detail about them here, because the names of different verse forms themselves are less important than feeling how their rhythmic patterns affect you physically. However, there are just a few terms that we'll be using in this chapter that you need to be familiar with for easy reference. They are:

- **Foot** – a foot is a unit of rhythm consisting of a regular pattern of stressed and unstressed syllables.

- **Iamb** – an iamb is a foot consisting of two syllables, in which the first syllable is unstressed and the second is stressed, giving it a 'ti **tum**' rhythm (like 'de**fend**', 'per**haps**' or 'the **first**'– in all three, the second syllable is stronger than the first).
- **Trochee** – a trochee is also a foot consisting of two syllables, but one in which the first syllable is stressed and the second syllable is unstressed, giving it a '**tum** ti' rhythm (like '**sec**ond', '**shoul**der', or '**beat** it' – in all three, the first syllable is stronger).
- **Metre** – a metre is a verse form consisting of the regular repetition of a specific number of feet in a line.
- **Pentameter** – a verse form that has five feet in a line. In **iambic pentameter**, for example, each of those feet is an iamb, creating verse lines of (normally) ten syllables.

Since most of the verse plays you are likely to encounter will be in iambic pentameter, we are going to focus on this verse form. Shakespeare, for example, uses primarily iambic pentameter. You can hear it in a line like: 'When **I** do **count** the **clock** that **tells** the **time**' from his Sonnet 12. Try speaking the line. Can you feel the ti **tum** ti **tum** ti **tum** ti **tum** ti **tum** rhythm? Speak it again and lean a little bit into the stressed syllables with your voice, tapping out the rhythm with your finger or foot as you go. Now go back to just speaking it. This line is often given as an example of iambic pentameter because the rhythm is very easy to hear. Even when you're just speaking it, not tapping or leaning into the rhythm, all of the strong syllables are more or less equally strong and all the weak syllables equally weak – it's a very regular pattern, and very effective at suggesting a beat like a clock. If, however, all lines of iambic pentameter were this regular, it would be mind-numbingly boring to listen to.

Fortunately, the conventions of iambic pentameter do not say that all strong stresses in a line have to be equally strong. The second syllable in a foot just has to be stronger than the first. Let's look at one of Romeo's line from *Romeo and Juliet*, 'But soft, what light through yonder window breaks?' When you're getting used to working with verse, it can help to start by identifying where the feet are since they don't always correspond to where the words are: 'But soft/what light/through yon/der win/dow breaks?' (The/marks the boundary between feet.) Now say it out loud, leaning into the rhythm with your voice and tapping it with your foot: 'But **soft**/what **light**/through **yon**/der **win**/dow **breaks**?' It helps to lean into the rhythm so that you can really feel the beat, but the fact is, no actor playing Romeo would ever speak the line this way; or if he did he would probably drive the audience out of the theatre in droves.

Now, just speak the line as if you were simply asking the question. Most likely, you gave a very strong stress to the words 'light' and 'breaks': they are, after all, the subject and the verb – the key parts of the sentence. You might also have given an extra little pulse to 'soft,' or maybe to the 'win' in 'window'. All those choices are open to you within the rhythm of the verse – those syllables all appear in positions of strong stress, but those strong stresses don't have to be equally strong. You probably did not, on the other hand, make 'but' more important than 'soft', or 'through' more important than 'yon.' Try doing it that way. It goes against the rhythm, doesn't it? And, just as important, it goes against the sense.

Just to make the point again: you will not encounter verse lines that naturally have a clock-like, completely uniform beat very often. This exercise of leaning into the iambic rhythm and tapping along with it is still a vital one, though, for several reasons.

FIRST: sometimes when we just speak a line normally, we break the rhythm without even knowing it – putting a strong stress where there should be a weak syllable or *vice versa*. Leaning into the rhythm can help you realize where you are breaking it. Although breaking the rhythm is not necessarily the worst thing in the world, Shakespeare in particular had an incredible instinct for rhythm and drama, so it's always worth considering what words he put into a stressed position and why.

There's a great example in Shakespeare's *Measure for Measure*. Angelo has sentenced Claudio to death, so Claudio's sister, Isabella, comes to Angelo to plead for his life. Angelo is desperately attracted to Isabella, so he tells her that if she will sleep with him, he'll free Claudio. She's very smart and tells him that if he doesn't free Claudio, she will tell everyone that he's made this indecent and illegal proposal. Angelo, however, has a reputation for being the most upstanding, law-abiding man in the city, so he tells Isabella that it won't make any difference because no one will believe her. He then leaves, and she says, 'To whom should I complain? Did I tell this//Who would believe me?' (The//is there to show where the new verse line begins.) Try speaking the lines as if you were asking the questions. Do it again, and notice which words you are stressing most strongly in the second sentence. Chances are they are 'tell', 'who' and 'believe'. Now try leaning into the iambic pentameter. 'Did **I**/tell **this**//Who **would**/be**lieve**/me?' You'll find that Shakespeare puts 'this' and 'would' in strong positions. That may feel awkward. Your job is then to figure out if you can make sense of this rhythm.

The first thing to remember is that 'tell' doesn't have to become an unimportant word – 'this' just needs to be more important. Try that: 'Did **I** tell **this**'. If you are playing Isabella, emphasizing 'this' gives you the chance to realize exactly how monstrous Angelo's proposition is as you say the word. Try it again. Now try making 'would' more important than 'who': 'Who **would** be**lieve** me?' Similarly, this gives you the chance to realize as you say the word 'would' that Angelo is right: you are completely trapped. Try it again – you may get chills. Many of us first go to a rhythm that essentially gives the lines the meaning, 'Wow, this is unbelievable.' Shakespeare uses a rhythm, however, that gives us the chance to *do* something *on* the language – to realize and absorb the horror of the situation – which has the potential to be much more interesting dramatically.

The SECOND reason to mark the rhythm of your text is to find out when you might come up a syllable short or have one syllable too many. You can then decide if there are simple adjustments that will make the rhythm regular again. Let's go back to Sonnet 12, which has the line 'When I behold the violet past prime.' Speak it once or twice out loud. Divide it into feet: 'When I/behold/the vio/let past/prime' – okay, first problem: we have only nine syllables. Now try speaking it and leaning into the iambic rhythm: 'When **I**/be**hold**/the **vio**/let **past**/prime' – wait a minute: 'past' is stressed and 'prime' isn't? That's hard to make sense of. When you feel your rhythm suddenly go wonky that way and find that your syllables are only adding up to nine, look and see if there's a word that could potentially be drawn out a bit. In this case, there's the word 'violet'. We usually say it with two syllables these days, but it was originally a three-syllable word. Try saying it with three syllables: 'vi-o-let'. Try saying it that way in the line: 'When **I**/be**hold**/the **vi**/o**let**/past **prime**.' There's your rhythm. It also adds emphasis to the word 'violet'. 'It's sad to see any flower past its prime,' the rhythm seems to say, 'but when it's the violet – well, that's a sorry sight indeed'. It's this need to keep the rhythm regular that leads to the final 'ed' in a word sometimes being pronounced as a separate syllable, for example '**bur**-i-**ed**' instead of just '**bur**ied'. Once you know that you're looking for ten-syllable lines with a regular beat, it's pretty easy to find where these belong.

When you find that you have one syllable too many, you first need to look at the rhythm to see if it's regular all the way but with one extra unstressed syllable at the end. For example: 'To **be**/or **not**/to **be**/that **is**/the **ques**tion.' This is a particular kind of line that we'll work with in the exercises – you don't need to worry about it now. If, however, you have eleven syllables and the rhythm goes wonky in the middle, you may find that you need to miss out a syllable. For example, going back to Romeo: 'It **is**/the **east**/and **Ju**/li**et**/is **the**/sun'. '**The** sun' – you can hear how that just doesn't make sense. If, however, you contract the word 'Juliet' into a quicker 'Julyet', the rhythm works: 'It **is**/the **east**/and **Jul**/yet **is**/the **sun**.' It's actually pretty natural to do this. We do it every day in conversational speech. For example, say, 'Um, Juliet, could you pass the salt?' You probably shortened the name to 'Julyet' as you spoke it. Technically, this reduction of the number of sounds or syllables in one word is called **elision**. This helps you keep an iambic rhythm. Tap it out as you repeat the sentence. A good writer will give you a rhythm that is as easy to speak as this. You will also find that the more time you spend doing this kind of work, the easier it gets. Before long, you can feel the bumps in the rhythm and how to adjust to them very quickly and easily.

The exercises below will give you the opportunity to practise finding and working with the rhythm of iambic pentameter. While many of the exercises in this book will (we hope) help you to make big, exciting discoveries about your text, most of those in this section are intended more to help you build up a particular skill – that of speaking effectively in metre. Think of them as the equivalent of playing scales on a musical instrument and come back to them regularly to build your verse muscles. So, even if you come across other forms of verse, you will find that the work you have done on iambic pentameter will help you identify and navigate the specific rhythm involved.

All this work on finding the rhythm of the language is something you should do very early in your process so that it feels natural and easy by the time you're performing. The very last thing you want to be thinking about when you're onstage is 'oh no, that "Juliet" is coming up; I have to remember to mush it into two syllables'. The rhythm is there to help move your thoughts, energy and intentions forward, not to tie you up in a straitjacket. The Shakespeare Police will not come and get you if you break it; it's just always worth investigating how the rhythm the author has used can serve you.

NOTE: For a fuller discussion of Shakespearean verse, please read our book, *The Shakespeare Workbook and Video* (see *Further Reading*).

Feeling the beat (20–30 minutes for the sequence of three exercises)

VIDEO LINK

Feeling the beat: https://vimeo.com/268972977

See *Suggested Texts* for some speeches that are particularly good for these exercises.

Get a pencil and your text and sit in a circle on chairs or on the floor.

As a group, first read the text out loud just to get the feel of it.

Go over any parts of the text that may not be clear and briefly review what the speech is about.

Read the text aloud again, this time leaning into the ti-**tum** of the iambic pentameter with your voice and tapping either your foot or pencil in rhythm with the strong stresses.

Whenever you get to a place where the rhythm goes off the iambic beat, stop and see if there's a word that needs to be cut down a bit or expanded to make the metre work. In a few cases, you may come across a line with an eleventh unstressed syllable at the end or a line that seems as if it should start with a strong stress to make sense. Don't worry about those – put a little star next to them and say them however you would naturally.

If you think it will help you keep track of the rhythm, you can put a little mark over each of the strong stresses.

Now try one of the following:

RHYTHM

I. Stand up and place one foot about half a metre in front of the other (more if you have long legs). Rock back and forth from one leg to the other. Start moving around the room at a trot or a slow gallop, the back foot propelling you forward. Don't feel like you have to go too fast. When you have the hang of it, grab your text and start speaking it as you gallop, lining up the strong stresses with the rhythm of your movement. It sounds complicated, but if you don't think about it too hard, it will come pretty intuitively. As you get into it, play with how you're galloping. Don't just go at the same pace in the same direction: explore changing direction on punctuation marks, or changing pace in response to the images. There are no right or wrong answers – it's about getting the rhythm into your body and using it creatively, not monotonously.

II. If you can easily get your hands on a basketball, or another good-sized bouncing ball, use it for this exercise; if not, just pretend you have one. Hold your text in one hand and start speaking it. Once you're a line or two into it, start bouncing the ball (real or imagined) with the other hand, hitting the ball on the strong stresses. As you get into it, you may find that you're hitting the ball more strongly on some stresses than others or that sometimes you're bouncing more rapidly than at others. When you get to the end, repeat the exercise moving around the room with the ball a bit, feeling where the bounces cover a lot of ground and where they stay confined to a smaller area. Again, there are no right or wrong answers – it's just about feeling the energy of the rhythm in your body. Did you discover anything interesting about the emotional life of the character in this way?

III. Sit facing a partner. Partner A, place one hand on your knee, palm up. Partner B, hold your text in one hand and rest your index finger in your partner's upturned palm. B, you will now read your speech out loud very gently tapping your partner's palm on each strong stress. Read the speech again focusing on the meaning and the images, rather than leaning into the rhythm, but still tap your partner's hand on each strong stress. The taps may speed up or slow down depending on what you're saying, and they may also get firmer or lighter from word to word, but you should still be able to feel that little pulse beating away. Switch partners and repeat with Partner A's text. Next, move away from each other a little. Partner B read your speech out loud, without leaning into the rhythm particularly hard; A, see if you can tap along with the strong stresses in your own palm as you listen. Switch and repeat for Partner A. Discuss any discoveries you made.

Scripted pauses (5–10 minutes each)

If you worked on the Romeo speech in the exercise above, you will have noticed that one of the lines only had three feet (six syllables) instead of the usual five (ten syllables). When you get a short line like this, it usually means that the author has written in a pause – in this case two feet long. When you get this kind of short line, you need to investigate where the pause is most effective for the scene – whether it's at the beginning or the end of the line. Often the line before or after will shed some light on where the pause will work best. The following exercises will help you to get a feel for this.

I. Take the following text from the balcony scene in *Romeo and Juliet*:

ROMEO
    It is my lady, O, it is my love.
    O that she knew she were!
    She speaks, yet she says nothing. What of that?

Get a partner, and read it out loud together, leaning into the rhythm, and find where the short line is.

You may have also noted that there's a stage direction to Juliet implied there ('She speaks, yet she says nothing.'). Pick one of you to play Juliet. Romeo, read the text again and take a two-foot pause (about as long as it would take you to speak half a line – don't worry about being too precise) **after** 'O that she knew she were!' During that pause, Juliet should perform whatever action is suggested to you by 'She speaks yet she says nothing'.

Now switch parts. This time the new Romeo will take the pause **before** 'O that she knew she were!' Juliet, you will now only have the ordinary break between lines to get in your action before Romeo says 'She speaks, yet she says nothing. What of that?'

Discuss these two options. The first probably went more smoothly – it seems likely that Shakespeare put the pause in just for that business to take place, but there may have been some comic value in the second that would be worth exploring. There aren't any rules; in fact, it's even possible that Shakespeare intended Romeo to draw out the three beats of 'O that she knew she were' as if they were five beats. What is important is that you think about how you want to use the pauses when an author gives them to you.

> *Teaching tip:* You might also wish to draw students' attention to Shakespeare's use of monosyllables in this extract.

II. Take the following text from Shakespeare's *All's Well That Ends Well*:

HELENA
    Then I confess
    Here on my knee, before high heaven and you,
    I love your son.
    My friends were poor but honest; so's my love.

Get a partner, and read it out loud together, leaning into the rhythm. Note that the first line is part of a full line that started earlier, so we're not going to count it as short. The short line is 'I love your son'. Helena has been pressured by the Countess into admitting that she loves the Countess's son, who is much higher in social class than Helena. Helena knows it's not appropriate for her to have these feelings, and really doesn't want to upset the Countess with her confession. Note the stage direction imbedded in the language: 'Here on my knee' – at some point Helena's going to have to get down on one knee.

One partner be Helena and the other the Countess. Helena, try taking your three-foot pause (that's a fairly long one) **before** 'I love your son'. What could you be doing or thinking during that time to justify the pause? Try it another time or two just to test out the possibilities.

Now switch parts. Helena, this time try taking your pause **after** 'I love your son'. What could you be doing or thinking here that would justify the pause? Try it another time or two.

You could also try taking a short pause before 'I love your son' and a further short pause after.

NOTE: Rebecca was once in a workshop with Dakin Matthews, a very accomplished American actor and director, when an actor asked about taking pauses other than those rhythmically built in by Shakespeare. Dakin thought about it and said, 'Well, you *could* take other pauses, but I'd want to make sure I was filling those extra pauses with something more interesting than Shakespeare's language'. Words to live by – you can pause whenever you want, but if the pause is not provided for in the rhythm of the speech or scene, make sure you have a darn good reason for taking it.

Shared rhythm (10–15 minutes for the sequence of two exercises)

If you ever think you've found a short line at the beginning of a speech, it's important that you count the syllables in the other character's line just before yours. And if you think you have a short line at the end of a speech, look at the other character's line just after. Sometimes Shakespeare and other verse authors will split the ten-syllable verse line between two or even more characters. In the *All's Well That Ends Well* example above, the Countess says 'Have to the full appeached' (six syllables) immediately before Helena says, 'then I confess' (four syllables). Together, the end of the Countess's speech and the beginning of Helena's make one complete verse line. When this happens, there's no room for pausing at all; on the contrary, the speeches need to flow together.

I. Try the following from *Romeo and Juliet* with a partner:

TYBALT
　I'll not endure him.
CAPULET
　He shall be endured.

If you think of it as one verse line, where do the five iambic beats fall?
　Lean into the rhythm a bit and feel how it propels you through the ten syllables from Tybalt's speech into Capulet's. Then ease off the rhythm and see if you can still feel the momentum.

II. In the following dialogue from *King John*, King John is speaking to the jailer, Hubert, about what he would like to see happen to a prisoner, a young boy, whom he perceives to be a political threat.

KING JOHN
　He lies before me. Dost thou understand me?
　Thou art his keeper.
HUBERT
　And I'll keep him so
　That he shall not offend your majesty.

KING JOHN
    Death.
HUBERT
    My lord.
KING JOHN
    A grave.
HUBERT
    He shall not live.
KING JOHN
    Enough.

With a partner try to piece together where the ten-syllable verse lines begin and end. Investigate different possibilities before reading further.

This one can be tricky. If you contract 'majesty' into two syllables ('maj'sty'), 'Death' can be the final syllable in that line. Then 'My lord' through 'Enough' makes a ten-syllable line. Try it that way.

Another possibility is that King John says 'Death' while Hubert is saying 'majesty' – they actually overlap. Try it that way.

Yet another possibility is that 'Death' is a verse line in itself with a nine-syllable pause before or after. Try that.

Finally, the verse line could start with 'Death' and be an eleven-syllable line (ending with 'Enough') with a syncopated rhythm. Try that.

The differences are subtle, but it's worth exploring in detail how rhythm can create drama.

Verse: Breaking the rhythm

As we said earlier, the main reason to establish a rhythm is so that you can then riff on it. Most authors of verse drama do a great deal of riffing – creating variations by breaking or modifying the rhythm they have established. Doing this can catch the ear of the listener, reveal the state of the speaker and make visceral the emotional undercurrents of a scene or speech. Let's look at a passage from Shakespeare's *King Lear* to see this at work. In this extraordinary tragedy, Lear banishes the one daughter who truly loves him, Cordelia, and then is made to suffer terribly at the hands of his two other daughters. Finally, he is reunited with Cordelia, who forgives him. Although they are now prisoners, he feels that nothing can take away the happiness that they feel just being together. At the very end of the play, however, Cordelia is hanged. Lear enters the stage with her body in his arms and says:

> Why should a dog, a horse, a rat have life
> And thou no breath at all? Thou'll come no more,
> Never, never, never, never, never.

Try beating out the rhythm as you speak the lines. You'll find that it's strongly regular until that last line. But the last line doesn't work with the same rhythm. You would probably never say 'ne**ver**'; it's just not how the word is pronounced. It has to be '**nev**er'. The rhythm has shifted from being iambic ('ti **tum**/ti **tum**/ti **tum**/ti **tum**/ti **tum**') to being trochaic ('**tum** ti/**tum** ti/**tum** ti/**tum** ti/**tum** ti').

This violates every expectation we, as the audience, have. It is the exact opposite of what we've been hearing all night. The rhythm is turned upside down, just as Lear's world is turned upside down in that moment when he truly realizes that Cordelia is dead. When Shakespeare changes the beat in this way, there is almost always some kind of reason why the character is off his rhythm and it almost always serves to jangle the audience's nerves a bit. You may not be able to explain the reason for the disruption, but somehow it makes sense – it has an emotional logic. Rhythmic disruptions get under your skin even if you don't consciously recognize them. The exercises that follow will help you to get a sense of how this can work.

Feminine endings (10–15 minutes including some discussion)

In the work on *Verse: Finding the Rhythm*, you might have come across a few lines that ended in an eleventh unstressed syllable; for example, Portia: 'And **that**/same **prayer**/does **teach**/us **all**/to **ren**der', where the '-der' is the eleventh unstressed syllable. These variations on the normal ten-syllable line are usually called 'feminine endings', and they are very common in Shakespeare. Normally they don't interrupt the overall rhythm of a speech very much – they get absorbed into the natural little shift of energy that comes at the end of verse lines anyway. Sometimes, however, they can have a particular effect. Take the following text:

HAMLET
    To be, or not to be: that is the question:
    Whether 'tis nobler in the mind to suffer
    The slings and arrows of outrageous fortune,
    Or to take arms against a sea of troubles,
    And by opposing end them? To die: to sleep;
    No more; and by a sleep to say we end
    The heart-ache and the thousand natural shocks
    That flesh is heir to, 'tis a consummation*   *ending*
    Devoutly to be wished. To die, to sleep …

Read through it aloud once.

Read it out loud again and tap out the rhythm. You may have noticed that the second line starts with a strong stress ('**whe**ther' – you'd never pronounce the word 'whe**ther**'); we'll talk more about this kind of rhythmic variation in the next exercise. You may also find that the fifth line works better rhythmically if you elide 'end them' to 'end th'm'. What you almost certainly noticed is that there are a good number of feminine endings in this passage.

Get up and try the galloping exercise from the *Verse: Finding the Rhythm* section. What is the effect of those feminine endings on the rhythm of your gallop? Next just try walking rhythmically as you read the passage. Where in the speech did you feel your walk had flow? Where did it feel more uncertain? Why do you think Shakespeare put all those feminine endings in a row? How might the rhythm reflect the state of Hamlet's mind?

Gallop apace indeed (20–30 minutes including discussion)

This speech from *Romeo and Juliet* offers great opportunity to explore the play between a very regular rhythm and periodic disruptions. In this speech, Juliet is waiting for night to fall so that Romeo can sneak into her bedroom and they can consummate their secret marriage, which took place earlier in the afternoon.

JULIET
    Gallop apace, you fiery-footed steeds,
    Towards Phoebus' lodging: such a wagoner [pronounced: **Fee**bus]

As Phaeton would whip you to the west, [pronounced: **Fay**uh**ton**]
And bring in cloudy night immediately.
Spread thy close* curtain, love-performing night,   *tightly shut*
That runaways'* eyes may wink and Romeo   *vagabonds*
Leap to these arms, untalked of and unseen.
Lovers can see to do their amorous rites
By their own beauties; or, if love be blind,
It best agrees with night. Come, civil night,
Thou sober-suited matron, all in black,
And learn me how to lose a winning match,
Played for a pair of stainless maidenhoods*:   *virginities*
Hood my unmanned blood, bating* in my cheeks,   *fluttering*
With thy black mantle; till strange love, grown bold,
Think true love acted simple modesty.
Come, night; come, Romeo; come, thou day in night;
For thou wilt lie upon the wings of night
Whiter than new snow on a raven's back.
Come, gentle night, come, loving, black-browed night,
Give me my Romeo; and, when he shall die,
Take him and cut him out in little stars,
And he will make the face of heaven so fine
That all the world will be in love with night
And pay no worship to the garish sun.

1. Start by reading the speech out loud without marking the rhythm and then discuss it to make sure you understand it.

2. Read the speech again leaning into the iambic pentameter. Take it slowly and mark with a star any line where:

- the rhythm goes wonky (too many or too few syllables or suddenly the wrong syllables are being stressed);
- the iambic rhythm forces you to mispronounce a word (like 'whe**ther**' in the Hamlet speech above);
- the iambic rhythm just feels wrong – it forces you to stress a word that it feels unnatural to stress.

Now go back and review those starred lines. In cases where the iambic rhythm forces you to mispronounce a word (people seldom say 'gal**lop**'), it's usually because Shakespeare is breaking the rhythm by deliberately replacing an iambic foot with a trochee.

For the other starred lines investigate whether they can be made regular by eliding or expanding a word? For example, 'runaways' could be elided to two syllables. You'll find that 'Romeo' goes back and forth from three syllables to two in this speech. You may feel that in some cases there is a good, dramatic reason not to contract or expand a word – that the irregular rhythm serves the line, which is a legitimate choice sometimes; just make sure you've tried it both ways and thought it through.

In cases where the rhythm just feels wrong – where it puts the stress on the wrong word, for example – try it both ways a couple of times. For example, 'Spread **thy**' and '**Spread** thy'. Given that Juliet hasn't been talking about anyone else's close curtain, it would be very odd for her to stress 'thy' more than the verb. Shakespeare has given you another trochee here.

3. Circle all of the trochees (feet that have a strong stress then a weak one: **tum** ti).

Stand up and read through the speech again, tapping your foot along with the strong beats, but whenever you come to a trochee, gently stomp your foot on the stressed syllable.

Read through the speech again, this time walking round the room as you speak. Don't worry about marking the rhythm, except when you come to a trochee. At those points, make some kind of strong physical gesture: you can stomp your foot again, or change direction, or throw your arms up to the sky – whatever comes out of the moment.

4. Sit down to discuss your discoveries. Why do you think Shakespeare uses so many trochees in this speech? Where in the verse line do they usually fall? Why do you think they're there? Does the rhythm tell us anything about Juliet's state of mind? What's the emotional logic of the disruptions?

Turbulence

(*Timing will depend on the size of the group – the preparatory stage will take about 8–10 minutes.*)

The three exercises below are useful for exploring any text that has more than a couple of rhythmic irregularities, or turbulence. They can be done in sequence, on their own or in any combination. We're going to start with Leontes, from *The Winter's Tale,* because much of his text is particularly rich in irregularities. In this passage, he has described to his chief advisor his conviction that his wife is having an affair with his best friend, the king of Bohemia. His advisor says there is nothing going on between them, and Leontes replies:

> Is whispering nothing?
> Is leaning cheek to cheek? is meeting noses?
> Kissing with inside lip*? stopping the career   *kissing intimately*
> Of laughter with a sigh (a note infallible
> Of breaking honesty)? horsing foot on foot*?   *playing footsy*
> Skulking in corners? wishing clocks more swift?
> Hours, minutes? noon, midnight? and all eyes
> Blind with the pin and web*, but theirs, theirs only   *an eye infection*
> That would unseen be wicked? Is this nothing?
> Why then the world, and all that's in't, is nothing,
> The covering sky is nothing, Bohemia nothing,
> My wife nothing, nor nothing have these nothings,
> If this be nothing.

This is basically a catalogue of all the things he believes he's seen his wife and best friend doing.

Read the speech out loud without marking the rhythm to get a feel for it. Talk over the content and make sure you have a basic understanding of it.

Read through the speech again, leaning into the rhythm. Whenever you find an irregularity – an extra syllable, including feminine endings; a place where the pronunciation and iambic rhythm are at odds or where a trochee makes more sense; or a place where the rhythm seems to disappear – stop and circle the word or words. Take it slowly; you're going to find some very unstable rhythms in this speech.

I. Read the speech again, whispering everything except the circled words; speak those on full voice.

II. Get in a circle of four to five people with one in the middle (you may have several circles depending on the size of your class).

Everyone hold your texts where you can see them.

The person in the middle will read the text out loud. Whenever she comes to a circled word, the person (or couple of people, it doesn't really matter) nearest to her will give her a little shove. NOTE: this should be gentle, nowhere near enough force to put her in any danger of losing her balance.

RHYTHM

Alternatively, as the person in the middle speaks the text, she will give the person next to her a gentle shove whenever she comes to a circled word.

Give as many people as would like, and as time permits, a chance to be in the centre of the circle.

III. Get in groups of four and get three *sturdy* chairs for each group. One person volunteer to try the exercise first, and arrange the chairs in a triangle far enough apart that when that person stands on a chair, he has to reach just a bit to step from one chair to another, but not so far that he is in any danger of falling between chairs as he steps.

Each of the other three people stand behind a chair and keep it steady.

The volunteer will then stand up on a chair and start reading the speech. Every time you comes to a circled word, step onto another chair **as you say the word**. If you step a bit before or after the word, go back and try it again.

Repeat this until everyone who wants to has had a chance. If you don't feel comfortable trying this exercise, that's fine; you can learn plenty by watching it.

After you've done any or all of the above exercises discuss them. How did punctuating the irregularities in this way make you feel as you read the speech? Did the rhythmic interruptions bring any words into particularly strong focus? What did the rhythm tell us about Leontes's frame of mind? Go back and read the speech out loud again. Can you still feel that turbulence running through the speech?

> *Teaching tip:* Clearly, *Exercise II* can only be done with groups that are mature and trust each other. You should only try *Exercise III* if you've done a health and safety check. Do not try it with chairs that are not very solid or do not have relatively flat seats – and make sure everybody has shoes on. If these exercises don't feel appropriate for your group, you can have the students punctuate the rhythmic irregularities by kicking an imaginary ball on them, walking and changing direction on them or punching an imaginary pillow on them.

Turbulent dialogue (15–20 minutes)

We'll use a scene between Macbeth and Lady Macbeth here – though this exercise works with many scenes that have rhythmic disruptions. This is the scene just after Macbeth has killed the king, Duncan. Donalbain is Duncan's son. Macbeth also talks about the two drugged guards whom they intend to frame for the murder.

MACBETH
   I have done the deed. Didst thou not hear a noise?
LADY MACBETH
   I heard the owl scream and the crickets cry.
   Did not you speak?
MACBETH
   When?
LADY MACBETH
   Now.
MACBETH
   As I descended?
LADY MACBETH
   Ay.
MACBETH
   Hark!
   Who lies i' the second chamber?
LADY MACBETH
   Donalbain.
MACBETH
   This is a sorry* sight.   (*Looking on his hands*) sorrowful
LADY MACBETH
   A foolish thought, to say a sorry sight.
MACBETH
   There's one did laugh in's sleep, and one cried 'Murder!'
   That they did wake each other: I stood and heard them:
   But they did say their prayers, and addressed
      them*   *made themselves ready for*
   Again to sleep.
LADY MACBETH
   There are two lodged together.

MACBETH
>One cried 'God bless us!' and 'Amen' the other;
>As they had seen me with these hangman's hands.
>Listening their fear, I could not say 'Amen,'
>When they did say 'God bless us!'

LADY MACBETH
>Consider it not so deeply.

MACBETH
>But wherefore could not I pronounce 'Amen'?
>I had most need of blessing, and 'Amen'
>Stuck in my throat.

LADY MACBETH
>These deeds must not be thought
>After these ways; so, it will make us mad.

Find a partner and decide who is Macbeth and Lady Macbeth. Read the passage out loud together without marking the rhythm to get a feel for it. Talk over the content and make sure you have a basic understanding.

Read through the text again, leaning into the rhythm. Whenever you find an irregularity – an extra syllable, including feminine endings; a place where the pronunciation and iambic rhythm are at odds or where a trochee makes more sense; an incomplete half line; or a place where the rhythm seems to disappear – stop and circle the word or words. Take it slowly; you're going to find some very unstable rhythms in this passage.

Read the passage again, whispering everything except the circled words; speak those on full voice.

Read the passage again on full voice. Whenever you say a circled word or phrase, move boldly away from your partner.

Try it again moving boldly towards you partner on all the circled words.

Take a moment to discuss any discoveries you made about how the rhythmic disruptions might contribute to the scene. What do they reveal about the characters' states of mind?

Verse: The energy of the line

In the work we've done on verse so far, we've mostly investigated the importance of the patterning of unstressed and stressed syllables. But another important characteristic of much verse is the verse line. A line of verse isn't just a pretty pattern of stressed and unstressed syllables. It also has a shape and energy that writers use to give shape to the thoughts they are expressing. The rhythmic journey of the verse line and the sense of the language can combine to give text interesting layers of meaning and emotion. For example, as we've seen, lines in iambic pentameter are generally limited to ten syllables. In many instances, the sentences or phrases are also ten syllables long, so when the thought energy of the language and the rhythmic energy of the line are in sync with each other, we get a very specific idea of the story of that line. Look at this example from *Romeo and Juliet:*

But soft, what light through yonder window breaks?

The line and the thought are the same length here, and we get a clear sense of a beginning ('But soft,'), middle ('what light') and end ('breaks?').
Now look at the next line:

It is the east, and Juliet is the sun.

Again, the sentence is exactly one line long. The thought energy of this metaphor is so active in Romeo's imagination, though, that it then extends over the next three lines:

Arise fair sun and kill the envious moon,
Who is already sick and pale with grief
That thou, her maid, art far more fair than she.

Look carefully at those last three lines; while the sentence stretches across all three, it *could* finish at the end of any one of them. There's some kind of turn in the thought at the end of each verse line – so the beginning of each line is the beginning of a new part of the thought.
Sometimes, however, the phrase is longer than the verse line. This happens later in Romeo's speech:

The brightness of her cheek would shame those stars
As daylight doth a lamp; her eye in heaven
Would through the airy region stream so bright
That birds would sing and think it were not night.

In this instance, the sentence stretches over four lines and there are no natural, grammatical breaking points at the ends of the lines. This poses an interesting challenge. If you stop your energy where the verse line stops, you risk breaking up the thought to such an extent that the meaning gets lost.

Speak the above lines as if there were a stop at the end of each verse line. You'll probably find that it's hard to follow what Romeo is saying and, as we discussed in Chapter 3, your primary job is to make sense of the language, so this approach is to be avoided. If, however, you don't moderate your energy at all at the end of the verse line, the 'pentameter' part of iambic pentameter gets lost; you're throwing away the form the author has given you and might as well be speaking prose. Again, there are no Shakespeare Police to come and cart you away if you do this, but you're losing an opportunity he gives you to play the two different energies off each other – the energy of the thought and the energy of the line.

You will often find if you look carefully that there is a profound emotional logic in how verse authors shape their line endings that can help you to find a much more truthful energy than if you simply drive from one complete thought to the next. The exercises in this section will help you discover these possibilities.

Sometimes, you will also find that one thought ends and another begins in the middle of a verse line. Later in the scene, Romeo says:

> Alack, there lies more peril in thine eye
> Than twenty of their swords. Look thou but sweet,
> And I am proof* against their enmity.   *protected*

Note the full stop in the middle of the second line. This kind of midline pause or change of direction in the thought is called a **caesura**. It creates a tension between the verse energy, which wants to drive forward, and the thought energy, which wants to stop.

As well as marking the end of one thought and the beginning of another, a caesura can also be a more subtle midline pause or change of direction in the thought: for example, in the line 'It is the east, and Juliet is the sun'. The sentence is exactly one line long, but it's composed of two thoughts which are joined in the middle. It's a journey made up of two stages, with a slight pause or break in the middle. Romeo could have ended his thought at 'east', but then the image of Juliet as the sun occurs to him and he completes the line. The caesura is like the tipping point in the middle of the see-saw line. Romeo climbs up one side of the see-saw on 'It is the east', where he gets to the discovery of the metaphor which tips him down the other side of the see-saw on 'and Juliet is the sun.'

Sometimes Shakespeare will add an extra unstressed syllable just before the caesura to heighten the tension at the tipping point, which is known as an **epic caesura**. After the caesura, the rhythm returns to normal. Let's look again at Hamlet's speech, particularly the fifth line:

HAMLET
To be, or not to be: that is the question:
Whether 'tis nobler in the mind to suffer
The slings and arrows of outrageous fortune,
Or to take arms against a sea of troubles,
And by opposing end them? To die: to sleep;
No more; and by a sleep to say we end
The heart-ache and the thousand natural shocks
That flesh is heir to, 'tis a consummation
Devoutly to be wish'd. To die, to sleep ...

You'll find several caesuras here; in fact the first line may have the most famous caesura of all. Earlier, we suggested that in the fifth line you might try eliding 'and by opposing *end th'm*' to make that line rhythmically regular. If, however, you say 'and by opposing end them', letting that extra unstressed syllable of the epic caesura dangle before moving forward into the iambic rhythm of the rest of the line, it gives extra momentum to the downside of the see-saw. Try saying it both ways.

In many instances, lines that seem rhythmically out of whack simply have an epic caesura – an extra unstressed syllable in the middle. Recognizing them will help you to realize how the energy of the thoughts and the energy of the verse are playing off each other in those lines. The exercises that follow will help you find a variety of ways of balancing those two energies. They will also give you an opportunity to explore how that tension between rhythm and meaning can help you find the emotional shape of the speech.

The last word (10–15 minutes)

> **VIDEO LINK**
>
> The last word: https://vimeo.com/268973276

This exercise can be done with any piece of verse text. It works best if partners are working with different speeches.

Read through your text out loud once to get a feel for it. Review any words or sections that are hard to understand.

Circle the last word in every verse line.

Read aloud the first circled word, and as you do so, make a gesture that embodies the image, meaning or energy of that word. For example, if the word were 'breaks' you might make a gesture of breaking something in two with your hands.

Repeat twice, allowing your gesture to grow in size until your entire body is involved. Then go on to the next circled word and repeat the process until you've worked through the whole speech.

Now find a partner. Partner A will listen and partner B will speak just the circled words in sequence, using as many of the accompanying gestures as he would like, to try to convey the story of the speech. Try to make your partner understand what the subject of your speech is, how you feel about it, and what you are trying to accomplish by speaking. Partner A feed back what you got from the circled words.

Switch partners so that partner B becomes the listener and repeat.

What discoveries did you make about these 'last words'?

Tap the balloon (about 5–10 minutes depending on the length of the speech)

This exercise is good for combating any tendency to let energy drop at the ends of verse lines. It works with any piece of verse text and particularly well with Restoration texts or speeches in rhyming couplets.

Read your text once out loud to get a feel for it. Review any difficult words or passages.

Read the text out loud again, walking around the space with energy and purpose as you do. On the last word of every line, pretend that a balloon is floating down towards you and gently tap it with the fingers of one hand back up into the air. Make sure you do this *as you say* the last word. Make sure too that you are just tapping, not lifting the balloon up with your hand; if you do this, you run the danger of your voice lifting up as well, making the end of every line sound like a question, which is not to be desired.

Whenever the last word of the verse line is also the last word of a sentence (i.e. is followed by a full stop, exclamation point or question mark), instead of tapping the balloon, take out an imaginary pin and pop it.

Read the speech again without the imaginary balloon, but still using that sense of energy moving forward on the last words of lines and coming to a conclusive ending at the full stops.

Discuss your experience with a partner or the rest of the group.

> *Teaching tip:* If your budget can stretch to it, you might like to use real balloons.

On your toes (10–15 minutes depending on the length of the text)

VIDEO LINK

On your toes: https://vimeo.com/268962517

This exercise works well with any verse text.

Read your text out loud to get a feel for it and go over any difficult bits for comprehension.

Walk around the room as you read your text out loud again, and *on the last word of every verse line* (not before or after) rise up on your toes. Sometimes you may pause there, but sometimes you will lift and then keep moving forward fluidly without stopping at all. This is a physicalization of what Cicely Berry has called an end-of-line 'poise', as opposed to a 'pause'.

Repeat the exercise once or twice until you can do it quite fluidly. Do it once more and take a bit more time on your toes, consciously exploring the possibility of there being a gathering of emotional energy at those moments.

Finally, read the speech again standing still, but working with a sense of energy gathering at the line endings.

Discuss your experience with a partner or the rest of the group.

> *Teaching tip:* This exercise could also be applied to exploring the tipping point of the caesura.

Our friend the chair (10–15 minutes)

Review the third *Turbulence* exercise in the *Verse: Breaking the Rhythm* section above. As in that exercise, get into groups of four and get three sturdy chairs for each group.

One person volunteer to try the exercise first, and arrange the chairs in a triangle far enough apart that that person has to reach just a bit to step from one chair to another, but not so far that he is in any danger of falling between chairs as he steps.

Each of the other three people stand behind a chair and keep it steady.

First volunteer, stand up on a chair and start reading the speech. At the end of every verse line step onto a new chair *as you say the last word*.

Repeat until everyone who wants to has had a chance. If you don't feel comfortable trying this exercise, that's fine; you can learn plenty by watching it.

Discuss your experience with your partners. What, if anything, did being a little off balance as you transitioned from one line to the next reveal to you about the emotional journey of the speech?

Teaching tip: Review the warnings for the first chair exercise.

Line by line (10–15 minutes)

Any piece of verse would work with this exercise, but it's more interesting with a piece that has a fair number of thoughts that begin at the caesura. See *Suggested Texts* for some ideas.

Everyone in the class stand in a circle.

Read the text out loud once in unison to get a feel for it and discuss what it is about.

Next, one person start reading the text and continue until he or she hits a punctuation mark (full stop, comma, dash etc.). The next person will pick up from there and read to the next punctuation mark, and so forth around the circle until the speech is done.

Read the speech again, but this time, the first person reads to the end of the verse line; the next person picks up at the beginning of the second verse line and reads to the end, and so forth through the speech. The only rule is that you *cannot breathe* in the middle of your line, only at the end of the line.

Discuss for a moment the differences between the two readings.

It's very possible that, the second time through, the thoughts were harder to understand. To help remedy that, *as you speak* the last word of the line, reach your hand out to the person who is about to start speaking as if you were offering him something in the palm of your hand. That person should be ready to start speaking without having to pause to find his place on the page or even breathe. Again, you cannot breathe in the middle of your line, but if you have a new thought beginning in the middle of the line, you can pause ever so slightly to let the energy of the new thought build.

Discuss for a moment what you got out of that reading. Were there any transitions between lines that struck you as particularly interesting?

RHYTHM

Were there any transitions between thoughts at the caesura that were interesting? Did you find any epic caesuras? How often does the character have a full stop at the end of a verse line? What does that tell you about the momentum of his thoughts?

Our friend the bag (5–10 minutes; longer if you do more than one text)

This works with any verse text.

Review the *Carry the Bag* exercise from Chapter 3.

Scatter bags around the floor, as in that exercise, and get your texts ready.

This time, you will pick up a bag on the first word of the speech and carry it until you get to a full stop. If the full stop comes in the middle of a verse line, do not put the bag down – instead switch it into the other hand. You'll also need to switch your paper over; keep your arms as high as you can while you make the switch.

If the full stop comes at the end of a verse line, put the bag down on the last word and go pick up another one as you start the next sentence.

When you finish, have a brief discussion about the different energies involved in switching hands midline and putting the bag down. Try it with a few different speeches and see what it reveals about whether characters come to a secure landing and have the time to gather energy for the next thought, or are moving more fluidly from thought to thought.

> *Teaching tip:* You may have noticed that we have a fair number of exercises that involve walking around with the text. We've been very inspired by Cicely Berry, who does a lot of work on getting the energy and rhythms of the text into the body. If your students are getting on well with these exercises, you can combine activities. For example, in the above, you could have students also go up on their toes at the ends of verse lines, or change direction on non-full stop punctuation marks.

Follow-up

Reflective practice questions:

- How has your understanding of rhythm in prose and in verse changed as a result of the work of this chapter?
- Which exercises have helped you get a physical sensation of rhythm?
- How would you describe your own rhythm of walking? Talking? Thinking? And how are these rhythms related to how you are feeling?
- Experiment with changing any of these personal rhythms. How does that affect how you think or feel?
- Try composing a sonnet in iambic pentameter, and share it in class.
- Try some of the rhythm exercises with a scene from a play you don't know. What does the rhythm work reveal to you about the characters and their relationships to each other?
- Pick a scene from a modern play. Working with a partner, discuss how you would 'translate' the scene into iambic pentameter. Where would you want to have shared verse lines? What words would you put at the ends of verse lines? Where would you break the rhythm? Read through the scene and see if you can incorporate some of your ideas about its rhythmic potential.

Suggested texts

Prose: Finding the rhythm

Riffing on repetition I

Samuel Beckett, *Happy Days*, Act I, Winnie: from 'There is of course the bag' through 'The old style! (*Smile off*.) And now?'
Jim Cartwright, *Two*, Moth: 'You're beautiful you'
Caryl Churchill, *Top Girls*, Act II Scene 3, Shona: 'My present job at present'

Lynn Nottage, *Sweat*, Act I Scene 1, Chris: 'I dunno. A couple of minutes'

Octavio Solis, *Santos & Santos*, Act I, Judge: from 'These boys, these boys' through 'its ugly head again again again'

Riffing on repetition II

William Shakespeare, *Othello*, Act I Scene 3, Iago: 'It is merely a lust of the blood'

William Shakespeare, *Romeo and Juliet*, Act III Scene 1, Mercutio: 'Nay, and there were two such'

Length of thought

Conor McPherson, *Dublin Carol*, Part II, Mary: 'I had this boyfriend'

Suzan-Lori Parks, *Topdog/Underdog*, Scene 1, Lincoln: 'I was riding the bus'

Harold Pinter, *Old Times*, Act II, Deeley: 'We've met before, you know'

August Wilson, *The Piano Lesson*, Act II Scene 5, Boy Willie: 'See now ... I'll tell you something'

Syllabic variations

Howard Barker, *Gertrude – The Cry*, Scene 5, Gertrude: 'Yes – And nothing he says', skip Cascan's next line and continue to 'You know my son'

George Etherege, *The Man of Mode*, Act I Scene 1, Dorimant: 'She means insensibly to insinuate'

Toni Morrison, *The Bluest Eye*, Act I Scene 4, Claudia, 'Cholly and Mrs. Breadlove fought each other'

Suzan-Lori Parks, *Devotees in the Garden of Love*, D., Odelin: 'At the hour there is silence'

Dialogue – sharing rhythm I

Samuel Beckett, *Waiting for Godot*, from Estragon: 'And what did he reply' through Vladimir: 'I think so too'

Jim Cartwright, *Road*, Act 1, Brenda and Carol from Brenda: 'Have you had 'owt eat'

Susan Glaspell, *Alison's House*, Act II Scene 2, from Ted: 'Sometimes I think I haven't just the mind' through Stanhope: 'Here'

Stephen Adly Guirgis, *In Arabia We'd All Be Kings*, Act I Scene 1, Lenny and Jake from Lenny: 'Say, Jake, where's the bartender'

Suzan-Lori Parks, *Topdog/Underdog*, Scene 1, Lincoln: 'Yr getting good at solitaire?' through Lincoln: 'Your luck will change'

Dialogue – sharing rhythm II

Noël Coward, *Hay Fever*, Act II, Simon, Sorel, Jackie, Judith, Richard, Myra and Sandy from Simon: 'Who'll go out?' through Sorel: 'Don't be too long'

George Etherege, *The Man of Mode*, Act III Scene 2, from Medley: 'Dorimant, you are luckily come' through Emilia: 'There are afflictions'

Quiara Alegría Hudes, *Elliot, A Soldier's Fugue*, 10/Fugue, Ginny, Grandpop, Pop and Elliot from the beginning through Ginny: 'A woman enters'

Tom Stoppard, *Arcadia*, Act I Scene 1, from Septimus: 'Well so much for Mr. Noakes' through Thomasina: 'a joke to make you mad'

Verse: Finding the rhythm

Feeling the beat

Christopher Marlowe, *Tamburlaine Part II*, Act III Scene 2, Tamburlaine: 'But now, my boys, leave off'

William Shakespeare, *Richard III*, Act I Scene 3, Margaret: 'And leave out thee'

William Shakespeare, *Romeo and Juliet*, Act II Scene 1, Romeo: 'He jests at scars'

William Shakespeare, *Merchant of Venice*, Act IV Scene 1, Portia: 'The quality of mercy'

Shared rhythm

John Ford, *'Tis Pity She's a Whore*, Act III Scene 2, Soranzo, Annabella and Giovanni from Soranzo: 'Have you not will to love' through Annabella: 'That is not mine to give'

Ben Jonson, *The Alchemist*, Act I Scene 1, from Face: 'Believ't I will' through Subtle: 'Do but collect, sir, where I met you first'

William Shakespeare, *The Merchant of Venice*, Act V Scene 1, from Lorenzo: 'The moon shines bright tonight' through Jessica: 'I hear the footing of a man'

Verse: Breaking the rhythm

Feminine endings

William Shakespeare, *Cymbeline*, Act III Scene 4, Imogen: 'True honest men'

William Shakespeare, *Troilus and Cressida*, Act II Scene 2, Troilus: 'I take today a wife'

Gallop apace indeed

Christopher Marlowe, *Doctor Faustus*, Act I Scene 1, Faustus: 'Settle thy studies'

William Shakespeare, *Henry VI Part 2*, Act I Scene 1, Gloucester: 'Brave peers of England' (note particularly from 'Or hath mine uncle Beaufort and myself')

Turbulence

William Shakespeare, *King Lear*, Act I Scene 2, Edmund: 'Thou nature art my goddess'

William Shakespeare, *The Tempest*, Act I Scene 2, Miranda: 'If by your art'

Turbulent dialogue

William Shakespeare, *As You Like It*, Act I Scene 3, Celia and Rosalind from Celia: 'O my poor Rosalind' through Celia: 'and not to banishment'

William Shakespeare, *Hamlet*, Act I Scene 1, Marcellus, Barnardo and Horatio from Horatio: 'Stay, speak' through Horatio: 'This bodes some strange eruption to our state'

Verse: The energy of the line

The last word

John Ford, *'Tis Pity She's a Whore*, Act II Scene 2, Hippolita: 'Do you know me now'

Christopher Marlowe, *Edward II*, Act V Scene 1, King Edward: 'Leicester, if gentle words might comfort me'

William Shakespeare, *As You Like It*, Act III Scene 5, Phoebe: 'I would not be thy executioner'

Tap the balloon

Hannah Cowley, *The Belle's Strategem*, Epilogue

T. S. Eliot, *Murder in the Cathedral*, Part I, Thomas: 'If the Archbishop cannot trust'

George Etherege, *The Man of Mode*, Prologue

William Shakespeare, *A Midsummer Night's Dream*, Act III Scene 2, Puck: 'My mistress with a monster is in love'

On your toes

Christopher Marlowe, *Edward II*, Act III Scene 2, Younger Spenser: 'Were I King Edward'

Sarah Ruhl, *Eurydice*, Second Movement Scene 1, Eurydice: 'There was a road, and a coldness'

William Shakespeare, *Julius Caesar*, Act II Scene 1, Portia: 'Is Brutus sick'

Octavio Solis, *Santos & Santos*, Act I, Vicky: 'What I said earlier'

Our friend the chair

T. S. Eliot, *Murder in the Cathedral*, Part I, Thomas: 'Peace. And let them be'

William Shakespeare, *The Merchant of Venice*, Act III Scene 1, Portia: 'I pray you tarry'

William Shakespeare, *The Winter's Tale*, Act III Scene 1, Hermione: 'Since what I am to say'

Line by line

William Shakespeare, *Othello*, Act IV Scene 3, Emilia: 'Yes, a dozen'
William Shakespeare, *Macbeth*, Act I Scene 7, Macbeth: 'If it were done'

Our friend the bag

William Shakespeare, *Julius Caesar*, Act II Scene 1, Brutus: 'It must be by his death'
William Shakespeare, *Romeo and Juliet*, Act V Scene 3, Romeo: 'Let me peruse thy face'

Further reading

Barton, John, *Playing Shakespeare*, Methuen, London, 1984. Chapter Two: Using the Verse, pp. 25–46.
Berry, Cicely, *The Actor and the Text* (revised edition), Virgin Books, London, 1993. Chapter 3: Metre and Rhythm, pp. 52–81; Chapter 7: Metre and Energy, pp. 171–178.
Berry, Cicely, *Text in Action*, Virgin Books, London, 2001. Chapter 8: Structures, pp. 155–161, 182–190.
Berry, Cicely, *From Word to Play*, Oberon Books, London, 2008. 'The Rhythm and Movement of Thought in Both Verse and Prose', pp. 78–89.
Carey, David and Rebecca Clark Carey, *The Shakespeare Workbook and Video*, Bloomsbury Methuen Drama, London, 2015. Chapter 3: Rhythm and Metre, pp. 111–178.
Cohen, Robert, *Acting in Shakespeare*, Mayfield Publishing Company, Mountain View, CA, 1991. Lesson 16: Scansion: A Primer and Lesson 17: Using Scansion, pp. 143–167.
Fenton, James, *An Introduction to English Poetry*, Penguin Books, London, 2002.
Hall, Peter, *Shakespeare's Advice to the Players*, Oberon Books, London, 2003. Part One, pp. 24–39.
Hobsbaum, Philip, *Metre, Rhythm and Verse Form*, Routledge, London, 1996.
Houseman, Barbara, *Tackling Text*, Nick Hern Books, London, 2008. 'Exploring Structures and Rhythms', pp. 72–104; 'Irregular Iambic Pentameter Lines', pp. 281–285; 'Shared Lines', pp. 285–288.
Linklater, Kristin, *Freeing Shakespeare's Voice*, Theatre Communications Group, Inc., New York, 1992. Chapter 6: The Iambic Pentameter, pp. 121–140; Chapter 8: Line Endings, pp. 153–172.

Rodenburg, Patsy, *The Need for Words*, Methuen, London, 1993. 'Verse', pp. 134–136; 'Exercises for the Iambic', pp. 136–139.
Rodenburg, Patsy, *Speaking Shakespeare*, Methuen, London, 2002. 'Rhythm', pp. 84–94; 'Pauses and Irregularities of Rhythm', pp. 95–102; 'The Line', pp. 103–107.
Weate, Catherine, *Modern Voice: Working with Actors on Contemporary Text*, Oberon Books, London, 2012. 'Stressing', pp. 27–34; 'Pacing', pp. 40–43; 'Rhythmic Research', pp. 122–124.

5
ARGUMENT

Framework

One of the driving motivations for young children to learn how to talk is to get what they want. Pretty early, we figure out that crying and cooing only get us so far and that the big people seem to be able to form sounds in a special way that gives them power. So we begin to imitate them, playing with sounds and rhythms as we try to make sense and communicate imaginatively, until eventually we crack the code. We put sounds and rhythm together with sense and image, and come up with our first word! And gradually, as our ability with language grows more and more sophisticated, so also does our ability to organize our thoughts and interact with the world. We move from the mastery of single words to phrases to complete sentences. Finally, we learn to put sentences together to tell stories, ask questions, make points and create arguments. As we emerge from early childhood, that ability to structure our thoughts ultimately gives us as much power to get what we want from the world as do the words themselves.

This process of identifying something we want and then structuring our language to get it eventually becomes so effortless that it can be easy to lose sight of the fact that, on an almost unconscious level, every time we speak we have a reason for choosing to talk and for choosing the words we use. Sometimes it's very clear why we choose to talk: we ask for directions because we want to know how to get somewhere. Sometimes what we want to accomplish can be a little more subtle: we chat with friends because we want to entertain them so they will give us approval and make us feel good about ourselves. Sometimes a part of us doesn't particularly want to talk, but another part wants to meet social expectations which dictate that shutting up in certain circumstances is not an acceptable option. There is always something that prompts us to start talking and then prompts us to keep going.

The problem with speaking from a play script is that when we are presented with words that are written down, they seem inevitable. It becomes very easy to lose touch with the fact that the words are a means to achieve an end, and to just keep talking because the script dictates that you do. It's vital, therefore, that as an actor you address the question of why you are talking as part of your preparation process. If you don't have a reason not only to talk, but also to say the exact things that you say, you are not going to find the right energy to sustain your argument and your audience is not going to have a reason to keep listening to you.

Various schools of acting give various names to that reason for talking – motivation, intention, goal, objective, action etc. For our purposes, it's less important what you call it than how you can find it in the structure of the language. In real life, this structure flows from the desire – the argument is fashioned in the way the speaker believes will be the most successful to accomplish what he wants. As an actor, you have to go backwards. You are given the structure, and by investigating *how* your character goes about pursuing her ends, you gain important insights into *what* those ends are. When you commit to the structural means that are in the language – the comparisons, builds, shifts, twists and turns – you will be convincing in your pursuit of your objective. Ignore how the language works and what it has to offer, however, and you may end up feeling like someone who is trying to eat soup with a fork.

In this chapter, we will look at a couple of the most common devices for structuring an argument and investigate how they can be used to move a character's intention forward. We will also explore how the impulses to speak or continue speaking are usually imbedded in the text, and how to keep them fresh and alive.

Exploration

I. Think of a time when you persuaded somebody to do something – lend you a car, go to a particular film, wash the dishes – whatever. Jot down some of the points that you made. Look at your list of points – did you spend more time focusing on the positive consequences of doing it or the negative consequences of not doing it? Which proved to be more successful in this case?

II. Get a friend to help you – someone who is not too much of a giggler. Your job is to try to make your friend laugh without touching him physically in any way. You can use any other resources at your disposal: language, gesture, facial expressions etc. Her job is to keep a straight face for as long as possible. What did you notice about the amount of energy you were putting into the activity as the game went on? What about your levels of inventiveness with language? Your willingness to behave ridiculously? Was there a build in frustration? How did that affect you?

III. Go back to the political speech you worked with in the *Rhythm* chapter *Explorations*, or find a new one – either a written copy or a video or audio clip. Write down, in one sentence or phrase, what you think the speaker is trying to convince his audience to do or believe. On a scale of 1 to 10, how persuasive do you think the speech is? Brainstorm what things you think the speaker does that work particularly well. Does he repeat things? Make the opposing side look ridiculous? Give lots of examples? If you're in a class, bring your list in and compare it with others; are there certain elements that appear repeatedly in different speeches?

Exercises

> *Teaching tip:* The exercises in this chapter are divided into three sections: *Contrasts, Builds* and *Why Are You Still Talking?* It makes little difference whether you begin with the first or the second section. The third starts to explore the interface between text work and acting and is good to come to whenever your students are feeling the need to explicitly apply what they have learned to a potential performance.

As with other chapters, many of the exercises that follow are physical, so you will want to wear loose clothes and warm up your body and voice before you begin. You will particularly need to spend some time on your breath support, resonance and pitch range. Some of the exercises will also require you to have a pencil to hand.

Contrasts

A colleague of ours in Oregon, Hilary Tate, often says that all unhappiness comes from making comparisons. You may or may not believe that to be true, but it is remarkable how much drama is built around them – at the heart of most plays is the contrast between what characters have and what they want, what they know and what they don't, what they love and what they hate. Not only does contrast drive plots, it is also to be found imbedded in the language of dramatic texts from all periods and all traditions.

Characters constantly build their arguments by pointing out the distinction between one position and another. Comparisons can be made not only between opposites (what is known as **antithesis**), but also between ideas that have some similarity to each other (what is sometimes called **parallelism**). For example, when Claudius in *Hamlet* describes his inability to pray effectively, he says: 'My words fly up, my thoughts remain below.' 'Fly up' and 'remain below' are direct opposites, but Claudius also compares his 'words' and his 'thoughts', which tend to have a relationship with each other. In this way, he creates a double contrast that expresses the inner conflict he is experiencing. As you will discover through the exercises, the energy generated by the tension between contrasting elements can be vast. That's why good writers of plays, poetry and speeches use them so often.

I love, I hate

> **VIDEO LINK**
>
> I love, I hate: https://vimeo.com/268972576

ARGUMENT

(*Allow up to 6 or 7 minutes depending on the group size – everyone should have at least one and no more than three goes.*)

Try this exercise with a partner or in a small group as a warm-up to any work on contrast in text.

The first person thinks of a dessert that has at least two words in it, say chocolate cake, and says, 'I love … chocolate cake (or whatever it is)'. The next person says, 'I hate chocolate cake, but I love … ', and here he has to change one word in the dessert, so he might say, 'I hate chocolate cake, but I love lemon cake'. The next person does the same thing, so she might say, 'I hate lemon cake, but I love lemon sorbet', and so forth. Pay attention to the words that you are contrasting – there's a contrast between 'love' and 'hate', but also a contrast between 'chocolate' and 'lemon'. What kind of vocal energy do you give to those contrasts to draw attention to them?

Crossing the line (about 10 minutes per variation)

VIDEO LINK

Crossing the line: https://vimeo.com/268972760

> *Teaching tip:* The core exercise is very effective in speeches such as 'Now is the winter of our discontent/Made glorious summer by this sun of York' from Shakespeare's *Richard III*, which are built around the act of comparing two things, but it can lead to wonderful discoveries in texts that might not be so obviously built around one central contrast. In fact, we have found that it will encourage students to engage strongly with the structure of most texts.

If you have a large group, you may want to have half watch while the other half do the exercise and then switch. Make sure there are never so many students on the floor that they can't avoid running into each other.

See *Suggested Texts* for some speeches that work particularly well with these exercises:

If you have masking tape, use it to make a line on the floor across the centre of the room. If not, then you can just imagine one.

If you are working with an unfamiliar text, read it out loud once or twice and take a moment to clarify any points of confusion about what it means with your teacher.

I. Stand on the centre line. Designate one end of the room as the 'positive' side and the other end as the 'negative' side. Start reading your text out loud, more slowly than usual, and with each word decide in which direction to move. On words that generally have a positive connotation (e.g. 'sunshine'), you will move towards that side of the room, and for words that generally have a negative connotation (e.g. 'brutal'), you will cross the line over to the other side. (Some words, such as 'the', 'and' etc. can be neutral and you don't have to move on them.) Sometimes you may be hopping back and forth from one side to the other quite frequently; don't be casual about it – really move with energy and purpose.

When in doubt about the value of a word, use the knowledge that you have of the circumstances to help you make a choice about whether something (or someone) is good or bad in the context of this speech. *Don't* make things too complicated ('Well, for some people "poison" could be good if they use it to hunt for food'), but don't worry about getting it 'right' – sometimes there are a couple of valid choices and you can learn a lot from the process of exploring each of them. Once you've worked through the speech this way, stop and talk about any discoveries you made.

You can then try reading the speech and crossing the line again, making more subtle choices about how you use the two sides. For example, consider *how* positive or negative the words are. You may have three negative words in a row, but the third one may be less negative to you than the other two, and so you would move closer to the midline, while staying on the negative side.

Once you've worked through the speech again, stop and talk about any further discoveries you made. You can then try reading the speech again without physically crossing the line but feeling the pulls in different directions that run through it. Of course, you wouldn't act it like this, but you will have discovered something about the character's intentions and how the dynamic of the language expresses them.

ARGUMENT

II. In some speeches, the character's idea of what might be positive or negative *for him/her* is different from usual definitions of good and bad. This comes up often with characters such as Richard III, Iago or Lady Macbeth, for whom 'murder', for example, could potentially be quite positive. With these characters, try the speech moving according to the conventional interpretation of the words (e.g. 'murder' = negative), and then try it again from the character's point of view.

Discuss afterwards: How at odds with the conventional view of the world is your character? What percentage of words would you say landed on the same side of the line both times? Were there words where you felt torn between the two sides? Think about the personal pronouns – for example, is 'We' always positive for your character, or always negative, or does it change?

III. In many speeches, characters are trying to make decisions or solve problems. This is particularly true of soliloquies – if you're not trying to solve a problem, then why would you be standing there talking with no other characters around? If you sense this is going on in your speech, try this variation, which is similar to work Patsy Rodenburg describes in *The Need for Words* (see *Further Reading*).

One student stand at the centre line. Determine what two possible choices that character could make. Designate one side of the room as one possibility, and half of the class line up at the wall on that side. The other half of the class line up at the wall on the other side, representing the other option.

The student in the centre will start reading and moving from one side to the other as the words pull her towards one decision or the other.

Students on either side, every time the reader says a word that you think might be used to convince her to come to your side, cheer her on by repeating the word back to her. There may be times when both sides are trying to use the same word and the person in the middle will have to choose which side to move to.

Discuss afterwards: Did one side feel stronger? Did you know that side would be stronger before doing the exercise? Did the cheers make it easier for you to find your way through the problem or did they distract and make it harder to figure out what to do?

IV. Some speeches and scenes explore contrasts other than positive and negative. Often characters speak of the difference between how things used to be and how they are now; between two people; between what they dream of and what they have etc. For any speech that focuses on such a contrast, you can work with a line and cross it every time you shift from talking about one thing to talking about the other.

This and that

(Allow 10–20 minutes depending on how much experience students have at identifying contrasts.)

Some texts are richer in contrasts than others, but once you start looking, you'll find them frequently. You can do this exercise for any contrast – even a single one in a short line of text. We'll use a speech from Oscar Wilde's *Lady Windermere's Fan* as an example. Lady Windermere believes her husband, Arthur, to be unfaithful and has written him a letter to tell him that she's leaving with another man who has professed his love to her. She's now waiting for her husband to come and try to win her back.

LADY WINDERMERE
Why doesn't he come? This waiting is horrible. He should be here. Why is he not here, to wake by passionate words some fire within me? I am cold – cold as a loveless thing. Arthur must have read my letter by this time. If he cared for me he would have come after me, would have taken me back by force. But he doesn't care. He's entrammelled by this woman – fascinated by her – dominated by her. If a woman wants to hold a man, she has merely to appeal to what is worst in him. We make gods of men and they leave us. Others make brutes of them and they fawn and are faithful. How hideous life! … Oh! it was mad of me to come here, horribly mad. And yet, which is the worst, I wonder, to be at the mercy of a man who loves one, or the wife of a man who in one's own house dishonours one?

Read through your speech once to get the sense of it.

Next, go through it, drawing a line between all the pairs of contrasting words or phrases that you can find. Some will be direct opposites, like 'cared' and 'doesn't care'. Others will be clearly antithetical – e.g. 'fire' and 'cold'; 'gods' and 'brutes'; 'leave us' and 'fawn and be faithful'. And some will be more subtle comparisons: 'passionate words' and 'loveless thing'; 'be at the mercy of' and '[be] the wife of'; 'a man who loves one' and 'a man who in one's own house dishonours one'. Remember you are looking for contrasts between two things – even small words can be compared to each other, as '**we** do **this,** and **others** do **that**'.

Put a '1' above the first word (or phrase) in each pair of comparisons you've found and a '2' above the second word (or phrase) in the pair. For example, 'cared' would have a 1 over it and 'doesn't care' would have a 2. 'Fire' would have a 1 over it and 'cold' a 2. You'll end up with at least half a dozen pairs of 1s and 2s. Here are our pairings (rather than drawing lines between pairs, we have given each pair a letter):

LADY WINDERMERE

Why doesn't he come? This waiting is horrible. He should be here. Why is he not here, to wake by *1A* passionate words some *1B* fire within me? I am *2B* cold – cold as a *2A* loveless thing. Arthur must have read my letter by this time. If he *1C* cared for me he would have come after me, would have taken me back by force. But he *2C* doesn't care. He's entrammelled by this woman – fascinated by her – dominated by her. If a woman wants to hold a man, she has merely to appeal to what is worst in him. We make *1D* gods of men and they *1E* leave us. Others make *2D* brutes of them and they *2E* fawn and are faithful. How hideous life! … Oh! it was mad of me to come here, horribly mad. And yet, which is the worst, I wonder, to be *1F* at the mercy of a man who *1G* loves one, or *2F* the wife of a man who in one's own house *2G* dishonours one?

Start in the middle of the room. As you approach your first 1, walk to the wall to your right and touch the wall *as you speak the word*. As you approach the 2 that goes with it, cross the room and touch the opposite wall *as you speak the word* (or words). Make sure you touch the wall firmly, with energy and purposefulness.

NOTE: sometimes you will get a couple of 1s in a row before you come to the corresponding 2s. When that happens, stay at the wall to the right and touch it on each of the 1s until you come to a 2 and have to cross the room.

Do the exercise again sitting across from a partner. Have your partner hold out her hands, palms up. Instead of touching the walls, this time tap your partner's left palm on all the 1s and right palm on all the 2s.

Finally, read through the speech just using the energy of your voice to bring out the contrasts, as you did in the *I Love/I Hate* exercise.

What have you discovered about the speech? How has this informed your understanding of the character's thoughts and feelings?

Colder/hotter (15–20 minutes)

Sometimes, characters are struggling with expressing their feelings about someone or something. Perhaps they want very strongly to have or be close to something or someone, but are embarrassed or afraid. Or maybe they know that they should try to stay away from something but find it hard to resist. Juliet, Cressida and others from *Suggested Texts* are all recommended for this exercise.

If you haven't worked with the speech before, read it out loud at least once and make sure you are clear about what the given circumstances of the speech are and what all the words mean.

Get a partner. Partner A will speak the text. Partner B will stand in front of A and represent the thing/person that A wants to get close to or wants to get away from, depending on the nature of the speech.

Partner A, as you read the speech, move closer to B when the words bring you closer to the thing you want (or want to avoid) and move farther away when the words put distance between you and that thing (or person).

When you move in one direction, move with purpose and conviction – don't let the fact that you know you'll be going in the other direction soon make you hesitant or anxious.

Repeat with B reading the speech.

Look at your text. Can you identify the points at which you stopped moving in one direction and started moving in another? Draw a slash right before the word on which you made the change.

Repeat the exercise as above, but this time, B read along and *on the slash* (so this will happen between words), make a loud, sharp sound –

ARGUMENT

something like slapping a book (not too hard!) on to a table or a wall works well. A, let that noise feed the energy of your switch from moving in one direction to moving in the other.

Repeat with B reading the text.

Discuss: How easy or hard was it to identify the moments when you switch from moving in one direction to moving in the other? How did the stimulus of the loud noise help you make the transitions? Usually when characters are torn this way, rather than being paralysed by anxiety they actually move fluidly between the two extremes, both linguistically and emotionally.

> *Teaching tip:* Partners will either have to work with the same text or they will need to have copies of each other's text to do the second part of the exercise.

He said/she said

(Allow 10–20 minutes depending on how experienced the students are at finding contrasts.)

Sometimes contrasts run between the dialogue of two characters. Often, this takes the form of straight contradictions: 'I said **this**', 'No, you said **that**'. But sometimes the contrasts are more complex. For this exercise, we'll use some dialogue between Richard of Gloucester (soon to become Richard III) and Lady Anne from Shakespeare's *Richard III*. Richard has killed Anne's husband and father-in-law. In this scene she confronts him and he attempts to win her over.

GLOUCESTER
Lady, you know no rules of charity,
Which renders good for bad, blessings for curses.
LADY ANNE
Villain, thou know'st no law of God nor man:
No beast so fierce but knows some touch of pity.

GLOUCESTER
   But I know none, and therefore am no beast.
LADY ANNE
   O wonderful, when devils tell the truth!
GLOUCESTER
   More wonderful, when angels are so angry.
   Vouchsafe*, divine perfection of a woman,   *grant, allow*
   Of these supposed-evils, to give me leave,
   By circumstance*, but to acquit myself.   *detailed description*
LADY ANNE
   Vouchsafe, defused* infection of a man,   *shapeless*
   For these known evils, but to give me leave,
   By circumstance, to curse thy cursed self.
GLOUCESTER
   Fairer than tongue can name thee, let me have
   Some patient leisure to excuse myself.
LADY ANNE
   Fouler than heart can think thee, thou canst make
   No excuse current*, but to hang thyself.   *generally believed*
GLOUCESTER
   By such despair, I should accuse myself.
LADY ANNE
   And, by despairing, shouldst thou stand excused;
   For doing worthy vengeance on thyself,
   Which didst unworthy slaughter upon others.

Get a partner and decide who is which character. Read through the scene together out loud once or twice to get familiar with it. If necessary, clarify the meaning of any unfamiliar words.

Next, go through it with a pencil and draw a line between any pairs of opposites, such as 'devils' and 'angels' or 'woman' and 'man'. Some pairs will be contained in one person's line, but some will be split between the two characters. Go through again and draw a line between parallel pairs of words or phrases that may not be direct opposites but are nonetheless contrasted. For example, 'divine perfection' and 'defused infection'; 'acquit' and 'curse'; 'tongue can name' and 'heart can think' etc. You'll find that there are a lot of

ARGUMENT

places where these parallels are shared between the two characters – places where one of the characters turns the other's words back on him or her.

Put a '1' above the first word (or phrase) in each pair of comparisons you've found and a '2' above the second word (or phrase) in the pair. For example, 'devils' would have a 1 over it and 'angels' would have a 2. 'Divine perfection' would have a 1 over it and 'diffused infection' a 2. You'll end up with at least a dozen pairs.

Get seven or eight smallish objects from around the room or from your bags, such as books, umbrellas, pencil cases, shoes – nothing too big, fragile or valuable. If you have a table, place them on the table all to one side and stand with the table between you. If you don't, sit on the floor facing each other and put the objects between you – all to one side.

Start reading the text, fairly slowly. When you get to a 1, *as you say the word or phrase*, pick up an object and move it to the other side of the space (or table) between you. Whenever the 2 that contrasts with that 1 comes up, the person who says it should pick up that object and move it back across the space. For example, if you were Richard, you would move an object from one side of the space/table on 'good' and move it back again on 'bad'. Further down, when Anne says 'devils', she would move an object, and when you say 'angels' you would move it back. Take your time with this.

There may be several 1s in a row before the corresponding 2s come up. If that happens, try to remember which object went with which word so you can move it back on that word's opposite. Don't worry too much about getting the right object if a lot of them have piled up, but do be energetic about putting those objects where you want them. If it feels a little frustrating that your partner keeps moving the objects back, that's okay.

After you've been through the text once, or even twice if you have the time, put the objects away and play the scene using the energy of the words to put the other character in his or her place.

NOTE: You can also do this exercise turning playing cards face side up and face side down again instead of moving objects.

Discuss any discoveries about how the language reflects the emotional dynamic between the characters.

Builds

Just as most drama starts with a contrast, the energy of most drama builds to a climax. Rare is the play, scene or speech where things become less important, less urgent or less interesting as the action moves on. The build isn't always one long, straight intensification, though. There can be platforms where the energy stays on one level for a while; cutbacks when it drops before spiking again; sharp accelerations; or slow, steady burns. Nor are builds always best expressed by simply getting louder. Getting progressively quieter can also be a kind of build – or slower, or faster, or higher or lower in pitch – or any combination of the above. How an individual build is constructed will largely depend on what tactics the character is using to get what he wants. The longer he goes without succeeding, the more energy he is going to give to those tactics – be they bullying, seducing, dazzling etc. – and there will be a build. The exercises in this section will help you learn to recognize builds and express their energy in a way that is true to the text.

Straight builds (2–3 minutes each)

We are indebted to Robert Cohen and Ursula Meyer for much of this work.

I. Get a partner. Count to 20 together, alternating numbers (the first partner says 'one'; the second says 'two'; the first says 'three' and so forth.) Try the following builds:

Start with a very quiet whisper and get a little louder with each number – do not, however, get so loud that you strain your voice!
Start quite loudly and get softer with each number.
Start with a long pause between 'one' and 'two', and then come in a little more quickly with each number.
Start with a very lethargic, depressed 'one', and become a little bit more enthusiastic with each number.
Start with a friendly 'one', and get a little less friendly and more threatening with each number.

II. Get a partner. Partner A, hold a very precious imaginary thing hidden in your hands. Partner B, ask in a low-key way if you can see

ARGUMENT

it. A, say, 'No'. B, offer to give A a pound (or whatever currency is relevant to you) if she'll let you see it. A, refuse again. B, continue offering more money, and A, continue refusing at least ten times (tap the exchanges out with your fingers). After ten exchanges, A can choose to either say a final 'no' and walk away or to say 'yes'. Try it both ways.

III. Take a monologue that you know by heart very well. As you start speaking it, walk around the room at a fairly slow pace, but as you continue, gradually speed up, so that by the end you are running around the room. If you peak too soon and are running at top speed two-thirds of the way through, or if you never really get to a good run, go back and try it again. Then try the speech standing still and see if you can still feel that sense of energy increasing without just talking faster and faster. NOTE: Only one person should do this exercise at a time.

I will die (about 15 minutes per student, or 30 for a pair)

This is based on an exercise Che Walker introduced us to – variations on it are used by many acting teachers.

Find a speech in which a character is trying to persuade another character of something or trying to solve a problem.

Find a partner and decide who will go first – that's partner A.

Partner B, get a pen and a piece of paper. Then ask partner A what he or she is trying to do in this speech.

A, explain to B in up to three or four sentences what you're trying to accomplish (e.g. persuade my troops to go back into battle; work up the courage to kill the king; convince my ex that I'm not attracted to him anymore – whatever it may be).

B, ask A, 'What will happen if you fail?'

A, tell B what the immediate consequences of your failing to meet this objective would be – i.e. what is the next thing that would happen (e.g. 'The army would have to retreat').

B, jot down a word or two to help you remember the gist of A's answer. Then ask A, 'And what would happen then?'

A, describe in a sentence or two what would happen next (e.g. 'The enemy would have control of the town, which would give them more supplies').

B, jot down a couple of words about that answer, then ask again, 'And what would happen then?' A, respond again. You can use your imagination to come up with a variety of different consequences – the only rule is that each consequence has to be worse than the one before. At no point can things get better.

Keep repeating this, with things getting worse and worse until eventually A comes to 'And then I would die'.

A, don't rush to the end – even in very high-stakes situations, there are at least a few steps before your life would have to come to an end. At the same time, don't resist things getting worse and worse. It may seem silly that failing to convince your ex that you're not attracted to him/her anymore would lead to your death, but even that failure could lead you to some very dark places if you let it.

When you've come to the last possible consequence of death, get up.

B, take your notes and stand next to A. A, start speaking the text, taking your time.

B, at regular intervals – particularly between sentences or when you sense A's energy starting to flag – whisper to A some of the bad things that could happen if he or she fails in this speech, getting worse as you go along (e.g. 'You'll lose your job', 'You'll be out on the street'). Use your notes for this.

A, let B's whisperings prompt you to try even harder to succeed as you go along in order to avoid the terrible consequences of failure.

Swap over and work with B's speech.

Discuss: Did thinking through the possible consequences of failing change how you approached this text? How did being reminded of them by your partner affect you as you read through it? Did the fact that they got worse and worse help you build your determination to avoid them?

You can also do this speech asking 'What will happen if you succeed?' with good consequences escalating to 'And my life will be happy forever'.

Lists (about 15 minutes)

VIDEO LINK

Lists: https://vimeo.com/268963127

ARGUMENT

Lists are everywhere in drama. We're going to work with a bit of text from Shakespeare's *The Merry Wives of Windsor* here, but you will find lists in many, many other texts.

In this speech, Ford has disguised himself to meet with Falstaff, the man he suspects is his wife's lover, and has confirmed that Falstaff is meeting with her at eleven o'clock. He little suspects that she is playing a trick on them both. Page is a friend of his who is more trusting.

FORD
    See the hell of having a false
    woman! My bed shall be abused, my coffers*   *money chests*
    ransacked, my reputation gnawn* at; and I shall not   *chewed*
    only receive this villainous wrong, but stand under
    the adoption of abominable terms*, and by him that
                                                  be called awful names
    does me this wrong*. Page is an ass, a secure ass: he
                                        by him who is stealing my wife
    will trust his wife; he will not be jealous. I will
    rather trust a Fleming with my butter, Parson Hugh
    the Welshman with my cheese, an Irishman with my
    aqua-vitae* bottle, or a thief to walk my ambling   *whisky*
    gelding*, than my wife with herself; then she
       plots,   *castrated horse*
    then she ruminates*, then she devises; and what
       they   *thinks over*
    think in their hearts they may effect*, they will   *make happen*
    break their hearts but they will effect. God be
    praised for my jealousy! Eleven o'clock the hour.
    I will prevent this, detect my wife, be revenged on
    Falstaff, and laugh at Page. I will about it;
    better three hours too soon than a minute too late.
    Fie, fie, fie! cuckold*! cuckold! cuckold!
                                      one whose wife has cheated on him

Read through the speech out loud a couple of times to get a feel for it. Notice that it's in prose, not verse.

Now read through the speech looking for lists. For example, at the beginning, Ford lists several things that he fears will happen to him:

'1) my bed shall be abused, 2) my coffers ransacked, 3) my reputation gnawn at; and I shall not only 4) receive this villainous wrong, but 5) stand under the adoption of abominable terms'. Then there's the cap to it all, which is that this is going to be inflicted on him 6) 'by him that does me this wrong'.

Write the number 1 over the first thing on the list, 2 over the second, and so forth.

When you find the next list (which is of people he would rather trust than his wife), do the same, starting with 1 again. Carry on in this way to the end of the speech until you've identified as many lists as you can.

When you've finished with your numbering, stand beside a wall and hold your text with the hand farthest from the wall.

Read through the speech out loud, including the numbers that you've added. When you get to the first 1, touch the wall at about hip height firmly and with purpose, and say '1, my bed shall be abused'. When you get to 2, touch the wall a bit higher, and say '2, my coffers ransacked'. When you get to 3, touch the wall higher still, and so forth.

When you come to the next 1, you can drop back down, but not as far as you were with the first 1. So if the first list started around your hip, the second list would start around your waist, the third list around your breastbone, and so forth.

Let the rising of your hand lift the energy you bring to your reading.

Just for fun, go back and read it again, this time putting a 1, 2 and a 3 before each 'fie' and each 'cuckold', so you'll be touching the wall on those as well – they may even pull you up to your tiptoes! These aren't lists as such, just repetitions; but repetitions can also build (and often do).

Finally try building the energy in the same way but without touching the wall.

Discuss any discoveries about the language and Ford's emotional state.

More lists (15–25 minutes)

Ford expresses his emotions to himself. Shylock, in the following speech from Shakespeare's *The Merchant of Venice*, is justifying his desire for revenge to one of his enemies, Salarino, who has just asked him what a pound of Antonio's flesh would be good for:

ARGUMENT

SHYLOCK
To bait fish* withal: if it will feed nothing
    else,   *to catch fish with bait*
it will feed my revenge. He hath disgraced me,
and hindered me half a million; laughed at my
losses, mocked at my gains, scorned my nation,
thwarted my bargains, cooled my friends,
heated mine enemies; and what's his reason?
I am a Jew. Hath not a Jew eyes? hath not a
Jew hands, organs, dimensions, senses,
affections, passions? fed with the same food,
hurt with the same weapons, subject to the
same diseases, healed by the same means,
warmed and cooled by the same winter and
summer, as a Christian is? If you prick us,
do we not bleed? if you tickle us, do we not
laugh? if you poison us, do we not die? and
if you wrong us, shall we not revenge? If we
are like you in the rest, we will resemble you
in that. If a Jew wrong a Christian, what is his
humility? Revenge. If a Christian wrong a Jew,
what should his sufferance* be by Christian
                                              patient endurance
example? Why, revenge. The villainy you teach
me, I will execute*, and it shall go hard but I will   *carry out*
better the instruction.

1. Read through the speech out loud a couple of times to get a feel for it. Notice that it's also in prose.

Now, as in the previous exercise, read through the speech looking for lists. For example, at the beginning, Shylock, a Jew, lists several insults that he has suffered from Antonio, a Christian.

When you've finished finding your lists, get a partner and compare notes. Why might there be some disagreement? What made you decide some phrases were part of a list or were on a separate list?

2. Now, A will speak the text, working with the lists as you chose them.

With each list, you are going to move your partner around the room in a new way. You may touch your partner, appropriately, but never with so much force that there is any possibility of hurting or pushing him off balance. For example, you may put a finger on your partner's collarbone and press him backwards as you speak one list. Or you may take him by the hand and pull him forward on another. Or you may take his elbow and move him off to the side. As you proceed through each list, let your movement become more firm and purposeful. And remember to change the way you are moving your partner with each new list.

3. Swap over, so that B, you will be speaking the text, working with the lists you've identified. This time, however, instead of moving your partner, with each list you yourself will move in a different way. You can back away from your partner on one list, turn your back on her and walk away on another, walk towards her, move in a circle around her etc. As you proceed through each list, let your movement be more firm and purposeful.

Discuss with your partner what each of these ways of speaking the text felt like. What did you discover about the different lists? Was there a different energy depending on whether you were moving your partner or moving on your own?

4. Each of you speak the text again, but this time you can choose whether to move your partner or move on your own as the language inspires you.

Discuss your choices. There is no right answer, but the different choices may bring out different dynamics in the lists. What did you discover about the overall build of the text? How did the different lists contribute to this?

> *Teaching tip:* In general, this is an exercise we would do only with groups that are mature and trust each other. We recognize that *The Merchant of Venice* is a contentious play for modern readers because of its casual anti-Semitism. While we would strongly condemn any form of racial hatred, Shylock's speech addresses the essential humanity of all human beings, and can open up a fruitful discussion about the treatment of any minority, the roots of hatred and the awful effects of any form of abusive behaviour.

> You may wish to assign same-sex pairs for this exercise as it involves some touching.

Spirals and stairs

(*Timing will depend on the number of students doing the exercise; it will take about 5 minutes per student once you get going.*)

This is a classic exercise taught in both British and American drama schools. We're going to work with some text from Bernard Shaw's *Man and Superman* for it. Shaw was a master of builds; his language drives forward with great energy, but creates fantastic patterns and rhythms along the way. This exercise also works well with speeches and scenes by Shakespeare and others.

TANNER
> The true artist will let his wife starve, his children go barefoot, his mother drudge for his living at seventy, sooner than work at anything but his art. To women he is half vivisector, half vampire. He gets into intimate relations with them to study them, to strip the mask of convention from them, to surprise their inmost secrets, knowing that they have the power to rouse his deepest creative energies, to rescue him from his cold reason, to make him see visions and dream dreams, to inspire him, as he calls it. He persuades women that they may do this for their own purpose whilst he really means them to do it for his. He steals the mother's milk and blackens it to make printers' ink to scoff at her and glorify ideal women with. He pretends to spare her the pangs of child-bearing so that he may have for himself the tenderness of fostering that belongs of right to her children. Since marriage began, the great artist has been known as a bad husband. But he is worse: he is a child-robber, a bloodsucker, a hypocrite, and a cheat.

Read the speech through once to yourself.

Next, form a circle and read around it, each person reading until he or she comes to a punctuation mark.

We worked with some Shaw in the *Rhythm* chapter, and you may already have noticed some rhythmic patterns emerging here – repetition of short or long sentences and phrases, for example. Builds are very much connected to rhythm.

Now, one or two students (depending on the size of the room) will take the floor.

Start in a corner of the room, and begin walking around the perimeter of the room in a large circle (or if there are two of you, walk around half the room).

As you read, start to spiral inward, so your circle gets progressively smaller – do this for the first three or four sentences so you get the feel of it.

Now start again. This time, you will start again moving in an inward spiral, but at any time you like, you may stop and change direction – switch from spiralling to the left to spiralling to the right. You may even spiral outwards for a while and then start spiralling inward again. You may change your speed and move from a very broad spiral into a very tight one. The only rule is that you land at the centre of your circle on (not before or after) the last word of the speech.

Try to be sensitive to the direction the language takes you in – don't change your movement just for the sake of change; do it when the thoughts seems to change direction, speed up or slow down.

When you've finished, talk a bit about how it felt doing the exercise and then the observers can comment on what they saw. Depending on time and desire, everyone can give it a try.

If you have access to some stairs, you can do a very similar exercise. Instead of spiralling go up and down steps. Start at the bottom, and from there you can go up several very quickly, slow down, go down steps from time to time, stay on one step for a while etc. Try to end up on the top step on the last word.

Why are you still talking?

Robert Cohen has made the point that in drama characters rarely start speeches intending to make speeches. Characters start speeches intending to accomplish something and, in most cases, would very much like to get the job done with the first sentence or two. It is because they do not succeed at first that they keep going. It may be that they don't succeed because the listener is resistant or downright hostile; it may be

ARGUMENT

that they don't succeed because they fail at first to make themselves clear; it may be that they kind of succeed but just can't trust their own success. Even characters who do intend to make a speech – say Brutus or Antony at Caesar's funeral – will gauge how well the speech is going and make adjustments along the way. In every case, there is a grain of dissatisfaction – a little feeling that the point hasn't quite landed, the argument isn't complete or the problem hasn't been solved. There is also a grain of hope that somehow more words can get the job done. These grains of hope and dissatisfaction keep the speaker talking.

The same principle is true in dialogues. In scenes that are full of conflict, it can be very clear that the characters aren't getting what they want, but even then the question remains, why are they talking instead of punching each other or walking out? In a love scene, where everything seems to be going wonderfully well, why aren't the characters just kissing instead of continuing to blab away? In the scene of conflict, the grain of dissatisfaction may, in fact, be a boulder, but the grain of hope is also there – hope that *somehow* the character will be able to walk away in a better position than she's in right now if she says just one more thing. In the love scene, the hope is usually huge, but the dissatisfaction is also there: 'This feels great, but wouldn't it be nice to get just a little more assurance, affection, etc.' Even in scenes that seem more ordinary, characters are constantly motivated by little grains of dissatisfaction and hope to try to alter their situations.

These grains lead to decisions. Good writers build those decisions into the script. They may be quite subtle, because in life we tend to make these decisions fluidly – almost without thinking about it. As an actor, however, it's usually a good idea to spend a little time thinking about where those decisions happen and why they get made the way they do. Once you have a good feel for the whens and the whys, you can play the making of the decisions quickly and easily. If you ignore them, however, you run the risk of continuing to talk just because there are more words on the page, not because you're actively responding to the need to accomplish something.

The work we did on using punctuation in Chapter 3 can help with finding those moments of decision to keep talking. Often they come at full stops and sometimes at commas, semicolons or colons. In a dialogue, they often happen while the other character is still speaking. There may be a key word or phrase that sparks the decision to reply.

Once you've found where the decision to say something new happens, you can investigate what kind of decision is made. Sometimes it's a decision to **intensify** what's just been said – to reinforce the point – and the work in the previous section on builds relates very much to this. Sometimes it's a decision to **clarify** – to offer more detail. Sometimes it's a decision to **qualify** – to modify what's just been said. Sometimes it's a decision to **change direction** and try a new point. Sometimes it's a decision to **back down** altogether.

In the exercises, we'll investigate how these decisions work dramatically – how they shape the energy of a speech or scene and give it life. In the chapter on *Rhythm*, we talked about 'emotional logic'. The same concept is applicable here: you'll be learning how to make sense of each new impulse to clarify, qualify, change direction or whatever the choice may be, but it won't necessarily be an intellectual sense. It would be a much tidier but much less interesting world if we always had a rational reason to say the things we say. Nevertheless, there is always some kind of reason – emotional or intellectual – and it makes some kind of sense to us in an intuitive way. Once you've found that sense, you can be active in choosing to keep talking. Speaking will then feel natural and fresh. Your breath will naturally drop in at the appropriate moments; you will find energy to drive to the ends of thoughts; and you won't have to worry about 'showing' what you are feeling or thinking because you will be doing what 'real people' do: moving from one impulse to the next.

Just walk away (8–10 minutes per partner)

For this exercise, find a speech in which you are clearly trying to have an effect on the person you are talking to – see *Suggested Texts* for some ideas.

Find a partner.

Partner A, speak your text to partner B with energy and commitment until you feel you have completed the first full thought. This may happen at the first full stop or it may take a couple of sentences to make the initial point. When you have finished that first thought, turn around and walk away. See how far you get before you feel an impulse, however slight, to follow it up with another thought. When you do, wheel back around and start the second thought, walking towards your partner.

ARGUMENT

When you have completed the second thought, turn your back to your partner and walk away again until you feel the need to come back and add more. If you're stopped by a door, you may even open and walk through it and then re-enter the room.

Continue this way until you get to the end of the speech. When you do, just stand in front of your partner and feel what it is to hold your ground in silence for a beat before coming out of the exercise.

> *Teaching tip:* As with other paired exercises, you can have all the pairs working in the room at once, but this can also be a particularly good exercise to have one pair working and the others watching.

Here's the deal

(*Allow about 10 minutes per partner depending on the length of the text.*)

This is a simple exercise that can help make the moment of choosing to speak or to continue speaking more alive and vivid for you. It can be used in dialogues as well as speeches.

Read through your text out loud once or twice if you're not familiar with it. Get a partner.

Now, before you start the text, look at your partner, take a breath in and say, 'Here's the deal.' Then launch into the speech. The energy of your 'Here's the deal' will be determined by the energy with which the speech starts. It can be confrontational, appeasing, matter of fact, seductive – anything at all.

Continue with the speech, and whenever a new point is about to be raised or the speech is becoming more insistent, or you feel like your energy is getting stale or stuck on one level, preface the next thing you say with 'Here's the deal', or 'So, here's the deal'. You will probably find yourself doing this often after full stops, but you don't have to after every full stop; and from time to time, you may find some kind of mid-sentence shift that calls for a 'Here's the deal'. The tone and energy of each 'Here's the deal' will change according to what you're saying and what you're trying to do at that point in the speech. Don't worry too much about 'getting it right'; just play and see what you discover.

Repeat the exercise – some 'Here's the deal's will probably appear in the same places, and may become stronger. Others may disappear this time, and some new ones may come in. You'll probably have a better sense of where and how they really serve you.

Switch over so your partner will now go through his speech twice.

Finally, both of you speak your text to each other again, but instead of saying, 'Here's the deal', use an in-breath to make a bit of space for those fresh intentions to form.

Discuss how the 'Here's the deal's helped you to feel the fresh impulse to say something new – both when you were speaking and when you were listening. Did they change your breathing? Your rhythm? What happened when you took them away again?

> *Teaching tip:* Other phrases can be used in this exercise to great effect. For example: 'Don't you see', 'The thing is', or even 'Dude' ('But soft what light through yonder window breaks? **Dude!** It is the east and Juliet is the sun'). Use variations to suit the speech and student.

Yes/No (timing will depend on the length of the dialogue)

You will need a partner and a piece of dialogue for this exercise.

Read the dialogue out loud together a couple of times and make sure that you are clear about the given circumstances of the scene.

Read the scene out loud again. This time, after the first line is spoken, you must preface every line be saying either 'Yes' or 'No' depending on whether you want to affirm what has just been spoken or oppose it. Don't think too hard about which it is – follow your impulses. You can also add a 'Yes' or a 'No' within your own line if you want to strengthen that affirmation or opposition.

ARGUMENT

As with 'Here's the deal', the energy of your 'Yes' and 'No' will depend on what is happening in the moment. They may be tentative, aggressive, flirtatious etc.

Try the scene again without saying 'Yes' or 'No', but remembering that little pulse of energy at the start of every line.

> *Teaching tip:* This exercise can also be done with speeches, with the student injecting 'Yes' and 'No' into the text wherever they are either gaining momentum in a certain direction or backing down and changing direction.

So what (5–8 minutes per partner)

See *Suggested Texts* for some possible speeches.

Get into pairs. Partner A, read your speech aloud to partner B.

A, read your speech to B again. Maintain eye contact as much as you can. This time, B, whenever you feel there is an appropriate break in A's line of thought, say 'So what?' Full stops and pauses are natural places for you to do this, but you don't have to on every one. You may also feel it's appropriate to interject in the middle of a long thought if it's not coming efficiently to the point. Aim to challenge A but not to bombard or undermine her.

A, whenever B says 'So what?' make sure that you take the time to receive that challenge and then push back against it with appropriate energy. That doesn't mean you have to take long pauses after the 'So what?' – we process the things that are said to us with lightning speed – but you have to let them affect you; you can't just ignore them. At the same time, don't feel that you always need to shout B down. Perhaps the challenge will prompt you to become more controlled and understated; you'll find the appropriate response in the moment.

Go through the text again. This time, B, instead of saying 'So what?', gently tap A on the arm (or knee if you're sitting) whenever you feel you want to challenge her. A, let that stimulus prompt you to give fresh energy to the next thing you say.

Switch partners.

When you've both finished, you can try delivering the speeches to each other again. Discuss how your performance has changed. What did it feel like to be challenged in that way? What have you discovered about the energy of the language?

> *Teaching tip:* Depending on the makeup of your class, you may want to assign partners for this exercise so that each student can work with someone who will present her with a level of challenge she can work with effectively.

Somebody listen (about 5 minutes per student)

This is an exercise we learnt from Cicely Berry, and works well with many speeches from classical and contemporary plays.

One student will take a piece of text. The other students should start walking around the space. Walk with purpose and energy; if you like, make up a little story for yourself about where you're going and why you need to get there promptly.

Once this is established, the student with the text will begin speaking and try to get someone to listen.

You can walk alongside someone for a while, for example; or stand in the space and try to get attention; or try to connect with each person who goes by. You may be loud and belligerent, or genial and understated. Try to match your tactics to what you are saying – for a long, complex thought, you may want to walk along with one person and try to draw her in. For a short, bold pronouncement, you may want to stand still and send your voice out strongly into the room. Stick with one tactic until you feel that you simply must try another.

NOTE: While you can get close to your classmates or even stand in their way, you cannot touch them.

If you are walking, remember that you need to get some place, but if something really grabs your attention, don't feel you have to ignore the speaker.

Repeat with a new speaker until everyone who would like to has had a turn.

Discuss: What were some moments when you really felt compelled to listen? What did it feel like to have to work so hard to get people to listen? Were there some moments when you felt you had to change tactics? Did the language suggest any new tactics to you? Did some things feel like they needed to be more private while others were better delivered to the whole group? Were there changes in rhythm? Builds?

Shadow dialogue (30–40 minutes)

Modern play texts from the last sixty years have often included scripted pauses and silences. Samuel Beckett's *Waiting for Godot* perhaps set the trend, but it was eagerly adopted by writers such as Harold Pinter and David Mamet. The following exercise will help you explore what may be happening in those silences, and why the characters may choose to speak again.

This exercise also works very well with monologues, working in pairs rather than groups of four. See *Suggested Texts* for ideas.

Read through the text as a class, and make sure you are clear about the given circumstances of the scene.

Now, get into groups of four and divide up the parts so that two people are designated as Character A (Estragon, say, from *Godot*) and two are designated as Character B (Vladimir). One Estragon and one Vladimir will have the text in front of them and will play it as scripted, taking all pauses or silences. The other partners are Shadow Estragon and Shadow Vladimir. They will put the text aside and sit beside or behind their character, listening actively to the dialogue. When Estragon and Vladimir come to a scripted pause or silence, their Shadows will speak the thoughts which they imagine the character is having during the pause or silence. These thoughts may be comments on the other character, feelings about themselves, distractions or just random observations. The only rule is that they should be in character and appropriate to the given circumstances.

Once you've played the scene like this once, swap over and do it again; so, the people who spoke the text the first time will now be the shadows and voice their character's thoughts, and vice versa.

Discuss what you've discovered about your character and the nature of the pauses and silences. What was the difference between a pause and a silence? What made a character choose to speak again?

Run the exercise another couple of times, so that each pair has a chance to voice the characters' thoughts, but this time explore how long you can let the pauses and silences last in the context of the scene.

Finally, each pair play the scene just speaking the text, while imagining their own character's internal thoughts.

Discuss what you've discovered about thought and language, and how the pauses and silences contribute to the dynamics of the scene.

Follow-up

- Watch a film or TV show and note any contrasts in the dialogue. Did the actors give them energy and focus? If so, how did they help move the scene forward?

- Watch a film or TV show and look for builds. What was the shortest build? And the longest? How were the builds created – through volume, pace, music, spatial relationship etc.?

- Think back to a sustained conversation you may have had over the last week. What first prompted you to engage in the conversation? What did you want going into it (perhaps just to catch up with a friend, relax, feel connected to somebody)? Did your intention and/or state of mind change during the course of the conversation? What prompted you to end it?

- Did you make any discoveries doing these exercises that surprised you? What did you find in the text that you had not seen before?

- Did any of the discoveries you made relate to rhythm? Image? Sound? Sense?

- In your experience, which exercises particularly served your acting? How?

Suggested texts

Contrasts

Crossing the line I

Aphra Behn, *The Rover*, Act IV Scene 3, Blunt: 'Cruel? Yes, I will kiss and beat thee'
Lorraine Hansberry, *A Raisin in the Sun*, Act III, Asagai: 'I live the answer'
Arthur Miller, *The Crucible*, Act IV, Hale: 'Let you not mistake your duty'
William Shakespeare, *Romeo and Juliet*, Act III Scene 2, Juliet: 'O serpent heart'

Crossing the line II

Eugene O'Neill, *The Iceman Cometh*, Act I, Mosher: 'Give him time, Harry'
William Shakespeare, *Richard III*, Act I Scene 1, Richard: 'Now is the winter'

Crossing the line III

Frances Ya-Chu Cowhig, *Snow in Midsummer*, Act I Scene 10, Rocket: 'Ghost of the Woman Dou Yi'
William Shakespeare, *The Two Gentlemen of Verona*, Act II Scene 6, Proteus: 'To leave my Julia'

Crossing the line IV

William Shakespeare, *As You Like It*, Act III Scene 5, Phoebe: 'Think not I love him'
Paula Vogel, *The Mineola Twins*, Scene 4, Myra: 'Well, it's like the story of Jacob and Esau'
August Wilson, *Seven Guitars*, Act II Scene 3, Floyd: 'I had seven ways to go'

This and that

James Baldwin, *Blues for Mister Charlie*, Act I, Meridian: 'I'm a Christian'
William Congreve, *The Way of the World*, Act II Scene 1, Mirabell: 'I have something more'

Nilo Cruz, *Anna in the Tropics*, Act I Scene 3, Conchita: 'Oh, I could see the husband'

Tennessee Williams, *The Glass Menagerie*, Scene 1, Tom: 'Yes I have tricks in my pocket' through 'I am the narrator of the play, and also a character in it'

Colder/hotter

Aphra Behn, *The Rover*, Act II Scene 2, Willmore: 'Yes I am poor'

William Shakespeare, *Romeo and Juliet*, Act II Scene 1, Juliet: 'Thou know'st the mask of night'

William Shakespeare, *Troilus and Cressida*, Act III Scene 2, Cressida: 'Hard to seem won'

John Webster, *The Duchess of Malfi*, Act I Scene 1, Duchess: 'Now she pays it'

He said/she said

Alan Ayckbourn, *Living Together*, Act II Scene 2, from Norman: 'You're dressed' through Ruth: 'happy without you, won't they?'

George Etherege, *The Man of Mode*, Act V Scene 1, from Dorimant: 'Women, when they would break' through Loveit: 'I knew you came'

Kate Hennig, *The Last Wife*, Act I Scene 14, from Henry: 'What you? A regent?' through Kate: 'Because you chose me as your wife'

Quiara Alegría Hudes, *The Happiest Song Plays Last*, Scene 1, Shar and Elliot from Shar: 'We better get credit for the stunts' through Shar: 'Julliard'

William Shakespeare, *Much Ado about Nothing*, Act I Scene 1, Beatrice/Benedick

Builds

Straight builds I, II and III

Lorraine Hansberry, *A Raisin in the Sun*, Act II Scene 2, Walter: 'You wouldn't understand yet, son'

Jose Rivera, *Cloud Tectonics*, Anibal: 'The closest is … I look up at an airplane'

Paula Vogel, *How I Learned to Drive*, Li'l Bit: 'You're getting old, Big Papa'

Tennessee Williams, *Summer and Smoke*, Part I Scene 1, Alma: 'I'm afraid that you and I move'

I will die

Tariq Ali and Howard Brenton, *Moscow Gold*, Act I Scene 5, Yeltsin: 'Comrades, we want the people'
Eisa Davis, *Bulrusher*, Act II, Madame: 'I got to have clean lines in my life'
Stephen Adly Guirgis, *Jesus Hopped the A Train*, Act I Scene 7, Angel: 'Where's my mother's full police escort'
Kate Hennig, *The Last Wife*, Act II Scene 19, Kate: 'This is love' skipping Henry's interjections

Lists

James Baldwin, *Blues for Mister Charlie*, Act I, Lorenzo: 'I don't want to be better than they are'
Bernard Shaw, *Man and Superman*, Act I, Tanner: 'I know it Ramsden'
Octavio Solis, *Santos & Santos*, Act I, Tomas: 'A thin white scar'
Tom Stoppard, *Rosencrantz and Guildenstern Are Dead*, Act II, Player: 'We're actors'

More lists

Howard Barker, *The Castle*, Act II Scene 1, Krak: 'He wants another wall'
Anne Devlin, *Ourselves Alone*, Act II Scene 3, Josie: 'Bus stop posts'
Sarah Kane, *4.48 Psychosis*, from 'Inscrutable doctors' through 'medical notes'
Eugene O'Neill, *The Iceman Cometh*, Act II, Hickey: 'Hello, what's this'

Spirals and stairs

Stephen Adly Guirgis, *Jesus Hopped the 'A' Train*, Act I Scene 7, Lucius: 'Like ya knew that it would'
David Hare, *Skylight*, Act II Scene 1, Kyra: 'Female? That's an odd choice of word'
Lynn Nottage, *Ruined*, Act II Scene 4, Mama: 'You men kill me'

Sarah Ruhl, *The Clean House*, Act I Scene 7, Virginia: 'I have my house cleaned' through 'Get a very large broom' skipping Matilde's lines

Why are you still talking?

Just walk away

Luis Alfaro, *Oedipus El Rey*, Scene 9, Jocasta: 'Well, you know what'
Hannah Cowley, *The Belle's Stratagem*, Act II Scene 1, Mrs. Rachet: 'And you I take to be a slanderous cynic'
Stephen Adly Guirgis, *Jesus Hopped the 'A' Train*, Act II Scene 1, Valdez: '"Saved?!" I am a good man'
Tom Stoppard, *Arcadia*, Act I Scene 3, Lady Croom: 'Mr. Hodge, you must speak to your friend'
August Wilson, *The Piano Lesson*, Act I Scene 2, Boy Willie: 'Now I'm going to tell you the way I see it'

Here's the deal

Edward Albee, *The American Dream*, Young Man: 'I hope so'
Phillip Kan Gotanda, *Ballad of Yachiyo*, Takamura: 'What did she tell you' (see *American Theatre Book of Monologues for Men*)
Lynn Nottage, *Sweat*, Act II Scene 3, Cynthia: 'Did you know that my mother gave birth to me'
Harold Pinter, *The Homecoming*, Act II, Teddy: 'You wouldn't understand'
Sarah Ruhl, *The Clean House* Act I.3, Virginia: 'People who give up the *privilege* of cleaning'

Yes/No

Frances Ya-Chu Cowhig, *Snow in Midsummer*, Act II Scene 1, from Madam Wong: 'This is their standard model' through Madam Wong: 'Do not let grief destroy your good memories'
Michael Frayn, *Copenhagen*, Act I, Bohr and Heisenberg from Bohr: 'Of course. I knew his father' through Bohr: 'I could see the expression on yours' omitting Margrethe's lines
Paula Vogel, *Desdemona: A Play about a Handkerchief*, Scene 11, Desdemona and Emilia

Oscar Wilde, *The Importance of Being Earnest*, Act II, Algernon and Cecily from Algernon: 'You are my little cousin' through Cecily: 'I shouldn't know what to talk to him about'

So what

Rajiv Joseph, *Guards at the Taj*, Scene 2, Humayun: 'I am tired of blasphemy'
Yasmina Reza, *Art*, Marc: 'It's a complete mystery to me'
Jose Rivera, *Cloud Tectonics*, Anibal: 'I made love with Debbie just last night'
August Wilson, *Fences*, Act II Scene 1, Rose: 'I been standing with you'

Somebody listen

Quiara Alegría Hudes, *The Happiest Song Plays Last*, Scene 8, Yaz: 'Thank you Miriam Moreno' through 'had not been cleaned in days'
Arthur Miller, *The Crucible*, Act IV, Danforth: 'Now hear me'
Eugene O'Neill, *The Iceman Cometh*, Act II, Hope: 'Bejees, I'm no good at speeches'
Jose Rivera, *Marisol*, Angel: 'I kick started your heart' (see *American Theatre Book of Monologues for Women*)

Shadow dialogue

Luis Alfaro, *Oedipus El Rey*, Scene 9, Jocasta and Oedipus from Jocasta: 'I'm not. It's just that, challenging the gods' to end of scene
Samuel Beckett, *Waiting for Godot*, Vladimir and Estragon
Kate Hennig, *The Last Wife*, Act I Scene 6, from Henry: 'It's a little hard to argue with you right now' through Kate: 'Yes'
Harold Pinter, *The Homecoming*, Act II, Ruth and Teddy from Teddy: 'I think we'll go back' through Teddy: 'I'll go and pack'
Monologues:
Howard Barker, *Gertrude – The Cry*, Scene 7, Hamlet: 'She's mad'
Samuel Beckett, *Krapp's Last Tape*, Krapp: from 'Nothing to say, not a squeak'
Jim Cartwright, *Two*, Old Man: 'Howdo (*Sups beer.*)'

Further reading

Berry, Cicely, *The Actor and the Text* (revised edition), Virgin Books, London, 1993. 'Antithesis', pp. 90–95.

Cohen, Robert, *Acting in Shakespeare*, Mayfield Publishing Company, Mountview, CA, 1991. Lesson 7: The Straight Build and Lesson 8: The Nature and Structure of Builds, pp. 38–50.

Houseman, Barbara, *Tackling Text*, Nick Hern Books, London, 2008. 'Language Patterns', pp. 127–138.

Kaiser, Scott, *Mastering Shakespeare*, Allworth Press, New York, 2003. Scene 4: Spoken Subtext.

Linklater, Kristin, *Freeing Shakespeare's Voice*, Theatre Communications Group, Inc., New York, 1992. 'Antithesis', pp. 82–92; 'The Ladder', pp. 95–98.

Rodenburg, Patsy, *Speaking Shakespeare*, Methuen, London, 2002. 'Antithesis', pp. 121–125.

6
PUTTING IT ALL TOGETHER

Through the book up to this point, we've worked primarily with monologues. This has given you the chance to work at your own speed and take one thing at a time. The reality is, however, that the vast majority of drama is written in dialogue. In this chapter, therefore, we're going to look at how you might go about putting together the work on sound, image, sense, rhythm and argument in scene work. The scenes we've chosen to work with are Act I, Scene 7 from Shakespeare's *Macbeth* and an extract from Act III of Oscar Wilde's *An Ideal Husband*. They are both scenes for one male and one female, but you should feel free to use women in the men's roles and vice versa if it suits your circumstances.

It's worth noting that if we were actually rehearsing these scenes for performance, we wouldn't necessarily go through all the exercises that we list here in order. Every rehearsal process has its own rhythms, and elements such as staging are as important as text work when preparing a scene or play. We believe it would be worth it, however, to spend some time exploring the scenes in at least some of the ways we describe. You may want to work your way through all the exercises we suggest for each of the scenes, or you may want to rehearse the scenes and draw from the exercises as they seem relevant to your process. Alternately, you may just want to read through this chapter for inspiration and then pick a scene of your own to work on, drawing on exercises from here and elsewhere in the book to bring the text to life as fully and creatively as possible.

Macbeth

Monologue work

The scene from *Macbeth* begins with a soliloquy. Macbeth and his wife have been plotting to kill the king, Duncan, but Macbeth is beginning to have second thoughts:

MACBETH

    If it were done when 'tis done, then 'twere well
    It were done quickly: if the assassination
    Could trammel up* the consequence, and catch   *tie up in a net*
    With his surcease* success; that but this blow   *death*
    Might be the be-all and the end-all here,
    But here, upon this bank and shoal* of time,   *shallow*
    We'd jump* the life to come. But in these cases   *risk*
    We still have judgement here; that we but teach
    Bloody instructions, which, being taught, return
    To plague the inventor: this even-handed justice
    Commends the ingredients of our poisoned chalice*   *cup*
    To our own lips. He's here in double trust;
    First, as I am his kinsman and his subject,
    Strong both against the deed; then, as his host,
    Who should against his murderer shut the door,
    Not bear the knife myself. Besides, this Duncan
    Hath borne his faculties so meek*, hath been   *managed his powers so gently*
    So clear in his great office, that his virtues
    Will plead like angels, trumpet-tongued, against
    The deep damnation of his taking-off;
    And pity, like a naked new-born babe,
    Striding the blast, or heaven's cherubim*, horsed   *angelic spirits*
    Upon the sightless couriers of the air,
    Shall blow the horrid deed in every eye,
    That tears shall drown the wind. I have no spur
    To prick the sides of my intent, but only

PUTTING IT ALL TOGETHER

> Vaulting ambition, which o'erleaps itself
> And falls on the other.

I. Get in a circle and read the text out loud a couple of times altogether, to get the feeling of the words in your mouth. Clarify the meaning of any words or phrases that you're not sure of.

Now, read the text out loud round the circle and change the speaker every time you reach a punctuation mark. So, speaker one will read 'If it were done when 'tis done'; speaker two will read 'then 'twere well / It were done quickly'; speaker three 'if the assassination / Could trammel up the consequence'; and so on to the end.

Discuss what you've discovered so far about what Macbeth is saying and doing in this speech. What do you notice about the length of sentences?

Teaching tip: You might find it useful to run this stage of the exercise a couple of times so that students get a clear hold of the basic shape of the thoughts. We also suggest more work on sense below.

II. Explore the rhythm of the text as you've done with previous speeches. Read through the text out loud altogether again, this time leaning into the ti-**tum** of the iambic pentameter with your voice and tapping your foot or a pencil in rhythm with the strong stresses. Whenever you find an irregularity – an extra syllable, including feminine endings and epic caesuras; a place where the pronunciation and iambic rhythm are at odds or where a trochee makes more sense; or a place where the rhythm seems to disappear – stop and circle the word or words.

Try any (or all) of the exercises on *Turbulence* in Chapter 4 (see pp. 139–41).

After you've done the exercises, discuss them. How did punctuating the irregularities make you feel as you read the speech? Do the rhythmic interruptions bring any words into particularly strong focus? What does the rhythm tell us about Macbeth's frame of mind? Go back and read the speech out loud again. Can you still feel that turbulence running through the speech?

III. Now, explore the energy of the lines. Read the text around the circle again, but this time change speaker at the end of every verse line. So, speaker one will read 'If it were done when 'tis done, then 'twere well'; speaker two will say 'It were done quickly: if the assassination'; speaker three 'Could trammel up the consequence, and catch'; and so on to the end. When you get to the last word of your line, make a gesture that embodies the image, meaning or energy of that word. For example, with the word 'assassination' you might make a gesture of stabbing somebody in the back. The only rule is that you cannot breathe in the middle of your line.

Discuss for a moment what you got out of that reading. What differences were there between this reading and the reading at stage one? Were there any transitions between lines that struck you as particularly interesting? Were there any transitions between thoughts at the caesura that were interesting? Did you find any epic caesuras (where there is an extra unstressed syllable at the caesura)? How did they affect the momentum of those lines? How often does Macbeth have a full stop at the end of a verse line? What does that tell you about the momentum of his thoughts?

IV. We'd now like you to explore the sounds of this speech. So, speak it through again, really enjoying all the consonant sounds. You might like to try whispering it as well, to focus more energy in the consonants. What patterns of alliteration and consonance can you feel? What sounds and clusters of sounds does Macbeth use most often? Does the balance of sounds shift at any point? Speak the passage through again, relishing the patterns of sounds you've discovered. What does this tell you about what Macbeth is experiencing?

V. Now, speak it again, really enjoying all the vowel sounds. You might like to say just the vowel sounds on their own, but make sure you pronounce them as they sound in the words themselves. What patterns of assonance can you feel? What kinds of vowel sounds does Macbeth use most often? Does the balance of sounds shift at any point? Speak it through again, relishing the patterns of sounds you've discovered. What does this tell you about Macbeth's experience?

VI. With this awareness of the sounds of the words, speak the text again, relishing each word. As you do so, notice in particular any words

PUTTING IT ALL TOGETHER

which have only one syllable (monosyllabic words) and any words which have more than two syllables (polysyllabic words). Monosyllabic words are usually uncomplicated, and often express a fullness of emotion. Polysyllabic words are often more cerebral, and tend to express abstract ideas. What patterns of monosyllables and polysyllables have you found in this speech? What does this tell you about how Macbeth is thinking and feeling?

VII. Move on to exploring the images in the text in more detail. Try *Line Painting One* from Chapter 2 (see p. 56). Painting the images in the air as you speak will slow you down considerably, which is fine. While this exercise came under the heading of *Literal Images*, it will also help you to connect to some of the more complex evocative images in this passage.

Next, pick one image that you find particularly vivid or unsettling or important (e.g. 'we but teach bloody instructions, which, being taught, return to plague the inventor'). Underline that passage and give your paper to a partner. Have your partner read you one word at a time. Take a moment to consider what each word means to you and then repeat the word, as in *One Word at a Time* from Chapter 2 (see p. 71). Do this with as many images from the speech as time allows, and then try speaking the text again, letting each word be vivid and specific.

VIII. By now, you probably have a good understanding of the sense of this speech, but the following exercises from Chapter 3 are good for exploring this speech further: *Twitter* (see p. 87), *Punctuation Play* (see p. 98), *Carry the Bag* (see p. 96) and *Subordinate Coo-Coo Clock* (see p. 91). At this point, however, we'd like you to look at the 'turning' words that Macbeth uses. Remember that turning words are any words that might mean the speaker is qualifying what he's said or is about to say – that is, he's taking his thought in a different direction or taking it to another level. Macbeth's first word 'If' is a very powerful turning word, for example.

Go through the text and look for turning words, circling any that you find. Then, read the speech aloud walking around the room, and each time you come to one of the circled words, change direction.

Experiment with how sharp your change of direction is. Do some words seem to pull you all the way round? Do others just knock you off course a little bit?

Try always going to the left on qualifying words ('but', 'however' etc.) and always going to the right on words that take things to the next level ('and', 'besides' etc.).

Stand still to read the speech again. Are there any patterns to the turning words? Does the balance shift at any point? What does this tell you about how Macbeth is thinking and feeling?

IX. To complete this sequence of exercises, run through the *Crossing the Line* exercise from Chapter 5 (see p. 163). Designate one side of the room as the positive side (where Macbeth's conscience lies) and the other side of the room as the negative side (where his murderous ambition is). Speak the text through again and, as you do so, cross the line from one side of the room to the other as the speech suggests. Does this tell you anything new about Macbeth's state of mind, his character?

> *Teaching tip:* The above sequence of exercises represents a fairly typical process in working on a speech, but feel free to change the order of the exercises, drop any which might become redundant, replace them with others or add further exercises depending on the level of the group. The whole sequence runs approximately 60–75 minutes.

Scene work

Macbeth is still debating with himself when Lady Macbeth enters. In the following scene, she becomes a further 'spur to prick the sides of [his] intent' to help him to fulfil his ambition.

MACBETH
    I have no spur
    To prick the sides of my intent, but only
    Vaulting ambition, which o'erleaps itself
    And falls on the other.

Enter **LADY MACBETH**

    How now! what news?
LADY MACBETH
    He has almost supped: why have you left the chamber?

MACBETH
    Hath he asked for me?
LADY MACBETH
    Know you not he has?
MACBETH
    We will proceed no further in this business:
    He hath honoured me of late; and I have bought
    Golden opinions from all sorts of people,
    Which would be worn now in their newest
        gloss*,   *surface brightness*
    Not cast aside so soon.
LADY MACBETH
    Was the hope drunk
    Wherein you dressed yourself? hath it slept since?
    And wakes it now, to look so green and pale
    At what it did so freely? From this time
    Such I account thy love. Art thou afeard
    To be the same in thine own act and valour
    As thou art in desire? Wouldst thou have that
    Which thou esteem'st* the ornament of life,   *considers*
    And live a coward in thine own esteem,
    Letting 'I dare not' wait upon 'I would,'
    Like the poor cat i' the adage*?   *proverb*
MACBETH
    Prithee, peace:
    I dare do all that may become a man;
    Who dares do more is none.
LADY MACBETH
    What beast was't, then,
    That made you break* this enterprise to me?   *share, disclose*
    When you durst* do it, then you were a man;   *dared*
    And, to be more than what you were, you would
    Be so much more the man. Nor time nor place
    Did then adhere*, and yet you would make both: *agree*
    They have made themselves, and that their fitness now
    Does unmake you. I have given suck*, and know   *suckled a baby*
    How tender 'tis to love the babe that milks me:
    I would, while it was smiling in my face,

Have plucked my nipple from his boneless gums,
And dashed the brains out, had I so sworn as you
Have done to this.

MACBETH
If we should fail?

LADY MACBETH
We fail!
But screw your courage to the
   sticking-place*   *wind your courage up tight*
And we'll not fail. When Duncan is asleep –
Whereto the rather shall his day's hard journey
Soundly invite him – his two chamberlains   *bedroom officers*
Will I with wine and wassail* so convince   *spiced ale*
That memory, the warder* of the brain,   *guard*
Shall be a fume, and the receipt* of reason   *receptacle*
A limbeck* only: when in swinish sleep   *an alchemical still*
Their drenchèd natures lie as in a death,
What cannot you and I perform upon
The unguarded Duncan? what not put upon
His spongy* officers, who shall bear the guilt   *drunken*
Of our great quell*?   *slaughter*

MACBETH
Bring forth men-children only;
For thy undaunted mettle* should compose   *character*
Nothing but males. Will it not be received,
When we have marked with blood those sleepy two
Of his own chamber and used their very daggers,
That they have done't?

LADY MACBETH
Who dares receive it other,
As we shall make our griefs and clamour roar
Upon his death?

MACBETH
I am settled, and bend up*   *strain*
Each corporal agent* to this terrible feat.   *bodily organ*
Away, and mock the time with fairest show:
False face must hide what the false heart doth know.

PUTTING IT ALL TOGETHER

I. Get into pairs and decide who is which character. Read the text out loud a couple of times together, to get the feeling of the words in your mouth. Clarify the meaning of any words or phrases that you're not sure of, but don't worry if it doesn't all make sense at this point.

II. You probably noticed that there are a lot of questions in this scene. Questions are provocative. Even when the speaker doesn't expect a verbal answer (i.e. is asking a rhetorical question), nonetheless she is intending to provoke some kind of thought or feeling response.

To start to explore the provocative power of the questions in this scene, stand on opposite sides of the room from your partner. As you run through the scene, whenever your character asks a question, take a step towards him or her. What does this tell you about their relationship?

Repeat the exercise but now also add a gesture on every question. In addition, when you respond to a question, make a choice whether to stand still and be firm or to back down and take a step away from your partner.

Discuss any further discoveries you've made about the dynamic of the scene.

III. Now we'd like you to explore the rhythmic turbulence in this scene.

Read through the text again with your partner, leaning into the rhythm. Whenever you find an irregularity – an extra syllable, including feminine endings and caesuras; a place where the pronunciation and iambic rhythm are at odds or where a trochee makes more sense; or a place where the rhythm seems to disappear – stop and circle the word or words. Take it slowly; you're going to find some very unstable rhythms in this scene.

Read the scene again, whispering everything except the circled words; speak those on full voice.

Read the scene again on full voice. Whenever you say a circled word or phrase, move boldly away from your partner.

Try it again, moving boldly towards you partner on all the circled words.

Take a moment to discuss any discoveries you made about how the rhythmic disruptions might affect the exchange. What do they reveal about the characters' states of mind, their relationship?

IV. You have probably noticed that there are a lot of shared lines in this scene. In fact, almost every speech finishes on a half-line which the other speaker completes. As we said in Chapter 4, where shared lines like this happen, there's no room for pausing at all; on the contrary, the speeches need to flow together.

Stand on opposite sides of the room from your partner again. As you run through the scene this time, whenever your character picks up a half-line, take a step towards her/him. How does this compare with the exercise on questions? Have you discovered anything new about the Macbeths' relationship?

V. We'd now like you to explore the sounds in the scene. So, speak it through again, really enjoying all the consonant sounds that your character uses. What patterns of alliteration and consonance can you feel? What sounds and clusters of sounds does each character use most often? For example, does one character use more stop consonants than the other? Does the balance of consonants shift at any point? Speak it through again, relishing the patterns of sounds you've discovered. What does this tell you about the characters' intentions?

VI. Now, play the scene again, really enjoying all the vowel sounds. What patterns of assonance can you feel? What kinds of vowel sounds does each character use most often? For example, does one character use more long vowels than the other? Does the balance of sounds shift at any point? Speak it through again, relishing the patterns of sounds you've discovered. What does this tell you about what the characters are experiencing?

VII. With this awareness of the sounds of the words, speak the text again, relishing each word. As you do so, notice in particular any patterns of monosyllables and polysyllables that each character uses. What does this tell you about how they are thinking and feeling?

VIII. You've probably noticed that there are some very vivid and disturbing images in this passage and that the Macbeths use these images to try to convince each other of their points. Macbeth, read your speech beginning 'We will proceed no further in this business', and as you do so, imagine the things and people you are talking about are right in front of you, as if frozen in a panorama. Take Lady Macbeth and point out to her each individual element of the scene as you talk about it, as in the *Take a Walk* exercise from the *Image* chapter

PUTTING IT ALL TOGETHER

(see p. 62). Lady Macbeth, do the same with your speech beginning 'We fail', physically pointing out to Macbeth what's going to happen to the guards as they give in to drunkenness etc. as you imagine it happening before you.

IX. As in the exercise *Sensual Imagery* from Chapter 2 (see p. 67), have your partner read your lines to you rather slowly. As he or she reads, find a way to physicalize any descriptions or images, such as 'Was the hope drunk wherein you dressed yourself?' You might want to embody individual words, like 'hope', 'drunk' and 'dressed', or you might act out the larger image, or just use your hands and arms to describe the energy of the thought in some way. Don't worry about getting it right – just think about giving physical expression to the energy of the image.

X. Join together with another pair of Macbeths. One pair will work with the text as scripted, while the other pair will be the Shadow Macbeths. They will put the text aside and stand beside or behind their character, listening actively to the dialogue. Whenever Macbeth and Lady Macbeth are about to answer each other, their Shadows will speak whatever thoughts they imagine their character is having before they speak. These thoughts may be comments on the other character, feelings about themselves, distractions or just random observations. The only rule is that they should be in character and appropriate to the given circumstances. For example, before she speaks her first line, Lady Macbeth's shadow might say something like 'What news does he think I'm bringing?' or 'What on earth is he doing out here talking to himself? Is he going crazy?' And no, you don't have to speak in iambic pentameter!

Once you've played the scene like this once, swap over and do it again, with the people who spoke the text the first time being the shadows and voicing their character's thoughts, and vice versa.

Discuss what you've discovered about your characters and the nature of their internal dialogue.

XI. Stay in groups of four as you explore some of the competing themes in the scene. Begin with the theme of courage (and its antithesis, fear or cowardice). Again, one pair will work with the text as scripted, while the other pair will be the Shadow Macbeths. They will put the text aside and stand beside or behind their character, listening actively to the dialogue. Shadows, whenever your character says a word or phrase which is connected with this theme of courage/cowardice, you should echo it – not so loudly as to drown out your partner, but loud enough for the words to be heard by each of you. The Macbeths don't need to make space for the echo but should be aware of it, nonetheless. You might like to try this a couple of times to give each pair a turn. There are no points for echoing and there are no right answers – it's more important that you focus on listening and responding to words that make you think of courage or cowardice.

Now, look at the related theme of man (and its antithesis beast). Work in the same way as above. You may find you're echoing the same words in some places, but you may discover other connections. Again try it a couple of times to give each pair a turn.

Discuss what you've discovered about your character, the relationship of the Macbeths and what changes in this scene.

XII. There is a further theme of appearances running through the scene. It's there at the beginning in words like 'opinions' and 'gloss'. Run the Shadow exercise once more, echoing any words or phrases which strike you as being connected to this theme.

What does this add to the scene, to the Macbeth's relationship, to your understanding of the play?

Teaching tip: Again, the above sequence of exercises represents a fairly typical process in working on a scene, but feel free to change the order of the exercises, drop any which might become redundant, replace them with others, or add further exercises depending on the level of the group. For example, you might find it useful to do some *Punctuation Play* (see p. 98) or *One Word at a Time* work (see p. 71). The whole sequence runs approximately 75–90 minutes.

An Ideal Husband

This play by Oscar Wilde was first performed in 1895, when the playbill described it as 'A New and Original Play of Modern Life'. The plot centres on Sir Robert Chiltern, a junior government minister who is widely admired and respected for his intelligence and integrity. As a young man, however, he made a considerable amount of money by selling secret information to a stock market speculator (i.e. he was guilty of what we would today call insider trading). Now, twenty years later, his past has returned to haunt him in the person of Mrs Cheveley, an unscrupulous woman who has acquired an incriminating letter with which she means to blackmail Sir Robert.

Scene work

The scene we're going to explore is taken from the middle of the play. Mrs Cheveley has confronted Sir Robert and his wife, Gertrude, with the evidence of his fraud, and has given them an ultimatum: either to agree to her terms or to face disgrace. Gertrude, who had been at school with Mrs Cheveley, is appalled that her 'ideal husband' – a man she took to be honest and noble – is little more than a common swindler. Their marriage is plunged into turmoil. Meanwhile, Mrs Cheveley visits Lord Goring, a close friend of Sir Robert's to whom she was briefly engaged at one time. She now offers Lord Goring Sir Robert's letter if Lord Goring will promise to marry her.

MRS CHEVELEY
I am tired of living abroad. I want to come back to London. I want to have a charming house here. I want to have a salon. If one could only teach the English how to talk, and the Irish how to listen, society here would be quite civilized. Besides, I have arrived at the romantic stage. When I saw you last night at the Chilterns', I knew you were the only person I had ever cared for, if I ever have cared for anybody, Arthur. And so, on the morning of the day you marry me, I will give you Robert Chiltern's letter. That is my offer. I will give it to you now, if you promise to marry me.
LORD GORING
Now?
MRS CHEVELEY
[*Smiling*] Tomorrow.
LORD GORING
Are you really serious?

MRS CHEVELEY
Yes, quite serious.
LORD GORING
I should make you a very bad husband.
MRS CHEVELEY
I don't mind bad husbands. I have had two. They amused me immensely.
LORD GORING
You mean that you amused yourself immensely, don't you?
MRS CHEVELEY
What do you know about my married life?
LORD GORING
Nothing: but I can read it like a book.
MRS CHEVELEY
What book?
LORD GORING
[*Rising*] The Book of Numbers.
MRS CHEVELEY
Do you think it is quite charming of you to be so rude to a woman in your own house?
LORD GORING
In the case of very fascinating women, sex is a challenge, not a defence.
MRS CHEVELEY
I suppose that is meant for a compliment. My dear Arthur, women are never disarmed by compliments. Men always are. That is the difference between the two sexes.
LORD GORING
Women are never disarmed by anything, as far as I know them.
MRS CHEVELEY
[*After a pause*] Then you are going to allow your greatest friend, Robert Chiltern, to be ruined, rather than marry some one who really has considerable attractions left. I thought you would have risen to some great height of self-sacrifice, Arthur. I think you should. And the rest of your life you could spend in contemplating your own perfections.
LORD GORING
Oh! I do that as it is. And self-sacrifice is a thing that should be

put down by law. It is so demoralizing to the people for whom one sacrifices oneself. They always go to the bad.

MRS CHEVELEY

As if anything could demoralize Robert Chiltern! You seem to forget that I know his real character.

LORD GORING

What you know about him is not his real character. It was an act of folly done in his youth, dishonourable, I admit, shameful, I admit, unworthy of him, I admit, and therefore ... not his true character.

MRS CHEVELEY

How you men stand up for each other!

LORD GORING

How you women war against each other!

MRS CHEVELEY

[*Bitterly*] I only war against one woman, against Gertrude Chiltern. I hate her. I hate her now more than ever.

LORD GORING

Because you have brought a real tragedy into her life, I suppose.

MRS CHEVELEY

[*With a sneer*] Oh, there is only one real tragedy in a woman's life. The fact that her past is always her lover, and her future invariably her husband.

LORD GORING

Lady Chiltern knows nothing of the kind of life to which you are alluding.

MRS CHEVELEY

A woman whose size in gloves is seven and three-quarters never knows much about anything. You know Gertrude has always worn seven and three-quarters? That is one of the reasons why there was never any moral sympathy between us. ... Well, Arthur, I suppose this romantic interview may be regarded as at an end. You admit it was romantic, don't you? For the privilege of being your wife I was ready to surrender a great prize, the climax of my diplomatic career. You decline. Very well. If Sir Robert doesn't uphold my Argentine scheme, I expose him. *Voila tout.**

that is all

LORD GORING

You mustn't do that. It would be vile, horrible, infamous.

MRS CHEVELEY
[*Shrugging her shoulders*] Oh! don't use big words. They mean so little. It is a commercial transaction. That is all. There is no good mixing up sentimentality in it. I offered to sell Robert Chiltern a certain thing. If he won't pay me my price, he will have to pay the world a greater price. There is no more to be said. I must go. Good-bye. Won't you shake hands?

LORD GORING
With you? No. Your transaction with Robert Chiltern may pass as a loathsome commercial transaction of a loathsome commercial age; but you seem to have forgotten that you came here tonight to talk of love, you whose lips desecrated the word love, you to whom the thing is a book closely sealed, went this afternoon to the house of one of the most noble and gentle women in the world to degrade her husband in her eyes, to try and kill her love for him, to put poison in her heart, and bitterness in her life, to break her idol, and, it may be, spoil her soul. That I cannot forgive you. That was horrible. For that there can be no forgiveness.

I. Get into pairs and decide on your character. Read the text out loud a couple of times together, to get the feeling of the words in your mouth. Clarify the meaning of any words or phrases that you're not sure of, but don't worry if it doesn't all make sense at this point.

II. We'll begin by doing some work on *Verbal Dynamics* from the first chapter (see pp. 34–6). Take each of the words from your character's list below and say it slowly and quietly to yourself two or three times, making sure that you don't rush through any of the sounds. You might even exaggerate the movement of your lips and tongue a bit as you relish each sound in the word. Say the word again, and this time perform a physical action suggested by the word. For some words the appropriate movement may be quite obvious; for others you may need to stretch your imagination. Don't think too hard about it; just let your body respond. Repeat the word and the movement twice more, using more energy in your voice and body each time. When you have finished, pick up the scene and read it with your partner. You don't have to move when you reach the words you've been working on, but be aware of the energy you felt in them.

PUTTING IT ALL TOGETHER

What did you learn about these characters and the way they use language to affect each other?

MRS CHEVELEY	LORD GORING
charming	serious
amuse	bad
immensely	fascinating
rude	challenge
disarm	demoralizing
perfections	folly
hate	war
romantic	vile
surrender	horrible
expose	infamous

III. With this awareness of the sounds of the words, speak the text again, relishing each word. As you do so, notice in particular any patterns of monosyllables and polysyllables that each character uses. At one point Mrs Cheveley accuses Lord Goring of using big words. Is this a fair claim? If so, why do you think he does so? Is she guilty of using big words too? What effect do they have? What effect does using shorter words have?

IV. At the beginning of the scene, Mrs Cheveley makes a very bold offer, which the two characters then talk around. To make sure that the information that is passing between them is as clear as possible, do the exercise *Question Time* from Chapter 3 (p. 88) with the text, starting at the beginning and working through to Lord Goring's line ending 'not his true character'. Each of you can be the questioner for the other. Ask one to three questions of each sentence your partner speaks – he or she must answer by repeating the text. When you have finished, read through that part of the scene again, trying to be as specific as possible with each thing you say so there could be no room for questions.

V. To get a stronger sense of the images, both literal and evocative, in the second half of the scene, take your text to a place in the room where you can work on your own. Starting with the line 'How you men stand up for each other!' if you are Mrs Cheveley or 'How you women war against each other!' if you are Lord Goring, read your first sentence silently to yourself. Lower your paper and breathe in fully but deeply as you think about that first sentence and picture what it's talking about. Mrs Cheveley, for your first sentence, you will be picturing your Lord Goring and an imaginary Robert Chiltern. What are they wearing? What kind of posture do they have? What in your picture suggested that they are standing up for each other? Lord Goring, you will be picturing your Mrs Cheveley and an imaginary Gertrude Chiltern. What are they wearing? What in their stance, facial expressions or actions reveals their warring? Once you have an image firmly in your mind, breathe in again and whisper that sentence. Breathe in again, and speak the sentence out loud. Continue this way with all of your text through to the end of the scene. When the sentences are long, you can go phrase by phrase. NOTE: a glove size of seven and three-quarters is just a bit larger than average.

VI. When you have finished the above, return to your partner. You're now going to try to make him or her see what you have seen as you speak the text. You will do this by embodying each thing you talk about, as in the *All the Parts* exercise from the *Image* chapter (see p. 60). When you talk about a person, you will adopt the physical stance of that person. When you talk about an action, you will perform that action – so in Mrs Cheveley's line, 'For the privilege of being your wife, I was ready to surrender a great prize ... ', you would, perhaps, pose like a bride and then make a gesture of giving up something valuable. Remember that you are physicalizing the things you are talking about in order to make them as clear as possible to the person you are talking to. Move only as much, or as little, as is necessary to do this.

VII. To get a further sense of the rhythm and structure of the scene, play through it stomping your foot on the last word of every sentence (not before and not after).

Play through the scene again, tapping your thumb on every word that you naturally stress as well as stomping on the last word of every sentence.

Are there any rhythmic 'hot spots' in the scene where the rhythm seems to gain momentum? Any places where it is particularly regular?

Play the scene again noting how the rhythm might shape the interaction between the two characters or reveal something about their intentions.

VIII. You may have noticed that there are a lot of contrasts in this scene. Take some time to go through the text with your partner drawing a line between each pair of contrasts that you find. Some may be within one character's line, while others may be shared between the two characters. Some may be clearly opposites, like 'charming' and 'rude'; others may be more subtle comparisons, like what Mrs Cheveley was hoping to get ('the privilege of being your wife') and what she was willing to give ('to surrender a great prize'). Write a '1' above the first part of each contrast and a '2' above the second. Don't worry too much about getting it right or finding them all – whatever you find will be useful. Next, gather a large collection of small objects on a table between you and move them back and forth with each pair of contrasts, as described in *He Said/She Said* in Chapter 5 (p. 169). What did working in this way reveal to you about these characters' relationship? What did it reveal to you about the tactics they use to get what they want from each other?

IX. Each of these two characters is driven through the scene by the need to affect the other person. To get a feel for this, try using the *So What* exercise from the chapter on *Argument* (p. 185). Read the scene out loud together, and any time the other character has a line with more than one sentence in it, you can jump in at any full stop to ask 'So what?' If there's a very long sentence, you can even throw in a 'So what?' at a comma. You don't necessarily have to do so at every opportunity, though – listen for those places where you feel the other character really hasn't gone far enough to convince you. Did you find it frustrating to be challenged so often? Did that frustration lead to a build in energy through individual speeches? Did the energy build through the scene as a whole? Read the scene again without challenging each other verbally but keeping a sense of how you have to keep working harder and harder to convince your partner that you are in the right.

Further reading

Barton, John, *Playing Shakespeare*, Methuen, London, 1984.
Berry, Cicely, *The Actor and the Text* (revised edition), Virgin Books, London, 1993.
Berry, Cicely, *Text in Action*, Virgin Book, London, 2003.
Berry, Cicely, *From Word to Play*, Oberon Books, London, 2008.

Carey, David and Rebecca Clark Carey, *The Shakespeare Workbook and Video*, Bloomsbury Methuen Drama, London, 2015.
Houseman, Barbara, *Tackling Text*, Nick Hern Books, London, 2008.
Kaiser, Scott, *Mastering Shakespeare*, Allworth Press, New York, 2003.
Linklater, Kristin, *Freeing Shakespeare's Voice*, Theatre Communications Group, Inc., New York, 1992.
Rodenburg, Patsy, *The Need for Words*, Methuen, London, 1993.
Rodenburg, Patsy, *The Actor Speaks*, Methuen, London, 1997
Rodenburg, Patsy, *Speaking Shakespeare*, Methuen, London, 2002.

Appendix 1
VOCAL WARM-UP

Following is a warm-up you can do in about 10–15 minutes to prepare your body and voice for text work. Most of the exercises in it can be found in the *Vocal Arts Workbook and Video,* which has another sample warm-up in the first appendix that would also work well before a text session. As you continue working after your warm-up, remember to keep monitoring your vocal usage. Take the time to shake out, stretch, yawn and focus if at any time you feel yourself losing the sensations of being balanced, open in the throat, soft in the jaw and neck, and having the energy of your breath and voice anchored in your lower torso.

1. Start by stretching and yawning. Reach your arms and hands up to the ceiling, out towards the walls, behind you, in front of you, down to the ground.

When you've finished stretching, stand upright with your feet about hip-width apart and your toes turned slightly outwards, your weight evenly distributed, knees soft and neck long.

Swing your right arm in a circle forward eight times and backwards eight times; repeat with the left arm, letting the momentum of the swing move through your body so that your knees bounce a bit with each one.

Widen your stance, and bend your knees in a deep *plié* (if you have knee problems, skip this step). While still in the deep *plié*, think of your head getting heavy and roll down your spine until your torso is hanging forward, hands brushing the floor. Leaving your hands on the floor as much as you can, straighten your knees and lift your bottom up in the air. Make a strong 'whoosh' noise with your out-breath as you do. As you breathe in, bend your knees again. Then straighten the knees and 'whoosh' again. Repeat this cycle two or three times, ending with the knees bent.

With knees bent and hands on the floor, make a figure of eight with your hips, so that you circle them over one foot and then over the other. Repeat three or four times.

Still rolled over, walk your feet in until they are about hip-width apart. Now imagine your tailbone getting heavy and the heaviness of the tailbone initiating a nice, slow roll up your spine. Feel your shoulder blades slide into place as you roll through your upper back. End with your head up, keeping the neck long (i.e. don't lift the chin).

2. Take a moment to feel your feet on the floor, your weight evenly balanced between them. Focus on your legs for a moment, imagining the muscles in them becoming softer and less 'held' as you breathe in and out a couple of times. Focus on your pelvis, imagining the muscles there becoming softer and less held as you again breathe in and out a couple of times. Focus on your lower abdomen, lower back, chest, upper back, shoulders, neck and jaw in turn – taking one or two breath cycles with each one to imagine the muscles becoming softer and less held.

Focus on your breath and imagine it freely dropping to your pelvis on the inhalation and floating up from the pelvis on the exhalation. Spend four or five breath cycles with this image.

Let your head gently roll forward. Without lifting or putting unnecessary tension in the shoulders, reach up and give your neck a little massage.

As you are massaging your neck, imagine a column of 'vvvvv' vibrations starting at your pelvis and running up through your torso to the back of your neck. Of course, you will really be creating the 'vvvvv' sound by softly tucking your bottom lip under your top teeth, but don't think of there being any effort in the mouth or tongue or jaw – keep them as soft as you can. Instead, think of the flow of energy coming up from the muscles at the base of your torso. Let the breath drop in whenever you need it.

After three or four cycles of 'vvvvv', stop massaging your neck, but leave the fingers of one hand resting there, your head still dropped forward. Turn your column of vibrations into a 'mmmm', imagining those vibrations coming up from your pelvis and hitting the back of your neck, just beneath your fingers. Stay with this for three or four breath cycles. Try a different pitch with each one.

Now, imagine that you have a mouth at the back of your neck. On your next out-breath, slide your fingers down your neck, and imagine that mouth opening. When it does, the 'mmmm' will become a 'mmaahhh'.

Repeat for three or four breath cycles, on a different pitch each time, and then lift your head up in the middle of the final 'mmaahhh'.

Release a nice, yawning sigh.

3. Give the muscles along the side of your jaw (the ones that pop out when you clench your teeth) a massage for 20–30 seconds. When you've finished, let your fingers slide down the sides of your face and the space between your back teeth gradually increase. You'll end up with your mouth open and your jaw muscles very soft.

Place one hand on the back of your neck to make sure you don't tense up there.

Without moving the jaw, flap your tongue in and out of your mouth (as if you were rapidly sticking your tongue out at someone and then letting it fall back in) for 7 seconds.

Next, stick your tongue out and move it rapidly from side to side for 7 seconds.

Finally, curl the tip of your tongue under your front bottom teeth and roll the rest of your tongue out and over – so the tip stays behind the teeth and the body of the tongue is pushed out. Alternate pushing the tongue out and letting it fall back into your mouth for 7 seconds, keeping the tip behind the bottom teeth.

Repeat this sequence two more times; your tongue will start to ache, which is the point.

4. Leaving your mouth gently open, make a sirening sound on a 'ng'. Siren up and down your pitch range. Open the siren onto a 'ngah' without moving your jaw – practice doing it just by moving the back of your tongue and your soft palate on many different pitches.

Leaving your mouth gently open, let your tongue slide out onto your bottom lip. Don't think of pushing it out – let it just kind of ooze forward and then rest lazily.

Now, without moving your tongue or jaw, try to say the nursery rhyme 'Humpty Dumpty'. It will, of course, be impossible to make most of the speech sounds without moving your tongue or jaw, so you will end up kind of chanting the tune, which is fine.

Notice how the energy of your voice focuses in the front part of your mouth and how little effort there is in the throat. Say the nursery rhyme again, gradually letting your tongue slide back into your mouth and start forming the sounds as you do. Try to keep the feeling of your voice energy being forward in your mouth.

5. Give your face a little massage.

Make some very silly faces, paying particular attention to scrunching and stretching the lips.

Rest your lips gently together (without closing the space between your back teeth), and then blow through them so that they make a fluttering sound. Repeat two or three times, adding some voice and gliding up and down your pitch range.

Let both your jaw and lips hang softly open. Put one hand at the back of your neck so that you don't tighten up there. Without moving your jaw, make a 'puh' sound – you'll have to use the muscles in your lips. Make a sequence of 'puh' sounds in a nice jazzy rhythm. Add some voice and make a sequence of 'buh' sounds.

Now using the tip of the tongue, not the jaw, make a series of 'tuh' sounds and then a series of 'duh' sounds.

Finally, using the back of the tongue, not the jaw, make a series of 'kuh' sounds followed by a series of 'guh' sounds.

Keeping the jaw gently open, say 'puh, tuh, kuh'. Speed it up. Now, do the same with 'buh, duh, guh'. Then, say 'kuh, tuh, puh'. Speed it up. And 'guh, duh, buh'. Go back and forth between the sequences using a firm, active muscularity in the lips and the tongue.

Appendix 2
RUDOLF LABAN

A pioneer in modern movement studies, Rudolf Laban (1879–1958) developed a way of describing physical movement known as **Laban Movement Analysis** which enables anybody to explore their expressive movement potential.

Laban's system provides a very detailed analysis of the components of human expressive movement. In this brief overview, however, we are going to focus on the key concepts of **Space, Time, Weight** and **Flow**. These are the four elements of motion which are present in any movement (even stillness).

Each element exists as a continuum of potential movement. The element of Space is concerned with how we relate to and affect the space around us. At one end of its continuum is **direct**, linear movement; at the other end is **indirect**, flexible movement. The element of Time is concerned with the duration of a movement, how long it lasts in relation to other events. Its continuum is between quick, **sudden** movements at one end and slow or **sustained** movements at the other. The element of Weight is concerned with the force of a movement, which exists on a continuum between **light** and **strong**. The element of Flow is concerned with the continuity of a movement: at one end of the spectrum, a movement may be performed in a confident and released way which is hard to stop, in which case it is said to be **free**; at the other end, it may be performed in a cautious and inhibited way which is easy to stop, in which case it is said to be **bound**.

In Laban's system, the first three elements of Space, Time and Weight combine to create eight **Basic Effort Actions** (also known as **Action Drives**), each of which is usually performed with either bound or free flow. **Effort** is the term Laban applied to the type of energy we bring to movement, and is related to our internal feelings and impulses which produce that energy (hence the alternative term, **Drive**).

The eight Effort Actions are:

1 **Pressing** – which is the combination of Space, Time and Weight that is *direct, sustained* and *strong*. It is performed with *bound* Flow.
2 **Flicking** – which is the opposite combination of Space, Time and Weight: *indirect, sudden* and *light*. It is performed with *free* Flow.
3 **Wringing** – which is *indirect, sustained* and *strong*. The Flow is usually *bound*.
4 **Dabbing** – which is *direct, sudden* and *light*. The Flow is usually *free*.
5 **Slashing** – which is *indirect, sudden* and *strong*. The Flow is *free*.
6 **Gliding** – which is *direct, sustained* and *light*. The Flow is usually *bound*.
7 **Punching** – which is *direct, sudden* and *strong*. The action can be either *free* or *bound* in Flow.
8 **Floating** – which is *indirect, sustained* and *light*. The action can be either *free* or *bound* in Flow.

Laban identified these Effort Actions as the basis on which to build a more detailed description of movement. However, the same principles can be applied to voice and text work, as we have suggested in Chapter 1. For a more thorough exploration of Laban's work, we refer you to Barbara Adrian's *Actor Training the Laban Way* (2008) and Jean Newlove's *Laban for Actors and Dancers* (1993), both of which offer further ways of adapting Laban's ideas to voice and text, and to a companion work in the Theatre Arts Workbooks series, *The Laban Workbook for Actors* by Katya Bloom, Barbara Adrian, Tom Casciero, Jennifer Mizenko and Claire Porter (2017).

Appendix 3
PUNCTUATION AND PARTS OF SPEECH

Punctuation

As we pointed out in Chapter 3, punctuation exists to help capture in writing what we naturally do with our voices when we speak. So, when it comes to reading a piece of written text out loud, punctuation marks can be your friend because they point up things that are important for speaking. What follows is a complete list of the punctuation marks we refer to in this book.

Marks which usually indicate the end of a complete thought:

- . The full stop. In American English, this is called a period. It comes at the end of a sentence and indicates that a thought has concluded.
- ! The exclamation mark or exclamation point. It usually comes at the end of a sentence, and indicates that the thought which precedes it should be spoken with some emotional strength. Sometimes, though, an author will throw an exclamation point into the middle of a thought to emphasize a particular word or idea.
- ? The question mark. This also usually comes at the end of sentences, and indicates that the thought which precedes it should be spoken as a question. Sometimes, however, an author will use question marks like commas in a series of short questions. It is also worth noting that, when reading a text out loud, a question mark doesn't always require you to raise the pitch of your voice at the end of

the thought. If a question begins with any of the following words – *why, what, when, where, how* (often referred to as WH-question words) – the pitch of the voice doesn't necessarily go up at the end of the thought. In fact, it is much more likely to drop slightly. This is because the WH-question words are enough to indicate that a question is being asked, without the addition of the rising inflection.

Marks which usually indicate a change of direction within a complete thought:

, The comma. Commas come in the middle of sentences. They break up a large thought into smaller chunks and help to show how those pieces relate to each other. They can also indicate changes of direction within a thought.

; The semicolon. Semicolons join together two thoughts that could stand on their own as complete sentences but are coming together to build a bigger thought.

: The colon. Colons can come before lists or examples – as if to say, 'This is what I'm talking about'. They are sometimes also used like semicolons to join thoughts that could stand on their own, especially when the second thought seems to flow consequentially from the first.

() Parentheses. Parentheses are used to mark out a separate but related thought within a sentence or paragraph, often providing a comment or an afterthought.

- The dash. Dashes will often be used in the same way as parentheses, but a single dash at the end of a sentence tends to indicate an interrupted or incomplete thought.

… The ellipsis. The three dots of an ellipsis are the conventional way of indicating that a writer or speaker has omitted something. In dramatic writing it is often used to indicate that a character is hesitating or is unable to complete their thought for some reason.

It's worth noting here that the punctuation in different editions of Shakespeare plays can vary quite a bit. Many of Shakespeare's plays were not published during his lifetime, and in most instances we can't be sure that what was published was exactly what Shakespeare had written, especially when it comes to the punctuation. Modern editors usually 'clean up' the punctuation a bit, and generally they do a good job of putting it in where it makes sense, so that it indicates where the pauses or changes in pitch would come if someone were speaking the text. Do note, however, that sometimes editors insert exclamation points in places where you, as an actor, may not feel it appropriate to exclaim, so you should never think of the punctuation as stage directions. Some people find it very useful to go to a facsimile edition of the First Folio, which was the first published collection of Shakespeare's plays, to see what the punctuation is there. The punctuation in any good edition will help you to understand the language, but it can be worth it to look at a couple of different versions just to see what the possibilities are.

For a humorous but detailed look at punctuation, we recommend *Eats, Shoots & Leaves* by Lynne Truss (see Bibliography).

Parts of speech

The other group of terms we want to review here are the different parts of speech (or word classes). Ever since scholars first started to describe language, they have recognized that different types of words perform different functions, and they have traditionally identified several parts of speech, including:

- **Nouns** and **pronouns**. A **noun** is a word which refers to a being, place or thing, for example, 'horse', 'Tewkesbury' or 'grief'. A **pronoun** is a word that stands in for a noun, for example, 'him' instead of 'King Richard' or 'it' instead of 'grief'. You usually need to know the context to understand precisely what a pronoun is referring to.
- A **verb** is an action word (i.e. something you do), or a being word, like 'am', 'is' and 'are'. Some verbs come in a couple of parts and so make a verb phrase, like 'She is thinking': 'is' and 'thinking' together make up the verb phrase in the sentence.
- **Adjectives** and **adverbs**. An **adjective** is a word which describes or modifies a noun, such as 'beautiful', 'crinkly' or 'wide'. An **adverb** is a word which describes or modifies the action of a verb, such as 'quickly', 'reluctantly' or 'elegantly'.

- **Connective** words – **prepositions** and **conjunctions**.
  A **preposition** is a word which indicates location or direction, for example, 'under', 'towards' or 'inside'. **Conjunctions** are words which create links between thoughts, such as 'and', 'although' and 'if'.

Knowing what type of word a word is and how it functions helps you understand its value in a sentence.

Appendix 4
CURRICULUM CHOICES

As we stated in the *Introduction*, we would suggest exploring the chapters in sequence, as generally the early chapters cover fundamental principles and the later chapters more complex issues. However, if we were constructing a year's programme in text work for drama students, this would be one possible curriculum:

Weeks 1–5 Exploring *Sound* and *Image* work through a focus on twentieth- and twenty-first-century poetry.
Weeks 6–10 Exploring *Image* and *Sense* work through a focus on classical folk tales.
Weeks 11–15 Exploring *Sense* and *Rhythm* work through a focus on Shakespearean sonnets and/or nineteenth-century poetry.
Weeks 16–20 Exploring *Sound, Image, Sense, Rhythm* and *Argument* work through a focus on Shakespearean and contemporary monologues.
Weeks 21–25 Exploring *Sound, Image, Sense, Rhythm* and *Argument* work through a focus on nineteenth- and twentieth-century political speeches and monologues by Bernard Shaw, with an emphasis on *Argument*.
Weeks 26–30 Exploring *Putting It All Together* through a focus on Shakespearean and contemporary duologues.

Alternatively, if you choose to focus on one particular type of text at a time, we would suggest working as follows:

Poetry

Poetry makes powerful use of sound and imagery. It usually involves an active use of rhythm, either through a regular metre or by working with a particular number of stresses or syllables per line of verse. And there may be a density of thought and feeling that expresses itself through complex sense and argument. We find that it helps comprehension to begin with a focus on *Sound* and *Image* exercises before undertaking some initial work on thoughts from the *Sense* chapter. It is then valuable to do some physical work on *Rhythm* before attempting a more detailed exploration of *Sense* and *Argument*, if necessary.

Storytelling

A traditional storyteller will make instinctive and creative use of all the elements of spoken language, weaving an artistic web of sound, image and rhythm in service of the communication of the story: its meaning, sense and argument. Folk tales and children's stories generally use vivid images and strong characters, and so it can be useful to begin with a focus on exercises from the *Image* chapter before exploring *Sound* and *Rhythm* work. More complex, adult stories and novels will also benefit from detailed exploration of *Sense* and *Argument*.

Political speeches

We find work on political speeches requires and encourages a strong engagement with sense and argument, but they also involve a sensitivity to sound, image and rhythm in order to achieve a compelling connection with an audience. It can be useful, therefore, to begin with work on *Sense* and *Argument* to develop a secure feeling for what the speech is trying to achieve, before progressing to an exploration of *Image* which can bring out the underlying emotional appeal, and finishing with some work on *Sound* and *Rhythm* to highlight the use of elements such as alliteration and repetition.

Shakespearean monologues and scenes

It is a commonplace to say that Shakespeare is one of the greatest playwrights of any language, but his particular ear for English in service of character, storytelling and political argument shouldn't be taken for granted. Like many voice and text teachers, we find Shakespeare offers some of the richest opportunities to explore language in all its creativity and complexity. However, because his language can now seem alien, old-fashioned or overly poetical, approaching a Shakespearean monologue or scene can be daunting. We find it useful to begin with work on *Sound* and *Image* in order to open up an oral and visual relationship with the language before engaging more specifically in *Sense* work. Exploring how Shakespeare's use of verse *Rhythm* supports, reveals or enhances characters' intentions can then follow. Finally, some detailed work on *Argument* is essential: Shakespeare's characters speak in order to effect change, either in other people or in themselves, and make full use of argument to do this. For both monologues and scenes, work on *Putting It All Together* will pay real dividends.

Other sixteenth- and seventeenth-century monologues and scenes

Like Shakespeare, many dramatists of the sixteenth and seventeenth centuries were also poets, and had a similar ear for the English language. Christopher Marlowe, Ben Jonson, and other Elizabethan and Jacobean writers, as well as the playwrights of the Restoration period, all require a heightened awareness of language. Taking a similar approach to that which we recommend for Shakespearean monologues and scenes will be helpful, but it is worth recognizing that punctuation in these texts may be closer to the original than it is in modern editions of Shakespeare's plays. So it is worth exploring in some detail, for example, a particular author's use of commas, dashes and colons, in order to develop a deeper relationship to the meaning and speaking of the text. Restoration playwrights also displayed a fine sense of wit, and so *Argument* work is particularly necessary. Again, for both monologues and scenes, work on *Putting It All Together* will pay real dividends.

Shaw, Wilde and their contemporaries

Bernard Shaw and Oscar Wilde were also much preoccupied with wit, as were many of their English-language contemporaries, and they shared a delight in the rhythms and sounds of English, coupled with well-chosen imagery. The progression of work described under *Political Speeches* applies well to these dramatists.

Modern verse drama

A number of modern poets have written verse dramas that have earned comparison with classical verse plays, including W. B. Yeats's *Cathleen Ni Houlihan* (1902), T. S. Eliot's *Murder in the Cathedral* (1935), Ted Hughes's 1969 version of Seneca's *Oedipus*, Derek Walcott's 1993 dramatized version of the *Odyssey* and Seamus Heaney's 2004 version of Sophocles's *Antigone*, entitled *The Burial at Thebes*. These writers make use of a variety of verse forms and styles which range from the highly poetic to the visceral or demotic. The progression of work described under *Poetry* and *Shakespeare* applies well to these dramatists.

Modern and contemporary drama

The range of modern and contemporary dramatists is immense – from Samuel Beckett to Lynn Nottage and from Tennessee Williams to Kwame Kwei-Armah – and each has his or her distinctive way of using language. The work of all these playwrights requires you to give full attention to the voices of their characters as expressed in the verbal rhythms, images, sound patterns and arguments they use. The implied order of work on *Rhythm, Image, Sound* and *Argument* does not rule out the need to look at *Sense* where necessary and at *Putting It All Together* in the end. Nor should you expect always to work in the same way with different dramatists: the pauses and silences which are characteristic of Beckett and Pinter, for example, are unlikely to play such an important role in a David Edgar play, and Howard Barker's individual style would be completely alien to August Wilson. Developing your sensitivity to language in general will help you appreciate the particular way each writer is making use of it. All our exercises are designed to help you achieve this.

Appendix 5
PROFESSIONAL HISTORIES

David Carey

David Carey trained during the 1970s as a speech and drama teacher at the Royal Scottish Academy of Music and Drama in Glasgow, where his voice teachers were John Colson, Jacqui Crago and Jim House. John was the husband of Greta Colson, Co-Director of the New College of Speech and Drama, London. Greta Colson was a graduate of the Central School of Speech and Drama and author or co-author of a number of books on voice, speech and phonetics. The New College of Speech and Drama, which was later absorbed by Middlesex Polytechnic (later to become Middlesex University), was one of a number of drama schools in the 1960s which were training voice teachers in the UK. Jacqui Crago and Jim House were both graduates of New College. Jacqui's classes in phonetics and poetry were a particular influence on David's decision to become a voice teacher.

However, David's initial introduction to voice and speech work was literally at his mother's knee. Elna Carey (née Graham) trained during the 1930s as a Speech teacher at the Central School of Speech and Drama under Elsie Fogerty. Gwynneth Thurburn and J. Clifford Turner were also on the Central faculty at this time. She married actor Brian Carey, who came from a theatrical family in Dublin, and so David was brought up with a deep awareness of the importance of voice, speech and articulate communication.

Following his training in Glasgow, David completed a BA degree in English Language and Linguistics at Edinburgh University before taking up a position as Lecturer in Voice and Speech at Queen Margaret College, Edinburgh, where he taught on the undergraduate drama programme for five years. His work at this time was strongly influenced by both Cicely Berry and Kristin Linklater through their seminal books, *Voice and the Actor* (first published in 1973) and *Freeing the Natural Voice* (first published in 1976). Berry had trained under and worked with Gwynneth Thurburn at the Central School of Speech and Drama (CSSD), while Linklater had trained under and worked with Iris Warren at the London Academy of Music and Dramatic Art (LAMDA). David found that the rigorous and muscular work of Berry was complemented by the more kinaesthetic and image-based approach of Linklater, and that a combination of the two was well suited to the needs of developing students.

David left Edinburgh in 1982 to join the Royal Shakespeare Company as Assistant Voice Director, working under Cicely Berry and alongside Patsy Rodenburg. The four years that David spent at the RSC were a rich period in the company's history. Judi Dench, Fiona Shaw, Juliet Stevenson and Harriet Walter, Kenneth Branagh, Brian Cox, Derek Jacobi, Alan Rickman and Antony Sher were all members of the acting company. In addition to Joint Artistic Directors, Terry Hands and Trevor Nunn, other directors included Bill Alexander, John Barton, Ron Daniels, Howard Davies, Barry Kyle and Adrian Noble. Notable plays and productions of this period with which David was associated were *Richard III* with Antony Sher, *Henry V* with Kenneth Branagh, and the world premieres of Christopher Hampton's *Les Liaisons Dangereuses* and Howard Barker's *The Castle.* David's understanding of voice, text and acting was deeply informed by the opportunity to observe these actors and directors, but most especially by the experience of watching Cicely Berry's unique collaboration with them. Her passion for language and its ability to express human experience, particularly in the work of Shakespeare, left an indelible impression on David and continues to influence his work to this day.

David left the RSC to take up the post of Senior Lecturer (later Principal Lecturer) in Voice Studies at the Central School of Speech and Drama, where he was responsible for developing and sustaining the School's postgraduate programme in Voice Studies, a course of professional development for graduates who wished to follow a career in voice teaching. David was responsible for all aspects of teaching and learning, from course design and admissions to assessment, timetabling and pastoral care. He taught modules in vocal anatomy, vocal pedagogy, voice and text, and phonetics, as well as supervising dissertations and independent practical projects.

Under his leadership, the course became recognized as a national and international benchmark in the field. British graduates were regularly employed by all of the leading Higher Education drama training institutions in England and Wales. As UK universities diversified their provision with respect to practice-based drama courses, graduates also found employment in this part of the sector. The course also served a worldwide demand for well-qualified teachers of voice and speech, attracting a regular number of international applicants from North America, Europe, Asia and Australia. Graduates went on to work at Yale University, Southern Methodist University, and the University of Utah, among others in the United States, and at drama training institutions in Australia, Canada, Japan, Singapore, South Africa, Holland and Denmark.

In his seventeen-year tenure, David was responsible for training over 200 voice teachers, many of whom are now at the top of their profession, including the Heads of Voice at the Royal Shakespeare Company, the Royal National Theatre in London, the Stratford Ontario Festival Theatre and the Oregon Shakespeare Festival.

Through the course at CSSD, David introduced a generation of voice teachers to the work of a wide range of practitioners, including Frankie Armstrong, Kevin Crawford, Meribeth Bunch Dayme, Catherine Fitzmaurice, Nadine George, Barbara Houseman, Gillyanne Kayes, Christina Shewell, Andrew Wade and Joanna Weir-Ouston.

In 2000, recognizing the need for a major resource facility that was designed to serve the professional development of teachers of voice and speech and to contribute to the wider international community in HE actor training, David established the International Centre for Voice at CSSD. During his term as Director of the Centre, he organized a number of events intended to support and influence colleagues.

David left Central in 2003, returning to the vocal training of actors as a senior voice tutor at the Royal Academy of Dramatic Art. In 2004 he revisited the RSC to coach their touring productions of *Julius Caesar* and *Two Gentlemen of Verona*. In 2005 he spent two months with the Oregon Shakespeare Festival as Voice and Text Director for productions of *The Philanderer* by Bernard Shaw and *By the Waters of Babylon* by Robert Schenkkan. He returned to Oregon in 2008 as Voice and Text

Director for productions of *Coriolanus* by William Shakespeare and *The Further Adventures of Hedda Gabler* by Jeff Whitty; and again in 2010 for a production of *Hamlet* by William Shakespeare. He also maintains a relationship with the Stratford Ontario Festival in Canada, where he was vocal coach for the 2007 production of Oscar Wilde's *An Ideal Husband*. He was an Associate Editor for the *Voice and Speech Review,* the journal of the Voice and Speech Trainers Association, from 2002 to 2009.

David left his position at RADA at the end of 2010 to become a Resident Voice and Text Director with the Oregon Shakespeare Festival, where he is currently responsible for voice, text and dialect for four to five productions each season. He also maintained his connection with the Royal Shakespeare Company for several years through work on the following productions: *Written on the Heart* by David Edgar (2011), *The Orphan of Zhao* by Ji Junxiang and adapted by James Fenton (2012), *King Lear* by William Shakespeare and adapted by Tim Crouch (2012), and *Antony and Cleopatra* by William Shakespeare and adapted by Tarell Alvin McCraney (2013).

David's pedagogy is an eclectic one which draws on the work of the leading voice teachers of today, such as Cicely Berry, Kristin Linklater and Patsy Rodenburg. His academic interest in linguistics – he has a master's degree in Contemporary English Language and Linguistics from Reading University – also informs his practice through a deep understanding of language, vocal anatomy, phonetics and dialects. He also draws actively on his experience of Alexander Technique and T'ai Chi. He places emphasis on exploring and developing the natural potential of the voice, with equal attention paid to physiological function and imaginative intention, so that fundamental work on breathing, alignment, resonance and articulation is integrated with expressive work on text and communication.

David was awarded a prestigious National Teaching Fellowship in 2007 by the UK's Higher Education Academy in recognition of his contribution to vocal pedagogy.

Rebecca Clark Carey

Rebecca Clark Carey received her BA in History and Literature from Harvard University. She focused particularly on the history of drama in Germany and wrote her undergraduate thesis on Weimar theatre. She went on to train as an actress in the University of California at Irvine's Master of Fine Arts programme, where her principal voice and speech teacher was Dudley Knight, on whose teaching she continues to draw heavily in her own work. Dudley himself studied voice with Kristin Linklater and Catherine Fitzmaurice, both of whom did their initial training in London – Kristin at the London Academy of Music and Dramatic Art with Iris Warren and Catherine at the Central School of Speech and Drama with Cicely Berry and Gwynneth Thurburn.

Rebecca's principal acting teacher at Irvine was Robert Cohen, author of *Acting Power, Acting One* and *Acting in Shakespeare*, among other titles. Robert's approach to Stanislavki-based actor training continues to influence Rebecca's approach to text work, and his emphasis on builds and keeping impulses fresh informed much of her contribution to Chapter 5: Argument.

While at Irvine, working with Joan Melton, Rebecca first read Kristin Linklater's *Freeing Shakespeare Voice*. Kristin's thoughts on the power of the individual word to open up a world of associations to both the speaker and the listener profoundly influenced Rebecca's understanding not only of language but also of what it is to act truthfully. Her master's thesis at Irvine focused on the encounter between speaker, word and listener. When teaching, she often tells her students that the essence of their job is to mean what they say, a creed which grew out of her thinking on this subject.

After leaving UC Irvine, Rebecca worked as a professional actress, primarily on the west coast of the United States. She gained skills in classical text particularly through her work with the California Shakespeare Festival, Shakespeare Santa Cruz and the Oregon Shakespeare Festival. While in Los Angeles, she also had the good fortune to study Shakespeare with Dakin Matthews at the Antaeus Company of classical actors. She was especially inspired by Dakin's thoughts on metre and line endings, and many of her exercises in Chapter 4: Rhythm grew out of the insights she gained at this time.

While still working as an actor, Rebecca was first invited to teach voice and text at Palomar College in San Diego County. She coached every Shakespeare play produced at the college for a number of years. When she decided to make the transition to teaching and coaching full time, she went to London to study at the Central School of Speech and Drama. While working on her MA in Voice Studies there, she had the opportunity to receive instruction from many prominent voice practitioners, including Cicely Berry, Andrew Wade, Joanna Weir-Ouston, Gillyanne Kayes and Meribeth Bunch Dayme. An edited version of her dissertation on speaking Shakespeare's late plays was published in *Voice and Speech Review: Film, Broadcast and Electronic Media Coaching* (2003). In preparing this, she drew heavily on the works of Cicely Berry and Patsy Rodenburg, and she still uses what she learned from them about embodied exploration of text.

Shortly after completing the Central course with distinction, Rebecca joined the Oregon Shakespeare Festival's (OSF) education department, headed by Joan Langley. Among her responsibilities was developing workshops with another actor-teacher, Kirsten Giroux, to be delivered by members of the company to the hundreds of students who visit the festival every year. The experience she gained in finding ways to actively engage young people with Shakespeare has been invaluable to her later teaching, and the work on laying out a programme of exercises so that other teachers could follow it was also excellent preparation for writing this book.

In her first year at OSF, Rebecca was invited to assist voice and text directors Scott Kaiser and Ursula Meyer on productions of *Handler* by Pulitzer Prize winner Robert Schenkkan, and *A Winter's Tale*. Their expertise and generosity continue to inform and inspire her coaching work. The following year she served as voice and text director on *Hedda Gabler* and *Wild Oats*. She returned regularly as a guest voice and text director and is currently the head of voice at OSF.

She has also worked in England as a voice teacher at the Central School of Speech and Drama, The Italia Conti Academy of Theatre Arts, The Oxford School of Drama and for five years as a senior voice tutor at the Royal Academy of Dramatic Art. She frequently coaches British actors on American accents and was the accent coach for the Royal and Derngate's productions of Tennessee William's *Spring Storm* and Eugene O'Neill's *Beyond the Horizon* and their revivals at the Royal National Theatre in 2010. She was also the accent coach for Robert Schenkkan's Tony Award-winning *All the Way* at the American Repertory Theatre and on Broadway.

BIBLIOGRAPHY

General reference

Adrian, Barbara, *Actor Training the Laban Way*, Allworth Press, New York, 2008.
Ashby, Patricia, *Speech Sounds* (2nd edition), Routledge, London, 2005.
Barton, John, *Playing Shakespeare*, Methuen, London, 1984.
Berry, Cicely, *The Actor and the Text* (revised edition), Virgin Books, London, 1993.
Berry, Cicely, *Text in Action*, Virgin Books, London, 2003.
Berry, Cicely, *From Word to Play*, Oberon Books, London, 2008.
Bloom, Katya, Barbara Adrian, Tom Casciero, Jennifer Mizenko and Claire Porter, *The Laban Workbook for Actors*, Bloomsbury Methuen Drama, London, 2017.
Burniston, Christabel and Jocelyn Bell, *Into the Life of Things*, English Speaking Board, Southport, Lancashire, 1972.
Carey, David and Rebecca Clark Carey, *Vocal Arts Workbook and Video*, Methuen, London, 2008.
Carey, David and Rebecca Clark Carey, *The Shakespeare Workbook and Video*, Bloomsbury Methuen Drama, London, 2015.
Carr, Philip, *English Phonetics and Phonology*, Blackwell Publishers, Oxford, 1999.
Cohen, Robert, *Acting in Shakespeare*, Mayfield Publishing Company, Mountview, CA, 1991.
Colaianni, Louis, *The Joy of Phonetics and Accents*, Drama Book Publishers, New York, 1994.
Crystal, Ben, *Shakespeare on Toast*, Icon Books, London, 2009.
Crystal, David and Ben Crystal, *Shakespeare's Words: A Glossary and Language Companion*, Penguin Books, London, 2004.
Fenton, James, *An Introduction to English Poetry*, Penguin Books, London, 2002.
Hall, Peter, *Shakespeare's Advice to the Players*, Oberon Books, London, 2003.

Hobsbaum, Philip, *Metre, Rhythm and Verse Form*, Routledge, London, 1996.
Houseman, Barbara, *Tackling Text*, Nick Hern Books, London, 2008.
Kaiser, Scott, *Mastering Shakespeare*, Allworth Press, New York, 2003.
Lessac, Arthur, *The Use and Training of the Human Voice* (3rd edition), Mayfield Publishing, Mountview, CA, 1997.
Linklater, Kristin, *Freeing Shakespeare's Voice*, Theatre Communications Group, Inc., New York, 1992.
MacArthur, Tom (ed.), *The Oxford Companion to the English Language*, Oxford University Press, Oxford, 1992.
Matthews, Dakin, *Shakespeare Spoken Here: A Handbook for Students, Actors, and Lovers* (6th edition), Andak Theatrical Services, Los Angeles, CA, 2009.
Newlove, Jean, *Laban for Actors and Dancers*, Nick Hern Books, London, 2001.
Onions, C. T., *A Shakespeare Glossary* (revised by Robert D. Eagleson), Oxford University Press, Oxford, 1986.
Rodenburg, Patsy, *The Need for Words*, Methuen, London, 1993.
Rodenburg, Patsy, *The Actor Speaks*, Methuen, London, 1997.
Rodenburg, Patsy, *Speaking Shakespeare*, Methuen, London, 2002.
Schmidt, Alexander, *Shakespeare Lexicon and Quotation Dictionary* (in 2 volumes, revised by Gregor Sarrazin), Dover Publications, New York, 1971.
Sharpe, Edda and Jan Haydn Rowles, *How to Do Accents* (revised edition), Oberon Books, London, 2009.
Sher, Anthony, *Year of the King*, Chatto & Windus: The Hogarth Press, London, 1985.
Shewmaker, Eugene F., *Shakespeare's Language: A Glossary of Unfamiliar Words in His Plays* (2nd edition), Checkmark Books, New York, 2008.
Truss, Lynne, *Eats, Shoots & Leaves*, Profile Books, London, 2003.
Usher, George, *Shakespeare A–Z: Understanding Shakespeare's Words*, Bloomsbury Publishing, London, 2005.
Weate, Catherine, *Classical Voice: Working with Actors on Vocal Style*, Oberon Books, London, 2009.
Weate, Catherine, *Modern Voice: Working with Actors on Contemporary Text*, Oberon Books, London, 2012.
Wells, J. C., *Accents of English* (3 volumes), Cambridge University Press, Cambridge, 1982.

Plays

Alfaro, Luis, *Oedipus El Rey*, Woolly Mammoth Theatre Company, Washington, DC, 2011.
Ali, Tariq and Howard Brenton, *Moscow Gold*, Nick Hern Books, London, 1990.

BIBLIOGRAPHY

Ayckbourn, Alan, *Living Together* included in *The Norman Conquests*, Samuel French, London, 1975.
Baldwin, James, *Blues for Mister Charlie*, Samuel French, New York, 1964.
Barker, Howard, *The Castle* and *Gertrude – The Cry* included in *Plays Two*, Oberon Books, London, 2006.
Beckett, Samuel, *Happy Days*, Faber and Faber, London, 1981.
Beckett, Samuel, *Krapp's Last Tape* from *Krapp's Last Tape and Embers*, Faber and Faber, London, 2006.
Beckett, Samuel, *Waiting for Godot*, Faber and Faber, London, 2006.
Beckett, Samuel, *Endgame*, Faber and Faber, London, 2009.
Behn, Aphra, *The Rover Part I* and *The Lucky Chance* included in *Five Plays*, Methuen, London, 1990.
Cartwright, Jim, *Road* and *Two* included in *Plays:1*, Methuen, London, 1996.
Churchill, Caryl, *Top Girls*, Methuen, London, 2001.
Churchill, Caryl, *Serious Money*, Methuen, London, 2002.
Churchill, Caryl, *The Skriker*, Nick Hern Books, London, 2003.
Congreve, William, *The Way of the World*, A&C Black, London, 1992.
Coward, Noël, *Hay Fever*, included in *Plays: One*, Methuen, London, 1979.
Cowhig, Frances Ya-Chu, *Snow in Midsummer*, Methuen, London, 2017.
Cruz, Nilo, *Anna in the Tropics*, Theatre Communications Group, New York, 2003.
David, Eisa, *Bulrusher*, Samuel French, 2009.
Devlin, Anne, *Ourselves Alone*, Faber and Faber, London, 1990.
Edgar, David (adaptor), *The Life and Adventures of Nicholas Nickleby*, Dramatists Play Service, Inc., New York, 1982.
Edgar, David, *Pentecost*, Nick Hern Books, London, 1994.
Eliot, T. S., *Murder in the Cathedral*, Faber and Faber, London, 1936.
Etherege, George, *The Man of Mode*, Ernest Benn Ld., London, 1979.
Ford, John, *'Tis Pity She's a Whore* included in *Webster & Ford: Selected Plays*, J. M. Dent & Sons, London, 1969.
Frayn, Michael, *Copenhagen*, Methuen, London, 1998.
Friel, Brian, *Faith Healer*, Faber and Faber, London, 1980.
Glaspell, Susan, *Alison's House*, Samuel French, New York, 1930.
Gotanda, Phillip Kan, *Ballad of Yachiyo*, Dramatists Play Service Inc., New York, 1998.
Guirgis, Stephen Adly, *In Arabia We'd All Be Kings*, Dramatists Play Service, New York, 2002.
Guirgis, Stephen Adly, *Jesus Hopped the 'A' Train*, Methuen Drama, London, 2002.
Gunderson, Lauren, *The Book of Will*, Dramatists Play Service, New York, 2018.
Hansberry, Lorraine, *A Raisin in the Sun*, Vintage, New York, 2004.
Hare, David, *Skylight*, Faber and Faber, London, 1995.

Hennig, Kate, *The Last Wife*, Playwrights Canada Press, Toronto, 2016.
Hudes, Quiara Alegría, *Elliot, A Soldier's Fugue*, Dramatists Play Service, New York, 2007.
Hudes, Quiara Alegría, *The Happiest Song Plays Last*, Theatre Communications Group, New York, 2014.
Jonson, Ben, *The Alchemist*, A&C Black, London, 1991.
Jonson, Ben, *Volpone or The Fox*, Methuen, London, 2003.
Joseph, Rajiv, *Guards at the Taj*, Oberon Books, London, 2017.
Kane, Sarah, *4.48 Psychosis* included in *Complete Plays*, Methuen, London, 2001.
Kushner, Tony, *Angels in America Parts One and Two*, Theatre Communications Group, New York, 2003.
Kushner, Tony, *Homebody/Kabul*, Theatre Communications Group, New York, 2005.
Kwei-Armah, Kwame, *Statement of Regret* in *Plays: 1*, Methuen, London, 2009.
Loomer, Lisa, *The Waiting Room*, Dramatists Play Service Inc., New York, 1998.
Mamet, David, *Glengarry Glen Ross*, Methuen, London, 1990.
Marlowe, Christopher, *Dido Queen of Carthage, Doctor Faustus, Edward II, Tamburlaine Part II* included in *The Complete Plays*, Penguin Books, London, 1973.
McPherson, Conor, *The Weir*, Nick Hern Books, London, 1998.
McPherson, Conor, *Dublin Carol*, Nick Hern Books, London, 2000.
Miller, Arthur, *The Crucible*, Penguin Books, New York, 1983.
Morrison, Toni, *The Bluest Eye*, adapted by Lydia R. Diamond, Dramatic Publishing, Woodstock, IL, 2007.
Nottage, Lynn, *Ruined*, Theatre Communications Group, New York, 2009.
Nottage, Lynn, *Sweat*, Theatre Communications Group, New York, 2017.
O'Neill, Eugene, *The Iceman Cometh*, Nick Hern Books, London, 1998.
Parks, Suzan-Lori, *Imperceptible Mutabilities in the Third Kingdom* and *Devotees in the Garden of Love* included in *The American Play and Other Works*, Theatre Communications Group, New York, 1995.
Parks, Suzan-Lori, *Topdog/Underdog*, Theatre Communications Group, New York, 2001.
Pinter, Harold, *The Homecoming* and *Old Times* included in *Plays: 3*, Faber and Faber, London, 1997.
Reza, Yasmina, *Art*, translated by Christopher Hampton, Faber and Faber, London, 1996.
Rivera, Jose, *Marisol* and *Cloud Tectonics* included in *Marisol and Other Plays*, Theatre Communications Group Inc., New York, 1997.
Ruhl, Sarah, *The Clean House* and *Eurydice* in *The Clean House and Other Plays*, Theatre Communications Group, New York, 2006.
Schenkkan, Robert, *The Kentucky Cycle*, Dramatists Play Service, New York, 1994.

Shakespeare, William: There are many good editions of Shakespeare's plays: The Arden Shakespeare, The New Cambridge Shakespeare and the Oxford Shakespeare offer helpful and scholarly editions of each play. The following are good editions of the complete works: The Arden Shakespeare, The Oxford Shakespeare, The Riverside Shakespeare and The RSC/Modern Library Shakespeare. http://shakespeare.mit.edu is a very good internet edition of the complete works.
Shaw, Bernard, *Heartbreak House*, Penguin Books, London, 2000.
Shaw, Bernard, *Saint Joan*, Penguin Books, London, 2003.
Shaw, Bernard, *Man and Superman*, Penguin Books, London, 2004.
Shepard, Sam, *A Lie of the Mind*, Plume, New York, 1987.
Solis, Octavio, *Santos & Santos*, Samuel French, New York, 2017.
Stoppard, Tom, *Rosencrantz & Guildenstern Are Dead*, Faber and Faber, London, 1980.
Stoppard, Tom, *Arcadia*, Samuel French, London, 1993.
Stoppard, Tom, *Salvage: The Coast of Utopia Part III*, Faber and Faber, London, 2002.
Thomas, Dylan, *Under Milk Wood*, J. M. Dent & Sons, London, 1979.
Vogel, Paula, *Desdemona: A Play about a Handkerchief*, Dramatists Play Service, New York, 1994.
Vogel, Paula, *How I Learned to Drive* and *The Mineola Twins* included in *The Mammary Plays*, Theatre Communications Group, New York, 1998.
Webster, John, *The Duchess of Malfi* included in *Webster & Ford: Selected Plays*, J. M. Dent & Sons, London, 1969.
Wertenbaker, Timberlake, *Our Country's Good*, Methuen, London, 1995.
Wilde, Oscar, *The Importance of Being Earnest, Lady Windermere's Fan* and *An Ideal Husband* included in *The Importance of Being Earnest and Other Plays*, Penguin Books, New York, 1986.
Williams, Tennessee, *Summer and Smoke* in *Four Plays*, Signet Classic, Penguin Books, New York, 1976.
Williams, Tennessee, *The Glass Menagerie*, Penguin Books, New York, 1987.
Wilson, August, *Fences*, Plume, New York, 1986.
Wilson, August, *Seven Guitars*, Samuel French, New York, 1996.
Wilson, August, *The Piano Lesson and Joe Turner's Come and Gone*, Penguin Books, London, 1997.

Recommended anthologies of monologues

Caldarone, Marina (ed.), *Classical Monologues for Men*, Nick Hern Books, London, 2006.
Caldarone, Marina (ed.), *Classical Monologues for Women*, Nick Hern Books, London, 2006.

Coen, Stephanie (ed.), *American Theatre Book of Monologues for Men*, Theatre Communications Group, New York, 2003.
Coen, Stephanie (ed.), *American Theatre Book of Monologues for Women*, Theatre Communications Group, New York, 2003.
Earley, Michael and Philippa Keil (eds), *The Classical Monologue: Men*, Methuen Drama, London, 1992.
Earley, Michael and Philippa Keil (eds), *The Classical Monologue: Women*, Methuen Drama, London, 1992.
Earley, Michael and Philippa Keil (eds), *The Contemporary Monologue: Women*, Methuen Drama, London, 1995.
Earley, Michael and Philippa Keil (eds), *The Contemporary Monologue: Men*, Methuen Drama, London, 1995.
Weate, Catherine, *The Oberon Book of Modern Monologues for Men*, Oberon Books, London, 2008.
Weate, Catherine, *The Oberon Book of Modern Monologues for Women*, Oberon Books, London, 2008.

Poetry and novels

Burns, Robert, *Selected Poems*, Penguin Classics, London, 2007.
Donne, John, *Selected Poems*, Penguin Classics, London, 2006.
Eliot, Thomas Stearns, *Selected Poems*, Faber and Faber, London, 1954.
Hopkins, Gerard Manley, *Poems and Prose* (edited by W. H. Gardner), Penguin Books, London, 1953.
Rossetti, Christina, *Goblin Market and Other Poems*, Dover Publications, Inc., New York, 1994.
Stevenson, Robert Louis, *Kidnapped*, Penguin Books, London, 2007.
Whitman, Walt, *Selected Poems*, Penguin Books, London, 2000.
Wordsworth, William, *The Prelude*, Penguin Books, London, 2004.

Recommended poetry anthologies

Astley, Neil (ed.), *Staying Alive*, Bloodaxe Books, Northumberland, 2002.
Astley, Neil (ed.), *Being Alive*, Bloodaxe Books, Northumberland, 2004.
Forbes, Peter (ed.), *Scanning the Century: The Penguin Book of the Twentieth Century in Poetry*, Penguin Books, London, 2000.
Heaney, Seamus and Ted Hughes (eds), *The Rattle Bag*, Faber, London, 1982.
Heaney, Seamus and Ted Hughes (eds), *The School Bag*, Faber, London, 1997.
Keegan, P. J. (ed.), *The New Penguin Book of English Verse*, Penguin Books, London, 2001.

Poetry websites

www.famouspoetsandpoems.com.
www.poemhunter.com.
www.poetryarchive.org.
www.poets.org.

Audio-visual resources

Cicely Berry, *The Working Shakespeare Library* (5 DVDs/2 Workbooks), available in Region 1 and 2 formats.
Patsy Rodenburg, *Brings You Shakespeare in the Present* (8 DVDs), available at www.shakespeareinthepresent.com.
Playing Shakespeare (DVD) with John Barton, available in Region 1 and 2 formats.

LINKS TO WORKBOOK VIDEO

To view a particular video, please use its URL below, or go to https://vimeo.com/channels/1391428

1. Introduction: https://vimeo.com/268960071
2. Poetic patterns: https://vimeo.com/268961230
3. On your toes: https://vimeo.com/268962517
4. Sandbox: https://vimeo.com/268962778
5. Lists: https://vimeo.com/268963127
6. Line painting: https://vimeo.com/268971556
7. Verbal dynamics: https://vimeo.com/268972017
8. Carry the bag: https://vimeo.com/268972242
9. I love, I hate: https://vimeo.com/268972576
10. Crossing the line: https://vimeo.com/268972760
11. Feeling the beat: https://vimeo.com/268972977
12. The last word: https://vimeo.com/268973276
13. Question time: https://vimeo.com/268973346

INDEX

accents 16–17, 19–21
Actors exercise 60
adjectives 87, 223
Adrian, Barbara 49, 220
adverbs 87, 223
affricates 25
Alfaro, Luis 111, 192, 193
Ali, Tariq 191
alliteration 38, 41, 42, 44, 45, 46, 198, 204, 226
All the parts exercise 60, 212
All's Well That Ends Well
    Helena 133–4
antithesis 162, 205
Antony and Cleopatra
    Cleopatra 69–70
    Enobarbus 56–8
Ashby, Patricia 49
assonance 38, 41, 46, 198, 204
Ayckbourn, Alan 190

Baldwin, James 77, 112, 189, 191
Barker, Howard 48, 77, 153, 191, 193, 228
Barton, John 157, 213
Beckett, Samuel 49, 96, 152, 153, 187, 193, 228
Behn, Aphra 48, 111, 189, 190
Bell, Jocelyn 34, 36, 49
Berry, Cicely 49, 79, 100, 108, 114, 149, 151, 157, 186, 194, 213
Breathe the image exercise 58, 76

Brenton, Howard 191
builds 160, 161, 172–4, 176, 179, 180, 182, 187, 188, 190, 213
Burniston, Christabel 34, 36, 49

caesura 145–6, 149, 150, 151, 197, 198, 203
    epic caesura 146, 151, 197, 198
Cameraman exercise 62–5, 77
Carr, Philip 49
Carry the bag exercise 96–8, 112, 151, 199
Cartwright, Jim 152, 153, 193
Churchill, Caryl 48, 49, 76, 123, 124, 152
Cohen, Robert 157, 172, 180, 194
Colaianni, Louis 49
Colder/hotter exercise 168, 190
Comedy of Errors, The
    Adriana 100–2
commas 97, 98, 122, 150, 181, 213, 221, 222, 227
Congreve, William 48, 113, 189
conjunctions 87, 224
consonance 38, 46, 198, 204
consonants 15–16, 17, 18, 21, 24–9, 31, 34, 35, 38, 39, 46, 198, 204
    Consonants and content exercise 27, 48
continuants 24, 25
contrasts 161, 162–3, 165, 166–71, 188, 189, 213

couplets 38, 39, 42, 44, 147
Coward, Noël 154
Cowhig, Frances Ya-Chu 78, 111, 113, 189, 192
Crossing the line exercises 163–6, 189, 200
Cruz, Nilo 76, 78, 190
Crystal, Ben 114
Crystal, David 114

Davis, Eisa 48, 111, 112, 191
descriptions 3, 53, 56–9, 68, 205
Devlin, Anne 77, 191
Dialogue-sharing rhythm exercise 124–5, 153, 154
Dramatic patterns exercises 39–40, 42–7

Edgar, David 95, 112, 228
The elements exercise 32–4, 67
Eliot, T.S. 66, 78, 156, 228
elision 129
ellipsis 98
emotional logic 136, 139, 145, 182
end-of-line 'poise' 149
Etherege, George 153, 154, 156, 190
exclamation point 97, 99, 122, 148, 221, 223
Extended imagery exercise 69–71, 78

fairy stories 59
Feeling the beat exercise 130, 154
feminine endings 136–7, 140, 143, 155, 197, 203
  Feminine endings exercise 136–7, 155
Fenton, James 157
Fill in the blanks exercise 94–6, 112
folk tales 59, 225, 226
Ford, John 92, 111, 154, 156
Frayn, Michael 192
Friel, Brian 76

Gallop apace indeed exercise 137–9, 155
Gotanda, Phillip Kan 77, 192
Greek messenger speeches 59
Guirgis, Stephen Adly 77, 154, 191, 192
Gunderson, Lauren 77, 113

Hall, Peter 157
Hamlet
  Hamlet 87, 137, 146
Hansberry, Lorraine 77, 189, 190
Hennig, Kate 112, 190, 191, 193
Henry V
  Chorus 62–4
Here's the deal exercise 183–4, 185, 192
He said/she said exercise 169–71, 190, 213
Hobsbaum, Philip 157
Hopkins, Gerard Manley 40–2
Houseman, Barbara 49, 79, 114, 157, 194, 214
Hudes, Quiara Alegria 77, 113, 154, 190, 193

iambic pentameter 126–30, 134, 136, 138, 140, 143, 144, 145, 146, 152, 197, 203, 205
Ideal Husband, An 195, 206–13
  Lord Goring and Mrs Cheveley dialogue 207–13
I love, I hate exercise 162–3, 168
indirect objects 86, 87
International Phonetic Alphabet 16
irregular rhythm 139
I will die exercise 173, 191

Jonson, Ben 48, 78, 111, 155, 227
Julius Caesar
  Brutus and Cassius dialogue 108–10
  Mark Antony 89–91, 102–4
Just walk away exercise 182, 192

INDEX

Kaiser, Scott 79, 114, 194, 214
Kane, Sarah 78, 191
Kidnapped 118–19
King John
    King John and Hubert dialogue 134–5
King Lear
    Lear 135–6
Kushner, Tony 48, 77, 78, 112, 113
Kwei-Armah, Kwame 113, 228

Laban Rudolf 21, 49, 50, 219–20
    Laban consonants exercise 21, 25–8
    Laban vowels exercise 20–1, 25–7
Lady Windermere's Fan
    Lady Windermere 166–8
The last word exercise 156, 167
Length of thought exercise 122–3, 153
Lessac, Arthur 50
Life and Adventures of Nicholas Nickleby, The
    Brooker 95
Line by line exercise 150–1, 157
Line painting one exercise 56–8, 76
Line painting two exercise 66–7, 77
Linklater, Kristin 71, 79, 157, 194, 214
Lists exercise 174–6, 191
Loomer, Lisa 76

Macbeth
    Lady Macbeth 165
    Lady Macbeth and Macbeth dialogue 142–3, 200–6
    Macbeth 38–9, 196–200
Mamet, David 113, 187
Man and Superman
    Devil 121–2
    Tanner 179–80
Marlowe, Christopher 112, 113, 154, 155, 156, 227
McPherson, Conor 77, 112, 153
Measure for Measure
    Isabella 127–8

Merchant of Venice, The
    Shylock 176–8
Merry Wives of Windsor, The
    Ford 175–6
metaphor 66, 69, 70, 144, 146
metre 8, 126, 129, 130, 225, 233
Meyer, Ursula 172
Midsummer Night's Dream, A
    Helena and Hermia dialogue 39–40, 42–3
    Hyppolita and Theseus dialogue 106–8
    Pyramus 44–5
Miller, Arthur 189, 193
monosyllables 124, 133, 199, 204, 211
More lists exercise 176–8, 191
Morrison, Toni 49, 76, 78, 153
Much Ado About Nothing
    Benedict 121–2

Narratives exercise 59–62, 76
nasals 24
Newlove, Jean 50, 220
Nottage, Lynn 76, 77, 153, 191, 192, 228
nouns 223

O'Neill, Eugene 48, 189, 191, 193
One word at a time I exercise 71–3, 78, 206
One word at a time II exercise 74–5, 78, 199, 206
Onions, C. T. 114
onomatopoeia 29, 39
    Onomatopoeia exercise 37–8
On your toes exercise 148–9, 156
Othello
    Othello 68
Our Country's Good
    Dabby and Mary dialogue 105–6
Our friend the bag exercise 151, 157
Our friend the chair exercise 149–50, 156

parallelism 162
parentheses 93, 98, 222
Parks, Suzan-Lori 112, 153, 154
parts of speech 86, 223–4
patterns of sound 16, 39, 46, 198, 204
Pinter, Harold 76, 96, 153, 187, 192, 193, 228
plosives 24, 25, 28, 29
Poetic patterns exercise 40–2, 49
political speeches 161, 225, 226, 228
polysyllables 199, 204, 211
'Prelude, The' 33–4
prepositions 87, 224
pronouns 165, 223
prose 117, 120, 145, 152, 175, 177
punctuation 86, 98–9, 122, 131, 150, 179, 181, 197, 221–3
Punctuation play exercise 98–9, 112, 199, 206

question marks 99, 221
Question time exercise 88–9, 111, 211

Rap the rhyme exercise 39–40, 48
repetition
  of sounds 16, 38
  of words 105, 120, 121
restoration 40, 59, 99, 147, 227
Reza, Yasmina 113, 193
rhyme 3, 16, 38–45
  rhyming couplets 42, 44, 147–8
Rhyming partners exercise 39
Richard III
  Gloucester 45–7
  Gloucester and Lady Anne dialogue 169–71
Riffing on repetition exercise 121–2, 152, 153
Rivera, Jose 48, 77, 190, 193
Rodenburg, Patsy 50, 74, 79, 114, 158, 165, 194, 214

Romeo and Juliet
  Capulet and Tybalt dialogue 134
  Juliet 66, 67, 82, 129, 132, 137–9, 145, 168, 184
  Romeo 67, 82, 126–7, 129, 132, 139, 144–6
Rossetti, Christina 22, 36
Rowles, Jan Haydn 17, 50
Ruhl, Sarah 156, 192

Sandbox exercise 61–2
Scene building exercise 55
Schenkkan, Robert 77, 78
Schmidt, Alexander 114
scripted pauses 132, 187
  Scripted pauses exercise 132
Sculptures exercise 59–60
Secret song exercise 22–4, 36
semicolons 98, 181, 222
Sensual imagery exercise 67–8, 77, 205
sentence fragments 96
Serious Money
  Jacinta 123
Shadow dialogue exercise 187–8, 193
Shakespeare, William 8, 16, 27, 38, 42–7, 48, 56, 59, 62–4, 68, 69, 82, 84, 86, 89, 96, 100, 112, 113, 114, 117, 121–2, 126–30, 132–7, 139, 146, 153–7, 163, 169, 175, 176, 189, 190, 195, 222–3, 225, 226–7
Shared rhythm exercise 134–5, 154
Sharpe, Edda 17, 50
Shaw, Bernard 112, 113, 121, 179–80, 191, 225, 227
Shepard, Sam 77
Shewmaker, Eugene F. 114
similes 65, 66, 69, 70
soliloquies 165, 196
Solis, Octavio 153, 156, 191
Somebody listen exercise 186–7, 193

INDEX

'Song of the Open Road' 71–2
sonnets 84, 126, 128, 152, 225
Sound and meaning exercise 30–1, 32
So what exercise 185–6, 193, 213
speech sounds 3, 15–17
Spirals and stairs exercise 179–80, 191
Spot the theme exercise 100–4, 113
'Spring' (Christina Rossetti) 22–3, 36
'Spring' (Gerard Manley Hopkins) 40
Stevenson, Robert Louis 118–19
Stoppard, Tom 112, 154, 191, 192
stops (phonetic). *See* plosives
storytelling 226
Straight builds exercise 172–3
stress (metric) 116–17, 119, 125–31, 136, 138–9, 197, 225
structure 4, 159–60, 163, 212
Subordinate cuckoo clock exercise 91–4, 112, 199
Syllabic variations exercise 123–4, 153

Take a walk exercise 62, 204
Tap the balloon exercise 147–8, 156
tempo 75, 116, 118, 120, 123, 124, 125
Themed dialogues exercise 105–10, 113
themes 100–10
This and that exercise 166–8, 189
Thomas, Dylan 37, 49, 78
'Tis Pity She's a Whore
    Richardetto 92–4
trochees 126, 139, 140, 143, 197, 203
Turbulence exercise 139–41, 155
Turbulent dialogue exercise 142–3, 155
Turning words exercise 99–100, 113
Twitter exercise 87–8, 199

Under Milk Wood 37, 49
unstable rhythms 140, 143, 203

unstressed syllables 116–17, 119, 120, 124, 125–6, 129, 130, 136, 144, 146, 198
Usher, George 114

Verbal dynamics I exercise 34–5, 210
Verbal dynamics II exercise 36, 48, 210
verb phrase 86–7, 90, 223
    verbs 90–1, 94–5, 127
verse 3, 5, 42, 83, 117, 118, 120, 123, 125–30, 134–7, 143–51, 152, 154–7, 228
    verse line 126–8, 134–5, 136, 139, 143–51, 152, 198
vocal warm-up 215–18
Vogel, Paula 48, 78, 113, 114, 189, 190, 192
vowels 15–17, 19–24, 25, 31, 34–5, 38, 41, 46–7, 198, 204

Waiting for Godot 153, 187, 193
weak syllables. *See* unstressed syllables
Weate, Catherine 158
Webster, John 113, 190
Wells, J.C. 19, 50
Wertenbaker, Timberlake 105
Whitman, Walt 71
Who's doing what? exercise 89–91, 111–12
WH-question words 222
Wilde, Oscar 112, 166, 193, 195, 206, 227
Williams, Tennessee 190, 191, 228
Wilson, August 1, 76, 77, 78, 153, 189, 192, 193, 228
Winter's Tale, The
    Leontes 27–9, 139–41
Wordsworth, William 33

Yeats, William Butler 228
Yes/No exercise 184–5

www.ingramcontent.com/pod-product-compliance
Lightning Source LLC
Chambersburg PA
CBHW051806230426
43672CB00012B/2657